Actor Network Theory and After

A selection of previous *Sociological Review* Monographs

The Sociology of Monsters†
ed. John Law
Sport, Leisure and Social Relations†
eds John Horne, David Jary and Alan Tomlinson
Gender and Bureaucracy*
eds Mike Savage and Anne Witz
The Sociology of Death: theory, culture, practice*
ed. David Clark
The Cultures of Computing
Ed. Susan Leigh Star
Theorizing Museums*
eds Sharon Macdonald and Gordon Fyfe
Consumption Matters*
eds Stephen Edgell, Kevin Hetherington and Alan Warde
Ideas of Difference*
eds Kevin Hetherington and Rolland Munro
The Laws of the Markets*
ed. Michael Callon
Actor Network Theory and After*
eds John Law and John Hassard
Whose Europe? The turn towards democracy*
eds Dennis Smith and Sue Wright
Renewing Class Analysis*
eds Rosemary Cromptom, Fiona Devine, Mike Savage and John Scott
Reading Bourdieu on Society and Culture*
ed. Bridget Fowler
The Consumption of Mass*
eds Nick Lee and Rolland Munro
The Age of Anxiety: Conspiracy Theory and the Human Sciences*
eds Jane Parish and Martin Parker
Utopia and Organization*
ed. Martin Parker
Emotions and Sociology*
ed. Jack Barbalet
Masculinity and Men's Lifestyle Magazines
ed. Bethan Benwell
Nature Performed
eds Bronislaw Szerszynski, Wallace Heim and Claire Waterton
After Habermas
eds Nick Crossley and John Michael Roberts

†Available from the Sociological Review Office, Keele University, Keele, Staffs ST5 5BG.
*Available from Marston Book Services, PO Box 270, Abingdon, Oxon OX14 4YW.

The Sociological Review Monographs

Since 1958 *The Sociological Review* has established a tradition of publishing Monographs on issues of general sociological interest. The Monograph is an edited book length collection of research papers which is published and distributed in association with Blackwell Publishing. We are keen to receive innovative collections of work in sociology and related disciplines with a particular emphasis on exploring empirical materials and theoretical frameworks which are currently under-developed. If you wish to discuss ideas for a Monograph then please contact the Monographs Editor, Rolland Munro, at *The Sociological Review*, Keele University, Newcastle-under-Lyme, North Staffordshire, ST5 5BG.

Actor Network Theory and After

Edited by John Law and John Hassard

Blackwell Publishing/The Sociological Review

Copyright © The Editorial Board of the Sociological Review 1999

First published in 1999
Reprinted 2004, 2005

Transferred to digital print 2006

Blackwell Publishing
108 Cowley Road, Oxford OX4 1JF, UK

and
350 Main Street
Malden, MA 02148, USA

All rights reserved. Except for the quotation of short passages for the purposes of criticism and review, no part of this publication may be reproduced, stored in a retrieval system or transmitted, in any form or by any means, electronical, mechanical, photocopying, recording or otherwise, without the prior permission of the publisher.

Except in the United States of America, this book is sold subject to the condition that it shall not, by way of trade or otherwise, be lent, resold, hired out, or otherwise circulated without the publisher's prior consent in any form of binding or cover other than that in which it is published and without a similar condition including this condition being imposed upon the subsequent purchaser.

British Library Cataloguing in Publication Data

A CIP catalogue record for this book is available from the British Library

Library of Congress Cataloging-in-Publication Data applied for

ISBN 0 631 21194 2

Printed and bound in Great Britain by
Marston Book Services Limited, Oxford

Contents

After ANT: complexity, naming and topology *John Law*	1
On recalling ANT *Bruno Latour*	15
Perpetuum mobile: substance, force and the sociology of translation *Steven D. Brown and Rose Capdevila*	26
From Blindness to blindness: museums, heterogeneity and the subject *Kevin Hetherington*	51
Ontological politics. A word and some questions *Annemarie Mol*	74
Who Pays? Can we pay them back? *Nick Lee and Paul Stenner*	90
Materiality: juggling sameness and difference *Anni Dugdale*	113
Staying true to the laughter in Nigerian classrooms *Helen Verran*	136
What is intellectual property after? *Marilyn Strathern*	156
Actor-network theory—the market test *Michel Callon*	181
Good passages, bad passages *Ingunn Moser and John Law*	196
A sociology of attachment: music amateurs, drug users *Emilie Gomart and Antoine Hennion*	220
Notes on Contributors	248
Index	253

After ANT: complexity, naming and topology

John Law

Abstract

What is a theory? Or, more broadly, what is a good way of addressing intellectual problems? This paper explores the tension central to the notion of an 'actor' – 'network' which is an intentionally oxymoronic term that combines—and elides the distinction between—structure and agency. It then notes that this tension has been lost as 'actor-network' has been converted into a smooth and consistent 'theory' that has been (too) simply and easily displaced, criticised or applied. It recalls another term important to the actor-network approach—that of *translation*—which is another term in tension, since (the play of words works best in the romance languages) to translate is to also betray (*traductore, tradittore*). It is suggested that in social theory simplicity should not displace the complexities of tension. The chapter concludes by exploring a series of metaphors for grappling with tensions rather than wishing these away, and in particular considers the importance of topological complexity, and the notion of fractionality.

> 'Today we have naming of parts. Yesterday,
> We had daily cleaning. And tomorrow morning,
> We shall have what to do after firing. But today,
> Today we have naming of parts. Japonica
> Glistens like coral in all of the neighbouring gardens,
> And today we have naming of parts.'
> (Henry Reed, *Lessons of the War*: 1)

The naming of parts

Notoriously, Michel Foucault said of his early work (was it *Histoire de la Folie*?) that it took them fifteen years to find a way of reducing it to a single sentence, whereas in the case of *Volonté de Savoir*, the

History of Sexuality, it took them only fifteen days. Perhaps, then, we are lucky. The naming of what we now call in English 'actor-network theory' took more than fifteen days. And its contraction to the status of 'ANT' took even longer. For the accolade of the three letter acronym is surely a mixed blessing. Yes, it is the contemporary academic equivalent of the Imperial Triumph, the glorious return to Rome. Yes, it is a good moment to rest, to bask in the glory. Perhaps it is a good moment return to the Paris chart-rooms and plan the subjugation of the next barbarian province. For the naming of the theory, its conversion into acronym, its rapid displacement into the textbooks, the little descriptive accolades—or for that matter the equally quick rubbishings—all of these are a sign of its respectability. Of its diffusion. Or, perhaps better, of its translation.

But if it is possible to build reputations this way, then the naming and the easy transportability of 'ANT' surely also sets alarm bells ringing. For the act of naming suggests that its centre has been fixed, pinned down, rendered definite. That it has been turned into a specific strategy with an obligatory point of passage, a definite intellectual place within an equally definite intellectual space.

There are many metaphors for telling of this tension between centring and displacement. One thinks, for instance, of Deleuze's and Guattari's distinction between arborescence and rhizome.[1] Or of some of their other metaphors, for instance: territoriality versus nomadism; or the difference between desire as lack and desire as intensity which grows from within. No doubt we need to be wary of their romanticism, to avoid the idea that freedoms and productivities are located in boundlessness and boundlessness alone. In the breaking of names and fixed places.[2] Yes, there are dangers in lionizing that which cannot be fixed.

But then again. The naming, the fixity and the triumphalism—I want to argue that in current circumstances these pose the larger danger to productive thinking—the larger danger to the chance to make a difference, intellectually and politically. My desire—and what I take to be the purpose of this volume—is to escape the multi-national monster, 'actor-network theory', not because it is 'wrong', but because labelling doesn't help. This means that there are several reasons why I do not wish to defend it against its critics. First, and quite simply, because this is not an interesting thing to do. Second, because it is not productive to defend a more or less fixed theoretical location, a location which is performed, in part, by the *fact* of its naming. And third, because it is not a good way of making a difference. Under current circumstances intellectual inquiry is not, should not be, like that. And, of course, actor-network theory was never *really* like that itself.

But this is, to be sure, the performance of an irony. The paradox is upon us. By putting it in this way I have made a fixed point in order to argue *against* fixity and singularity. I also turn myself into a spokesperson for this name, the 'theory of the actor network', 'ANT'. I seek to tell you how it really is.

Well, in this introduction I am going to have to live with this paradox because I want (as they say) to make progress, and I need to make it quickly. I want to make some claims about actor-network theory, what it really is, because I also want to commend some possibilities that don't have to do with triumphalism and expansion. That don't have to do with fixed points. That rather have to do with displacement, movement, dissolution, and fractionality.

Actor-Network theory was...

Some stories about actor network theory.

First story. Actor network theory is a ruthless application of *semiotics*. It tells that entities take their form and acquire their attributes as a result of their relations with other entities. In this scheme of things entities have no inherent qualities: essentialist divisions are thrown on the bonfire of the dualisms. Truth and falsehood. Large and small. Agency and structure. Human and non-human. Before and after. Knowledge and power. Context and content. Materiality and sociality. Activity and passivity. In one way or another all of these divides have been rubbished in work undertaken in the name of actor-network theory.

Of course the theory is not alone. There are cognate movements in feminist theory, cultural studies, social and cultural anthropology, and other branches of post-structuralism. But even so, we shouldn't underestimate the shock value, nor indeed the potential for scandal. Sacred divisions and distinctions have been tossed into the flames. Fixed points have been pulled down and abandoned. Humanist and political attachments have been torn up. Though, of course, it is also a little more complicated, and the scandal may sometimes be more metaphysical than practical. For this precise reason: it is not, in this semiotic world-view, that there *are* no divisions. It is rather that such divisions or distinctions are understood as *effects or outcomes*. They are not given in the order of things.

© The Editorial Board of The Sociological Review 1999

There is much that might be said about this. To take the notorious human/non-human divide, much ink has indeed been spilled over the importance or otherwise of the distinction between human and non-human.[3] Or, for that matter, the machinic and the corporeal. But this is not the place to reproduce such set-piece debates. Instead, I simply want to note that actor-network theory may be understood as a *semiotics of materiality*. It takes the semiotic insight, that of the relationality of entities, the notion that they are produced in relations, and applies this ruthlessly to all materials—and not simply to those that are linguistic. This suggests: first that it shares something important with Michel Foucault's work; second, that it may be usefully distinguished from those versions of poststructuralism that attend to language and language alone; and third (if one likes this kind of grand narrative) that it expresses the ruthlessness that has often been associated with the march of modernity, at least since Karl Marx described the way in which 'all that is solid melts into air.'

Relational materiality: this catches, this names, the point of the first story.

The second story has to do with *performativity*. For the semiotic approach tells us that entities achieve their form as a consequence of the relations in which they are located. But this means that it also tells us that they are *performed* in, by, and through those relations. A consequence is that everything is uncertain and reversible, at least in principle. It is never given in the order of things. And here, though actor-network studies have sometimes slipped towards a centred and no-doubt gendered managerialism (more on this below), there has been much effort to understand *how it is* that durability is achieved. How it is that things get performed (and perform themselves) into relations that are relatively stable and stay in place. How it is that they make distributions between high and low, big and small, or human and non-human. Performativity, then, this is the second name, the second story about actor-network theory. Performativity which (sometimes) makes durability and fixity.

Actor-Network theory became . . .

So that is two stories, two forms of naming, stories which tell of *relational materiality* on the one hand, and *performativity* on the other. The two, of course, go together. If relations do not hold fast by themselves, then they have to be performed.

But what of the naming of 'actor-network theory'? The term started in French as *acteur reseau*. Translated into 'actor-network', the term took on a life of its own. And other vocabularies also associated with the approach—'enrolment' or 'traduction' or 'translation' got displaced. For, like some kind of monster, the term 'actor-network' grew, and it started, like a theoretical cuckoo, to throw the other terms out of the nest. Which, with the privilege of hindsight, seems both significant and ominous.

'Actor-network'. This is a name, a term which embodies a *tension*. It is *intentionally oxymoronic*, a tension which lies between the centred 'actor' on the one hand and the decentred 'network' on the other. In one sense the word is thus a way of performing both an elision and a difference between what Anglophones distinguish by calling 'agency' and 'structure'. A difference, then, but a difference which is, at the same time a form of identity.

There is much to be said about this, about this notion of the '*actor ... network*'. Yes, actors are network effects. They take the attributes of the entities which they include. They are, of course, precarious. But how is the network assembled? Here there are answers, but many of them lead us into well-rehearsed machiavellian or managerialist difficulties. Or they are posed in a language of strategy. No doubt the sacred texts of ANT are more complex and oxymoronic than this quick naming suggests.[4] However, if we draw on a set of discourses that have to do with strategy, then the gravitational pull of those discourses is primarily about the struggle to centre—and the struggle to centre and order *from* a centre. And as we know, this brings problems that may be told in a number of ways.

- One: as Leigh Star notes, yes we are all heterogeneous engineers, but heterogeneity is quite different for those that are privileged and those that are not.[5] The point is a little like Rosi Braidotti's in relation to Deleuze: to celebrate a body without organs is all very well, but less than attractive if life has always been about organs without a body.[6]
- Two: we may talk of 'heterogeneous strategies' or 'heterogeneous engineering'. But what about *non*-strategic orderings? What about relations that take the shape or form that they do for other reasons?[7]
- Three: materials may be heterogeneous, but what of heterogeneity in the sense intended by a writer like Jean-François Lyotard? Heterogeneity, in one way or another, as Otherness, that which is unassimilable? As difference? Whatever has happened to this?[8]

Perhaps then, the ordering of 'actor . . . networks' tends to ignore the hierarchies of distribution, it is excessively strategic, and it colonizes what Nick Lee and Steve Brown call the 'undiscovered continent' of the Other.[9] Perhaps it tends to suck the tension out of the term 'actor . . . network', to defuse its oxymoronic charge. All this is well known. But there are other problems, for instance to do with the term 'network'. For this is deceptively easy to think. We live, or so they tell us, in 'social networks'. We travel using the 'railway network'. And, as historians of technology remind us, we are surrounded by 'networks of power'.[10] But what are we doing when we use such a vocabulary? What metaphorical bag and baggage does it carry?

No doubt there are various possibilities. Marilyn Strathern asks us to attend to the links between notions of network and the assumptions build into Euroamerican notions of relatedness.[11] Another (indeed linked) way of tackling the issue is to think topologically. Topology concerns itself with spatiality, and in particular with the attributes of the spatial which secure continuity for objects as they are displaced through a space. The important point here is that spatiality is not given. It is not fixed, a part of the order of things. Instead it comes in various *forms*. We are most familiar with Euclideanism. Objects with three dimensions are imagined to exist precisely within a conformable three dimensional space. They may be transported within that space without violence so long as they don't seek to occupy the same position as some other object. And, so long as their co-ordinates are sustained, they also retain their spatial integrity. In addition they may be measured or scaled. They may be piled on top of one another. All of this is intuitively obvious.

Another version of Euclideanism is that of regionalism. Here (and again the point is obvious) the idea is that the world takes the form of a flat surface which may then be broken up into principalities of varying sizes. Regionalism, then, is a world of areas with its own topological rules about areal integrity and change.

Arguably, these topological understandings underpin many of the discourses and practices of the socio-technical. But studies of exotic societies suggest that there are other spatial possibilities[12]—and so too does actor-network theory. Indeed, the notion of 'network' is itself an alternative topological system. Thus in a network, elements retain their spatial integrity *by virtue of their position in a set of links or relations*. Object integrity, then, is not about a volume within a larger Euclidean volume. It is rather about holding patterns of links stable—a point explored by Bruno Latour in his work on immutable mobiles.[13]

So, and I thank Annemarie Mol for this observation, we may imagine actor-network theory as a machine for waging war on Euclideanism: as a way of showing, *inter alia*, that regions are constituted by networks. That, for instance, nation states are made by telephone systems, paperwork, and geographical triangulation points. It isn't the only literature that does this: one thinks, for instance, of writing in the new area between geography and cultural studies.[14] However, posing the point generally, actor-network theory articulates some of the possibilities which are opened up if we try to imagine that the sociotechnical world is *topologically nonconformable*; if we try to imagine that it is topologically complex, a location where regions intersect with networks.

Of course it is not the only such attempt.[15] When Deleuze and Guattari talk of 'the fold' they are also wrestling with the idea that relations perform or express different and non-conformable spatialities. But—big but—*this sensibility for complexity is only possible to the extent that we can avoid naturalizing a single spatial form, a single topology.*

How does all this relate to the notion of the network? Perhaps there are two possibilities. One is to insist, robustly, that the term is indeed relatively neutral, a descriptive vocabulary which makes possible the analysis of different patterns of connection which embody or represent different topological possibilities. This is indeed a perfectly sustainable position, and no doubt one that underpins the coword approach to scientometrics. The alternative is to say, as I have above, that the notion of the network is itself a form—or perhaps a family of forms—of spatiality: that it imposes strong restrictions on the conditions of topological possibility. And that, accordingly, it tends to limit and homogenize the character of links, the character of invariant connection, the character of possible relations, and so the character of possible entities.

Indeed, this is the position that I want to press. Let me express this carefully. Actor-network is, has been, a semiotic machine for waging war on essential differences. It has insisted on the performative character of relations and the objects constituted in those relations. It has insisted on the possibility, at least in principle, that they might be otherwise. Some, perhaps many, of the essentialisms that it has sought to erode are strongly linked to topology, to a logic of space, to spatiality. They are linked, that is, to volumetric or regional performances of space. Examples here would include many versions of scale, of big and small, and (again in their many regional versions) such alternates as human and non-human, or material and social. So actor-network theory has indeed helped to destabilize Euclideanism: it has shown that what appears to be topographically natural, given in the order of the world, is in fact produced in networks which perform a quite different kind of spatiality.

But the problem is this: it has been incredibly successful. Successful to the point where *its own topological assumptions have been naturalized*. Which, if you take the position that I'm pressing, has had the effect of limiting the conditions of spatial and relational possibility. And, in particular, of *tending to homogenize them*.

So this is the sceptical diagnosis. When it started to think about relations, actor-network theory set off with a notion of translation—as I noted above, one of the terms that later tended to become submerged. For translation is the process or the work of making two things that are not the same, equivalent.[16] But this term translation tells us *nothing at all about how it is that links are made*. And, in particular, it assumes nothing at all about the similarity of different links. Back at the beginning of actor-network theory the character of semiotic relations was thus left open. The nature of similarity and difference was left undefined, topologically—or in any other respect. Which means, no doubt, that it might come in many forms. Or, to put it differently, there was *no assumption that an assemblage of relations would occupy a homogeneous, conformable and singularly tellable space*.

So my suggestion is that the naming has done harm as well as good. The desire for quick moves and quick solutions, the desire to know clearly what we are talking about, the desire to point and name, to turn what we now call ANT into a 'theory', all of these things have done harm as well as good. 'Have theory, will travel.' Easy use of the term 'actor-network' has tended to defuse the power and the tension originally and oxymoronically built into the expression. And the further abbreviation, ANT, removes this productive non-coherence even further from view. The blackboxing and punctualizing that we have witnessed as we have named it have made it easily transportable. They have made a simple space through which it may be transported. But the cost has been heavy. We have *lost the capacity to apprehend complexity*, Lyotardian heterogeneity.

What I am trying to do is to attack simplicity—and a notion of theory that says that it is or should necessarily be simple, clear, transparent. Marilyn Strathern has talked about audit in the context of British university teaching and research.[17] One of the things that she says was that transparency is not necessarily a good. She says of teaching students (I paraphrase): 'Sometimes it is good to leave them puzzled, uncertain about what is being said. Even confused.' She is, I think, questioning the assumption which is embedded in the practice of teaching audit, at least in the United Kingdom, that clarity about aims and objectives is a good in and of itself. That it is possible to make explicit, in as many words, what one is on about, what a topic is all about. This assumption means, of course, that one way of failing in (British) university teaching is to be unclear about the purpose of what one is doing. Or to leave students with undefined questions in their minds.

No doubt teaching audit is a peculiarly British disease. But the point is more general. It applies, or so I am arguing, to *thinking theory*, or *thinking research*, just as much as it does to thinking teaching. For as we practise our trade as intellectuals, the premiums we place on transportability, on naming, on clarity, on formulating and rendering explicit what it is that we know—this premium, though doubtless often enough appropriate, also imposes costs. And I am concerned about those costs. I believe that they render complex thinking—thinking that is not strategically ordered, tellable in a simple way, thinking that is lumpy or heterogeneous—difficult or impossible.[18]

Fractionality

The title of this book is 'Actor Network Theory and After'. The concern is neither with arguments 'for' nor 'against' actor-network theory. These are not necessarily very interesting in and of themselves. What *is* interesting are matters, questions, and issues arising out of, or in relation to, actor-network and the various approaches to thinking materiality, ordering, distribution and hierarchy with which it interacts. The book, then, is not a balance sheet: it is a report of heterogeneous work in progress.

One of the most important matters arising has, as I've been suggesting, to do with complexity. It has to do with complexities that are lost in the process of labelling. A simple and matter-of-fact way of making the point is to revisit, once again, the question of naming—of what it is that we are doing when we talk of a theory like 'actor network theory', when we make a label in this way.

So, yes, we have a name. So to speak, a fixed tag. The theory has been reduced to a few aphorisms that can be quickly passed on. But there is also a diaspora. Thus actor-network theory (and here, no doubt, it is like everything else) is diasporic.[19] It has spread, and as it has spread it has translated itself into something new, indeed into many things that are new and different from one another. It has converted itself into a range of different practices which (for this is the point of talking of translation) have also absorbed and reflected other points of origin: from cultural studies; social geography; organizational analysis; feminist STS. So actor-network theory is diasporic. Its parts are different from one another. But they are also (here is the point) *partially connected*. And this, of course, is another way of talking of the problem of naming, the problem of trying to discern or impose the 'ANT'-ness of ANT. Or, indeed, any of the single-line versions of actor-network theory, the 'have theory, will travels' which have proliferated.

The point, then, is both practical and theoretical. For these attempts to convert actor-network theory into a fixed point, a specific series of claims, of rules, a creed, or a territory with fixed attributes also strain to turn it into a single location. Into a strongpoint, a fortress, which has achieved the double satisfactions of clarity and self-identity. But all of this is a nonsense for, to the extent that it is actually alive, to the extent that it does work, to the extent to which it is inserted in intellectual practice, this thing we call actor-network theory also transforms itself. This means that there is no *credo*. Only dead theories and dead practices celebrate their self-identity. Only dead theories and dead practices hang on to their names, insist upon their perfect reproduction. Only dead theories and dead practices seek to reflect, in every detail, the practices which came before.

So there is, there should be, no identity, no fixed point. Like other approaches, actor-network theory is not something in particular. But then again (and this is the point of talking about complexity) neither is it simply a random set of bits and pieces, wreckage spread along the hard shoulder of the superhighway of theory. But how to *say* this? How to *talk* about something, how to name it, without reducing it to the fixity of singularity? Or imagining, as if we were talking of the Roman Empire in the sixth century, that something that used to be coherent has simply fallen apart? How to talk about objects (like theories) that are more than one and less than many? How to *talk about* complexity, to *appreciate* complexity, and to *practice* complexity?

I want to suggest that these are the most important theoretical and practical questions which we confront: how to deal with and fend off the simplicities, the simplifications, implicit in an academic world in which: 'Have theory, will travel' makes for easy progress. How to resist the singularities that are usually performed in the act of naming. How to defy the overwhelming pressures on academic production to render knowing simple, transparent, singular, formulaic. How to resisting the pressure of playing the God-trick. How to make a difference in ways that go against the grain of singularity, simplicity, or centring.

Well, the 'after' in the actor network and after holds out promise. In other places Donna Haraway and Marilyn Strathern talk of *partial connections*.[20] Donna Haraway also tells stories about cyborgs and prostheses, about internal but irreducible connections which perform oxymoronic tensions. Marilyn Strathern, in a contribution to this volume, considers the ways in which asymmetries grow, again, within the symmetries of the networks. Bruno Latour wishes to recall the theory in order to rid it of some of the common-sense divisions implied in talking of 'actors', 'networks' and 'theories'. Michael Callon shows us how the making of economic simplicity is indeed a complex task. Steve Brown and Rose Capdevila explore some of the philosophical moves—and circulations—implied in actor network theory. Annemarie Mol starts to explore some of the questions arising in the ontological politics opened up by complex semiotics and Kevin Hetherington find ways of recovering the non-conformability of heterogeneity. Nick Lee and Paul Stenner talk of the necessary tension between the continuities and discontinuities implied in belonging. Emilie Gomart and Antoine Hennion talk in a related way of movement between agency and passivity—or between agency and 'structure'. Ingunn Moser and John Law are similarly concerned with movements between continuity and discontinuity, and Anni Dugdale again explores oscillations, this time between the single and the multiple implied in decision-making, while Helen Verran considers the tensions implied in thinking non-reductively about the encounter of different knowledge traditions. The sense of theory in tension runs through all these contributions and suggests a power-house of difficult and irreducible metaphors, metaphors which make complexity and resist simplicity. Metaphors which resist the call to turn themselves into theories which may be summarised and travel easily. But—and again I borrow from Marilyn Strathern—the metaphor with which I would like to conclude is that of the *fractal*.

For here is the problem. The objects we study, the objects in which we are caught up, the objects which we perform, are always *more than one and less than many*. Actor-network theory is merely an example. Yes, it is more than one. It is not a single thing. It is not singular. But neither is it simply a random heap of bits and pieces. Which means that it is not a *multiplicity*. But neither—as Annemarie Mol shows—is it a *plurality*. The single on the one hand and the plural on the other, this is the dualism that we need to try to avoid, a dualism which is written into and helps to perform vicious limits to the conditions of intellectual and practical possibility. A dualism which, of course, also helps to define what will count as simple, and what is taken to be impossibly complex. Irreducible.

Which is why it is interesting to work with the metaphor of the fractal. The relevant and lay part of the mathematics is straightforward. A fractal is a line which occupies more than one dimension but less than two. So a fractional object? Well, this is something that is indeed *more than one and less than many*. Somewhere in between. Which is difficult to think because it defies the simplicities of the single—but also the corresponding simplicities of pluralism of laissez faire, of a single universe inhabited by separate objects. So the thinking is difficult—no, it is not transparent—precisely because it *cannot* be summed up and reduced to a point, rendered conformable and docile. It is difficult because what we study cannot be arrayed in a topologically homogeneous manner either as a single object or as a plurality within a single space. It is difficult because the act of naming does not simplify—it does not substitute the assemblage with a neat label.

Is it too dramatic to say that, despite the best efforts of many of its practitioners, actor-network theory has been broken on the altar of transparency and simplicity? Of rapid transportability? I don't know. The God eye is alive and well and seemingly incurable in its greed for that which is flat and may be easily brought to the point. But, or so I firmly believe, the real chance to make differences lies elsewhere. It lies in the irreducible. In the oxymoronic. In the topologically discontinuous. In that which is heterogeneous. It lies in a modest willingness to live, to know, and to practise in the complexities of tension.

Acknowledgements

To resist the demands of simplicity one needs friends. Here are some of those friends: Brita Brenna, Michel Callon, Bob Cooper, Anni Dugdale, Mark Elam, Donna Haraway, Kevin Hetherington, Bruno Latour, Nick Lee, Ivan da Costa Marques, Doreen Massey,

After ANT: complexity, naming and topology

Annemarie Mol, Ingunn Moser, Bernike Pasveer, Vololona Rabeharisoa, Sandy Stone, Marilyn Strathern, Sharon Traweek and Helen Verran. I thank them all.

Notes

1 Developed, in particular, in Deleuze and Guattari (1988).
2 A point which Ingunn Moser and I explore through empirical materials about disability in this volume.
3 See, for instance, the acrimonious exchange in Picking (1992).
4 This would, for example, be the case for Latour's study of Pasteur. See Latour (1988).
5 See Star (1991).
6 See Braidotti (1994).
7 Although she presents this in somewhat different terms, this is one of the concerns of Annemarie Mol in her work on the problem of difference. See Mol (1999). It has also been addressed in a different mode by Bruno Latour (1996).
8 This was one of the objects of the ethnography of managers reported in Law (1994). On heterogeneity see Lyotard (1991).
9 See Lee and Brown (1994).
10 The term is Thomas Hughes'. See Hughes (1983).
11 See Strathern (1996).
12 See Strathern (1991).
13 As discussed in Latour (1987).
14 Three rather different examples here would be Harvey (1989), Jameson (1991) and Thrift (1996).
15 See the papers by Steve Brown and Rose Capdevila, and Nick Lee and Paul Stenner, in this volume. See also Cussins (1997), Hetherington (1997), Mol and Law (1994) and Strathern (1991).
16 Perhaps this is in certain respects a little too limiting. Equivalence? Why equivalence?
17 See Strathern (1997).
18 For further discussion of the indirection of allegory see Law and Hetherington (1998).
19 I explore this point in greater detail in Law (1997).
20 The term appears in Donna Haraway's important but often misunderstood essay (Haraway, 1991), and is explored in Strathern (1991).

References

Braidotti, Rosi (1994), *Nomadic Subjects: Embodiment and Sexual Difference in Contemporary Feminist Theory*, Gender and Culture, New York: Columbia University Press.
Cussins, Adrian (1997), 'Norms, Networks and Trails', A paper delivered at the Actor Network and After, Centre for Social Theory and Technology, Keele University, 1997.

Deleuze, Gilles, and Félix Guattari (1988), *A Thousand Plateaus: Capitalism and Schizophrenia*, London: Athlone.
Haraway, Donna (1991), 'A Cyborg Manifesto: Science, Technology and Socialist Feminism in the Late Twentieth Century', pages 149–181 in Donna Haraway (ed.), *Simians, Cyborgs and Women: the Reinvention of Nature*, London: Free Association Books.
Harvey, David (1989), *The Condition of Postmodernity: an Enquiry into the Origins of Cultural Change*, Oxford: Blackwell.
Hetherington, Kevin (1997), 'Museum Topology and the Will to Connect', *Journal of Material Culture*, 2: 199–218.
Hughes, Thomas P. (1983), *Networks of Power: Electrification in Western Society, 1880–1930*, Baltimore: Johns Hopkins University Press.
Jameson, Frederic (1991), *Postmodernism, or, the Cultural Logic of Late Capitalism*, London: Verso.
Latour, Bruno (1987), *Science in Action: How to Follow Scientists and Engineers Through Society*, Milton Keynes: Open University Press.
Latour, Bruno (1988), *The Pasteurization of France*, Cambridge, Mass.: Harvard.
Latour, Bruno (1996), *Aramis, or the Love of Technology*, Cambridge, Mass.: MIT Press.
Law, John (1994), *Organizing Modernity*, Oxford: Blackwell.
Law, John (1997), *Traduction/Trahison: Notes on ANT*, Oslo: University of Oslo. TMV Working Paper, 106.
Law, John, and Kevin Hetherington (1998), 'Allegory and Interference: Economies of Representation and Sociology', submitted.
Lee, Nick, and Steve Brown (1994), 'Otherness and the Actor Network: the Undiscovered Continent', *American Behavioural Scientist*, 36: 772–790.
Lyotard, Jean-François (1991), *The Inhuman: Reflections on Time*, Cambridge: Polity.
Mol, Annemarie (1999), *The Body Multiple: Artherosclerosis in Practice*, Durham, N. Carolina: Duke University Press, forthcoming.
Mol, Annemarie, and John Law (1994), 'Regions, Networks and Fluids: Anaemia and Social Topology', *Social Studies of Science*, 24: 641–671.
Pickering, Andrew (ed.) (1992), *Science as Practice and Culture*, Chicago and London: University of Chicago Press.
Star, Susan Leigh (1991), 'Power, Technologies and the Phenomenology of Conventions: on being Allergic to Onions', pages 26–56 in John Law (ed.), *A Sociology of Monsters? Essays on Power, Technology and Domination, Sociological Review Monograph*, 38, London: Routledge.
Strathern, Marilyn (1991), *Partial Connections*, Savage Maryland: Rowman and Littlefield.
Strathern, Marilyn (1996), 'Cutting the Network', *Journal of the Royal Anthropological Institute*, 2: 517–535.
Strathern, Marilyn (1997), ' "Improving Ratings": audit in the British University system', *European Review*, 5: 305–321.
Thrift, Nigel (1996), *Spatial Formations*, London, Thousand Oaks and New Delhi: Sage.

On recalling ANT

Bruno Latour

Abstract

The paper explores one after the other the four difficulties of actor-network theory, that is the words 'actor', 'network' and 'theory'—without forgetting the hyphen. It tries to refocus the originality of what is more a method to deploy the actor's own world building activities than an alternative social theory. Finally, it sketches some of its remaining potential.

I will start by saying that there are four things that do not work with actor-network theory; the word actor, the word network, the word theory and the hyphen! Four nails in the coffin.

The first nail in the coffin is I guess the word 'network', as John Law indicates in his paper in this volume. This is the great danger of using a technical metaphor slightly ahead of everyone's common use. Now that the World Wide Web exists, everyone believes they understand what a network is. While twenty years ago there was still some freshness in the term as a critical tool against notions as diverse as institution, society, nation-state and, more generally, any flat surface, it has lost any cutting edge and is now the pet notion of all those who want to modernize modernization. 'Down with rigid institutions,' they all say, 'long live flexible networks.'

What is the difference between the older and the new usage? At the time, the word network, like Deleuze's and Guattari's term rhizome, clearly meant a series of *transformations*—translations, transductions—which could not be captured by any of the traditional terms of social theory. With the new popularization of the word network, it now means transport *without* deformation, an instantaneous, unmediated access to every piece of information. That is exactly the opposite of what we meant. What I would like to call 'double click information' has killed the last bit of the critical cutting edge of the notion of network. I don't think we should use it anymore at least not to mean the type of transformations and translations that we want now to explore.

The second nail that I'd like to hammer into the coffin is the word 'actor' in its hyphenated connection with the notion of 'network'. From day one, I objected to the hyphen because inevitably it would remind sociologists of the agency/structure cliché, or, as we say in French, of the *'pont aux ânes'* of social theory. Most of the misunderstandings about ANT have come from this coupling of terms, one that is much too similar to the traditional divides of social theory.

The managerial, engineering, Machiavellian, demiurgic character of ANT has been criticised many times. More exactly, critiques have alternated, quite predictably, between the two hyphenated poles: one type of critique has turned around the actor, the other turned around the network. The first line of criticism has insisted on the Schumpeterian, male-like, hairy gorilla-like character of ANT; the second line of criticism has focused instead on the dissolution of humanity proposed by ANT into a field of forces where morality, humanity, psychology was absent. Thus, the actor-network was split into two: demiurgy on one side; 'death of Man' on the other.

No matter how prepared I am to criticise the theory, I still think that these two symmetrical critiques are off target even though the very expression of 'actor-network' invites this reaction. The original idea was not to occupy a position in the agency/structure debate, not even to *overcome* this contradiction. Contradictions, most of the time and especially when they are related to the modernist predicament, should not be overcome, but simply ignored or bypassed. But I agree that the hyphenated term made it impossible to see clearly the bypass operation that had been attempted.

Let me try to refocus the argument. Let us abandon the words 'actor' and 'network' for a moment and pay some attention to two operations, one of *framing* (see the chapter in this volume by Michel Callon) and one of *summing up*.

It is not exactly true that social sciences have always alternated between actor and system, or agency and structure. It might be more productive to say that they have alternated between two types of equally powerful *dissatisfactions*: when social scientists concentrate on what could be called the micro level, that is face to face interactions, local sites, they quickly realize that many of elements necessary to make sense of the situation are already in place or are coming from far away; hence, this urge to look for something else, some other level, and to concentrate on what is not directly visible in the situation but has made the situation what it is. This is why so much work has been dedicated to notions such as society, norms, values, culture, structure, social context, all terms that aim at designating what gives shape to micro interaction. But then, once this new level has been reached, a second type of dissatisfaction begins. Social scientists now feel that something is missing, that the abstraction of terms like culture and structure, norms and values, seems too great, and that one needs to reconnect, through an opposite move, back to the flesh-and-blood local situations from which they had started. Once back to the local sites, however, the same uneasiness that pushed them in the direction of a search for social structure quickly sets in. Social scientists soon realize that the local situation is exactly as abstract as the so called 'macro' one from which they came and they now want to leave it again for what holds the situation together. And so on *ad infinitum*.

It seems to me that ANT is simply a way of paying attention to these two dissatisfactions, not again to overcome them or to solve the problem, but to follow them elsewhere and to try to explore the very conditions that make these two opposite disappointments possible. By topicalizing the social sciences' own controversies. ANT might have hit on one of the very phenomena of the social order: may be the social possesses the bizarre property of not being made of agency and structure at all, but rather of being a *circulating* entity. The double dissatisfaction that has triggered so much of the conceptual agitation of the social sciences in the past would thus be an artefact: the result of trying to picture a trajectory, a movement, by using oppositions between two notions, micro and macro, individual and structure, which have nothing to do with it.

If this bypassing strategy is accepted then perhaps a few things are clarified: ANT concentrates attention on a movement—a movement well demonstrated by the successive shifts of attention of the dissatisfied social scientist. This movement has many peculiar features. The first one is the redescription of what was earlier perceived as having to do with the macro-social. As it has been understood even, I think, by the harshest critics of ANT, the network pole of actor-network does not aim at all at designating a Society, the Big Animal that makes sense of local interactions. Neither does it designate an anonymous field of forces. Instead it refers to something entirely different which is the *summing up* of interactions through various kinds of devices, inscriptions, forms and formulae, into a very local, very practical, very tiny locus. This is now well known through the study of accounting, managerial practice (Power, 1995), organization studies (Czarniawska, 1997), some sociolinguistics (Taylor, 1993), panoptica (or what I now call 'oligoptica', Latour and Hermant, 1998), economics, the anthropology of markets, and so on. Big does not mean 'really' big or 'overall', or 'overarching', but connected, blind, local, mediated, related. This is already an important contribution of ANT since it means that when one explores the structures of the social, one is not led away from the local sites—as it was the case with the dissatisfied social scientist—but *closer* to them.

The second consequence is less well developed but equally important: actantiality is not what an actor does—with its consequence for the demiurgic version of ANT—but what *provides* actants with their actions, with their subjectivity, with their intentionality, with their morality. When you hook up with this circulating entity, then you are partially provided with consciousness, subjectivity, actoriality, etc. There is no reason to alternate between a conception of social order as made of a Society and another one obtained from the stochastic composition of individual atoms. To become an actor is as much a local achievement as obtaining a 'total' structure. I will come back to this aspect in a moment, but the consequence is already important: there is nothing especially local, and nothing especially human, in a local intersubjective encounter. I have proposed 'interobjectivity' as a way of phrasing the new position of the actor (Latour, 1996).

The third and very puzzling consequence is that, by following the movement allowed by ANT, we are never led to study social order, in a displacement that would allow an observer to zoom from the global to the local and back. In the social domain there is no change of scale. It is so to speak always flat and folded and this is especially true of the natural sciences that are said to provide the context, the frame, the global environment in which society is supposed to be located. Contexts too flow locally through networks, be these geography, medicine, statistics, economics, or even sociology. This is where ANT has used the insights of sociology of science—including of course the sociology of the social sciences—as much as possible: economies emerge out of economics; societies out of sociologies; cultures out of anthropologies; etc. The topology of the social, John Law is right, is rather bizarre, but I don't think it is fractal. Each locus can be seen as framing and summing up. 'Actor' is not here to play the role of agency and 'network' to play the role of society. Actor and network—if we want to still use those terms—

designates two faces of the same phenomenon, like waves and particles, the slow realization that the social is a certain type of circulation that can travel endlessly *without* ever encountering either the micro-level—there is never an interaction that is not framed—or the macro-level—there are only local summing up which produce either local totalities ('oligoptica') or total localities (agencies).

To have transformed the social from what was a surface, a territory, a province of reality, into a circulation, is what I think has been the most useful contribution of ANT. It is, I agree, a largely *negative* contribution, because it has simply rendered us sensitive to a fourth consequence which is also the most bizarre: if there is no zoom going from macro structure to micro interactions, if both micro and macro are local effects of hooking up to circulating entities, if contexts flow inside narrow conduits, it means that there is plenty of 'space' in between the tiny trajectories of what could be called the local productions of 'phusigenics', 'sociogenics' and 'psychogenics'.

'Nature', 'Society', 'Subjectivity' do not define what the world is like, but what circulates locally and to which one 'subscribes' much as we subscribe to cable TV and sewers—including of course the subscription that allows us to say 'we' and 'one'. This empty space 'in between' the networks, those *terra incognita* are the most exciting aspects of ANT because they show the extent of our ignorance and the immense reserve that is open for change. But the benefit that can be drawn from this vast empty space 'in between' network trajectories is not clear yet because of a third difficulty that I now have to tackle.

The third nail in the coffin is the word theory. As Mike Lynch said some time ago, ANT should really be called 'actant-rhizome ontology'. But who would have cared for such a horrible mouthful of words—not to mention the acronym 'ARO'? Yet, Lynch has a point. If it is a theory, of what it is a theory?

It was never a theory of what the social is made of, contrary to the reading of many sociologists who believed it was one more school trying to explain the behaviour of social actors. For us, ANT was simply another way of being faithful to the insights of ethnomethodology: actors know what they do and we have to learn from them not only what they do, but how and why they do it. It is *us*, the social scientists, who lack knowledge of what they do, and not *they* who are missing the explanation of why they are unwittingly manipulated by forces exterior to themselves and known to the social scientist's powerful gaze and methods. ANT is a way of delegitimating the incredible pretensions of sociologists who, to use Bauman's forceful expression (Bauman, 1992), want to act as legislators and to open yet another space for interpretive sociology. Far from being a theory of the social or even worse an explanation of what makes society exert pressure on actors, it always was, and this from its very inception (Callon and Latour, 1981), a very crude method to learn from the actors without imposing on them an *a priori* definition of their world-building capacities. The ridiculous poverty of the ANT vocabulary—association, translation, alliance, obligatory passage point, etc.—was a clear signal that none of these words could replace the rich vocabulary of the actor's practice, but was simply a way to systematically avoid replacing their sociology, their metaphysics and their ontology with those of the social scientists who were connecting with them through some research protocol—I use this cumbersome circumlocution to avoid the loaded term 'studying', because ANT researchers cannot exactly be said to 'study' the other social actors.

I agree that we have not always been true to the original task, and that a great deal of our own vocabulary has contaminated our ability to let the actors build their own space, as many critiques have charitably shown (Chateauraynaud, 1991; Lee and Brown, 1994). This weakness on our part does not mean, however, that our vocabulary was too poor, but that, on the contrary, it was not poor enough and that designing a space for the actors to deploy their own categories is a much harder task than we thought at first—and this applies of course to this notion of deployment itself. From the very beginning, ANT has been sliding in a sort of race to overcome its limits and to drop from the list of its methodological terms any which would make it impossible for new actors (actants in fact) to define the world in their own terms, using their own dimensions and touchstones. John Law and Annemarie Mol have used the word fluid (Mol and Law, 1994), Adrian Cussins, the word trails (Cussins, 1992), Charis Cussins, the word choreography (Cussins, 1996). All of these words designate in my view what the theory should be and what the excessive diffusion of 'double-click' networks has rendered irretrievable: it is a theory that says that by following circulations we can get more than by defining entities, essence or provinces. In that sense, ANT is merely one of the many anti-essentialist movements that seems to characterize the end of the century. But it is also, like ethnomethodology, simply a way for the social scientists to access sites, a method and not a theory, a way to travel from one spot to the next, from one field site to the next, not an interpretation of what actors do simply glossed in a different more palatable and more universalist language.

I have often compared it to perspective drawing (Latour, 1997), because of this peculiar relation between an empty construction that is nonetheless strictly determined but which has no other aim than disappearing once the picture is left to deploy its own space. I am well aware of the limits of this metaphor since there is hardly a more constraining method than three dimensional perspectival drawing! Yet the image has its advantage: ANT does not tell anyone the shape that is to be drawn—circles or cubes or lines—but only how to go about systematically recording the world-building abilities of the sites to be documented and registered. In that sense, the potentialities of ANT are still largely untapped, especially the political implications of a social theory that would not claim to explain the actors' behaviour and reasons, but only to find the procedures which render actors able to negotiate their ways through one another's world-building activity.

The fourth and last nail in the coffin is the hyphen that relates and distinguishes the two words 'actor' and 'network'. As I have indicated above, it is an unfortunate reminder of the debate between agency and structure into which we never wanted to enter. But it is also a place holder for a much bigger problem, one that we have become aware of only very slowly, and whose impact will be very much felt in the future. By dealing simultaneously with human and non-human agencies, we happened to fall into an empty space between the four major concerns of the modernist way of thinking. We were not conscious of this coherence at first, but learned it the hard way when we began to understand that those who should have been most interested in our work, that is social scientists, including those of SSK (the Sociology of Scientific Knowledge), turned out to be its harshest critics (Collins and Yearley, 1992; Bloor, 1998). Their social explanation did not seem to us to hold water: the very definition of society was part of the problem not part of the solution. How could that be possible, and how could sociology of science trigger such entirely different research programs?

ANT slowly drifted from a sociology of science and technology, from a social theory, into another enquiry of modernity—sometimes called comparative, symmetrical, or monist anthropology (Descola and Palsson, 1996). The difference between ANT and the masses of reflection on modernity and post-, hyper-, pre- and anti-modernity, was simply that it took to task all of the components of what could be called the modernist predicament simultaneously.

The reason why it could not stick to a theory of social order is that the whole theory of society soon appeared to be enmeshed in a much more complex struggle to define an epistemological settlement about: (a) what the world is like *outside* without human intervention; (b) a psychology *inside*—an isolated subjectivity still able to also comprehend the word out there; (c) a political theory of how to keep the crowds at bay without them intervening with their unruly passions and ruining the social order; and finally (d) a rather repressed but very present theology that is the only way to guarantee the differences and the connections between those three other domains of reality. There is not one problem of deciding what society is, a second of explaining why there is a psychology, a third of defining politics, and a fourth of accounting for the deletion of theological interests. Instead there is only *one* single predicament which, no matter how entangled, has to be tackled at once. To sum it up in one simple formula: 'out there' nature, 'in there' psychology, 'down there' politics, 'up there' theology. It is this whole package that by happenstance ANT called into question at once.

There is no room here to review the whole question—I have done so elsewhere (Latour, 1999)—but only to indicate the consequences for one possible future of ANT. ANT is not a theory of the social, any more than it is a theory of the subject, or a theory of God, or a theory of nature. It is a theory of the space or fluids circulating in a non-modern situation. What type of connection can be established between those terms, other than the systematic modernist solution? This is, I think, clearly the direction of what is 'after' ANT and what would begin to solve a number of the worries expressed in the contributions to this book.

Let us not forget that the first thing we made circulate is nature and reference, that is the 'out there' box. I was struck to see that none of the writers, in this book or at the conference from which it derived, mentioned social constructivism and the recent Science Wars. Clearly the treatment of the collective of scientific reality as a circulation of transformations—is it even necessary to say again that reference is real, social and narrative at once?—is now, if not taken for granted, at least clearly articulated. If ANT can be credited with something, it is to have developed a science studies that entirely bypasses the question of 'social construction' and the 'realist/ relativist debate'. It is not, it never was, a pertinent question, even though it still amuses many people who are not familiar with either science studies or ANT. Social theory is now allowed to have as many points of contact, as many correspondences, with a bountiful reality as there are circulating references. ANT can gorge itself on realities without having to spend a single moment excusing itself for not believing in an 'outside' reality. On the contrary, it is now able to explain why on earth the modernist had the bizarre idea of making reality 'outside'.

What I call the 'second wave' of science studies has offered (is offering) the same sort of treatment to the other sphere—'in there'. Subjectivity, corporeality, is no more a property of humans, of individuals, of intentional subjects, than being an outside reality is a property of nature. This new tack is so well represented in the papers in this book that there is no need to develop the point here (see the chapter by Annemarie Mol). Subjectivity seems also to be a circulating capacity, something that is partially gained or lost by hooking up to certain bodies of practice. Madeleine Akrich's work, the chapter by Emilie Gomart and Antoine Hennion for this book, the work I am doing on ethnopsychiatry (Latour, 1996), the work of Charis Cussins, the new book by Marc Berg and Annemarie Mol (Berg and Mol, 1998), all have the character of, so to speak, redistributing subjective quality *outside*—but of course, it is a totally different 'outside' now that epistemology has been turned into a circulating reference. The two movements—the first and the second wave, one on objectivity, the other on subjectivity—are closely related: the more we have 'socialized' so to speak 'outside' nature, the more 'outside' objectivity the content of our subjectivity can gain. There is plenty of room now for both.

What is next? Clearly the 'down there' aspect of the modernist predicament, namely political theory as indicated by a small but growing body of work (see work by Dick Pels). Not a single feature of our definition of political practice escapes the pressure of epistemology ('out there') and psychology ('in there'). If we could elicit the specificity of a certain type of circulation that is turning the Body Politic into one, that is, some type of circulation that 'collects' the collective, we would have made an immense step forward. We would have at last freed politics from science—or more exactly from epistemology (Latour, 1997)—a result that would be quite a feat for people who are still often accused to have politicized science beyond repair! From the recent work in political ecology, or in what Isabelle Stengers call 'cosmopolitics' (Stengers, 1996; Stengers, 1997), I am rather confident that this will soon come to fruition. The political relevance that academics always search for, somewhat desperately, cannot be obtained without a relocation of the extraordinary originality of political circulation.

Bruno Latour

What about the half hidden sphere above, that has been used as a guarantee for the rest of the modernist systems? I know this is a very risky territory since if there is anything worse than dabbling with non-humans, it is to take theology seriously. This line of work is not represented at all, I agree, in this book. Yet, I think that it is in theology that the notion of circulation is the most rewarding, precisely because it quickly rejuvenates a tissue of absurdities (what has become a tissue of absurdities) because of the shadow cast by the notion of a Science and by the notion of Society. Morality that seems totally absent from the engineering dreams of ANT, may be very abundant if we care to take it also for a certain type of circulation.

The point on which I want to conclude is somewhat different from that of John Law. In his chapter, he asks us to limit ANT and to tackle complexity and locality seriously and modestly. As with several of us, he is somewhat terrified by the monster that we have begot. But you cannot do to ideas what auto manufacturers do with badly conceived cars: you cannot recall them all by sending advertisements to the owners, retrofitting them with improved engines or parts, and sending them back again, all for free. Once launched in this unplanned and uncharted experiment in collective philosophy there is no way to retract and once again be modest. The only solution is to do what Victor Frankenstein did *not* do, that is, not to abandon the creature to its fate but continue all the way in developing its strange potential.

Yes, I think there is life after ANT. Once we have strongly pushed a stake into the heart of the creature safely buried in its coffin—thus abandoning what is so wrong with ANT, that is 'actor', 'network', 'theory' without forgetting the hyphen!—some other creature might emerge, light and beautiful: our future collective achievement.

References

Bauman, Z. (1992), *Intimations of Postmodernity*. London: Routledge.
Berg, M. and A. Mol (1998) (eds), *Differences in Medicine: Unravelling Practices, Techniques and Bodies*, Durham, North Carolina: Duke University Press.
Bloor, D. (1998), 'Anti-Latour.' *Studies in History and Philosophy of Science*.
Callon, M. and B. Latour (1981), 'Unscrewing the Big Leviathan: How Do Actors Macrostructure Reality'. *Advances in Social Theory and Methodology. Toward an Integration of Micro and Macro Sociologies*. K. Knorr and A. Cicourel. London: Routledge, 277–303.
Chateauraynaud, F. (1991), 'Forces et faiblesses de la nouvelle anthropologie des sciences.' *Critique* (529–530): 458–478.

Collins, H. and S. Yearley (1992), 'Epistemological Chicken'. *Science as Practice and Culture*. A. Pickering. Chicago: Chicago University Press, 301–326.
Cussins, A. (1992), 'Content, Embodiment and Objectivity: The Theory of Cognitive Trails.' *Mind* 101(404): 651–688.
Cussins, C. (1996), 'Ontological Choreography: Agency for Women Patients in an Infertility Clinic.' Pages 166–201 in M. Berg and A. Mol, *Differences in Medicine*, Durham, N. Carolina: Duke University Press.
Czarniarwska, B. (1997), *Narrating the Organization*, Chicago: The University of Chicago Press.
Descola, P. and G. Palsson (eds) (1996), *Nature and Society. Anthropological Perspectives*. London: Routledge.
Latour, B. (1996), 'On Interobjectivity—with discussion by Marc Berg, Michael Lynch and Yrjo Engelström.' *Mind, Culture and Activity* 3(4): 228–245.
Latour, B. (1996), *Petite réflexion sur le culte moderne des dieux Faitiches*. Paris, Les Empêcheurs de penser en rond.
Latour, B. (1997), 'Socrates' and Callicles' Settlement or the Invention of the Impossible Body Politic.' *Configurations* Spring(2): 189–240.
Latour, B. (1997), 'The Trouble with Actor Network Theory.' *Soziale Welt* 47: 369–381.
Latour, B. (1999), *Pandora's Hope. Essays on the reality of science studies*. Cambridge, Mass.: Harvard University Press.
Latour, B. and E. Hermant (1998), *Paris ville invisible*. Paris, La Découverte-Les Empêcheurs de penser en rond.
Lee, N. and S. Brown (1994), 'Otherness and the Actor-Network: the Undiscovered Continent.' *American Behavioral Scientist* 37(6): 772–790.
Mol, A. and J. Law (1994), 'Regions, Networks, and Fluids: Anaemia and Social Topology.' *Social Studies of Science* 24(4): 641–672.
Power, M. (ed.) (1995), *Accounting and Science: National Inquiry and Commercial Reason*. Cambridge: Cambridge University Press.
Stengers, I. (1996), *Cosmopolitiques—Tome 1: la guerre des sciences*. Paris, La découverte and Les Empêcheurs de penser en rond.
Stengers, I. (1997), *Power and Invention*. Minneapolis: University of Minnesota Press.
Taylor, J.R. (1993), *Rethinking the Theory of Organizational Communication: How to Read an Organization*. Norwood, New Jersey: Ablex Publishing.

Perpetuum mobile: substance, force and the sociology of translation

Steven D. Brown and Rose Capdevila

'There are optical errors in time as there are in space'
                          Marcel Proust *The Fugitive*

'One takes force as it is or one produces it'
                        Michel Serres *Turner Translates Carnot*

Abstract

Going after means taking up a position with regard to something and the active pursuit of that same thing. It is the critical move *par excellence*, but also an act of appropriation. This essay suspends the urge to *go after* in preference for an exploration of the trajectory of that body of texts known as the sociology of translation. The figure of the *perpetuum mobile* is put into circulation through these texts in order to trace some of their more unusual and unfamiliar connections. These include a whole series of parallels with seventeenth century classical philosophy and with nineteenth century 'social energetics'. Connections are drawn out by using three 'test signals', which are sent on through the ANT canon: substance, force and time. Pivotal to each is the sense of how very different events and apparently diverse territories can be brought into contiguity, or folded up together. This contiguity needs to be *performed* rather than *described*, placed *in translation* rather than simply *presented*. The chapter concludes by tracing a way from the strange folds of ANT to the equally peculiar forms of early Psychology.

Unbelievable lightness

What does it mean to be 'after' actor-network? It means, at the very least, that we know what this phrase 'actor-network' designates. And that we can come to some form of judgement about the kind of relationship we desire with the referent. That relationship will be one where we suppose ourselves to have surpassed or gone beyond its limitations. It means that we know in advance much of what we—those who come 'after'—would want to say about 'actor-network'. Such are the usual modes of critique. In this essay we want to try something different. We are mindful that there are a number of, as Latour calls them, 'obvious criticisms' of actor-network theory. Like the observation that the actor-network approach can become itself a peculiar obligatory points of passage through which something broadly resembling a liberal-humanist agenda is played out (Lee and Brown, 1994). We are also mindful that this observation is no less totalizing than the approach it seeks to critique. It knows in advance what it wants to say about actor-network theory. How then to read critically without totalizing? And, perhaps more importantly, how to work with and against actor-network without lapsing into simple appropriation?

Let's start somewhere off centre. In Kurt Vonnegut's *Hocus Pocus*, Eugene Debs Hartke, newly appointed physics teacher, makes a surprising discovery in the attic of a campus building: a number of perpetual motion machines. He takes these machines to be evidence of the 'foolish' and ill-educated ambitions of the college's founder, Elias Tarkington:

'I brought them downstairs and into the 20th century. Some of my students and I cleaned them up and restored any parts that had deteriorated during the intervening 100 years. At least they were exquisite jewelry, with garnets and amethysts for bearings, with arms and legs of exotic woods, with tumbling balls of ivory, with chutes and counterweights of silver. It was as though dying Elias hoped to overwhelm science with the magic of precious materials. The longest my students and I could get the best of them to run was 51 seconds. Some eternity!' (Vonnegut, 1990: 13–14)

In cleaning the machines, Hartke and his students revive the ambitions of the long deceased Tarkington. They participate, albeit briefly, in his attempt to overthrow conventional knowledge with riches. The irony of such participation is not lost on Hartke. Tarkington is a private college, specializing in 'lightweight' pedagogic programmes for the 'ineducable' offspring of the preposterously wealthy. Hartke is engaged in ensuring the inept heirs to great fortunes ascend to their rightful position. He keeps cultural capital in perpetual motion. Indeed, the whole college is effectively a machine set off by the push of nineteenth century 'new money', designed to overwhelm fate and preserve in perpetuity a suddenly found advantage.

Tarkington is, of course, a network, and there are doubtless many translations to be understood in the course of tracking how such an institution is able to make itself irreversible. But it is not this that interests us here. It is rather the machines themselves, or more precisely the idea of something which, once set in operation, *goes on beyond the time and place of its inception*.

The notion of a perpetual motion machine, or *perpetuum mobile*, dates from at least the eighteenth century, and is of a piece with the fascination for automata that gripped that period. In a Newtonian universe, clockwork devices, especially timekeeping machines, stand for linear order and precision (Mayr, 1986), submitting the social to the discipline of natural lawfulness. One need only think of the role of bells and chimes in Foucault's *Discipline and Punish*, or of the translations that were shortly to occur in the military term 'organization' as biology began to emerge from natural history (Jacob, 1973). The ticking hand of the clock and the chirruping of mechanical birds as a wake-up call to the fast approaching dawn of modernity.

Amongst all these familiar images it is the *perpetuum mobile* which jars. For a while the ambition to discover the principle behind the construction of a machine which once set in motion would run for all eternity came to take on an almost hermetic status. The French Academy of Sciences even offered a prize for the victor (Rabinbach, 1990). What differentiates the *perpetuum mobile* from a simple automaton is that whilst it is a product of human labour, once it begins to operate it effectively becomes cause-of-itself. The *perpetuum mobile* is a pure going-on, a demonstration of how an entirely self-enclosed mechanism may persist in being without any dependence or perhaps cognisance of the universe around it. This is the dream that the emerging strands of materialism and nationalism would seek to turn into political destiny.

All of this, then, is what Eugene Debs Hartke becomes suddenly very close to: eighteenth century Western Europe, nineteenth century North America pioneer country. So where are he and his students now? Crouched around the machines in a twentieth century backwoods campus, or somewhere else? In a sense it doesn't matter, or at least it is not decisive to fix Hartke and company in clearly marked time and place. What is important here is that in rediscovering the machines they enter into proximity with otherwise distant events, regions and ideas. The machine inscribes a fold in space and time, like a blunt scissors edge run across paper, such that what were distant points suddenly become neighbours. Things, to borrow Michel Serres' (1995) felicitous term, get crumpled up together.

Let us now turn back to actor-network theory, or to use the proper generic, the sociology of translation. We have indicated that we aware that any attempt to uncover some as yet unrevealed inner principle at the core of this heterogeneous series of texts—which could serve as the object of sweeping rebuttal—is utterly misguided. This would be to posit some axiom in advance which would then serve as the basis by which the sociology of translation might be critically decoded. We believe that no ready axiom exists. The approach, in its less programmatic guises, is a method in and of translation. It is constructed around a near formal requirement that it does not remain the same as it unravels in its own convoluted networks (Law, 1997). But in order for anything to go on as actor-network theory it is necessary that *something* remains in circulation to forge and order relations between the various texts. It is not immediately obvious precisely what it is that circulates in this manner. The sociology of translation would seem well able to proceed in the absence of a solitary mobile actor (it lacks a single 'guru'), methodology (despite the promotion by Callon *et al.*, 1986 of co-word analysis; and Latour's methodological prescriptions, 1987) or indeed theory (compare, say, Law's symbolic-interactionist Daresbury study, 1994; with Callon's semiotic readings of DGRST, 1980).

But to ask what is proper to a condition 'after actor-network' is already to have some sense of the *trajectory* of what circulates, even if we are as yet unclear about just what that something is. We can perhaps grasp this in two non-equivalent ways. First, that the circulation is something like a 'translation drift' (cf. Latour, 1987), where a body of texts and concerns moves progressively further away from its natal interests in the process of network building. This understanding would be grist for an actor-network analysis of the sociology of translation itself. Second, that the goings-on that constitute the trajectory are themselves the very *essence* of ANT. For the moment we would like this contention to stand with all the horror that such classical statements induce in the poststructuralist imaginary.

Yet there are problems with this term 'drift'.[1] It implies a kind of weightlessness to ANT, as though it could simply spin its networks through the social sciences without solidifying or forming 'hard segments' (cf. Deleuze and Guattari, 1984) of procedural and theoretical dogma. As though it could make itself irreversible without becoming an obligatory point of passage for social theory. This apparent belief in the power of an approach to seemingly reinvent itself with every repeated application provides a great source of hope for those who would seek to utilize it. But it also disguises the proprietary aspects of such utility. In order to use ANT, one must accept or allow that whatever circulates pass through one's own work.

So one reason why we use the term *essence* (there are others we will mention later) is to suggest an unsettling mixture of insubstantiality (as with pure extract) and heavy burden (the acceptance of a proprietary obligation) that we find appropriate in considering the goings-on of ANT. Essence adds weight, the burden of being-the-same, the idea that there is some-thing which remains throughout the many modifications contained within the drift.

There is then a particular mode of circulation characterizing the drift that is 'actor-network and after'. This we will refer to as essence. Now to explore this circulation-as-essence, it is necessary to make some kind of connection which brings us into proximity with the sociology of translation. We require something which will make a fold. For this we choose the *perpetuum mobile*. At the same time, circulation is not granted without cost. It demands that we—as social psychologists—labour to product connections along which whatever circulates may pass through us. In all this the *perpetuum mobile* can work as something like a 'test signal'. We will set it in motion through the texts of ANT and by seeing what emerges gain some understanding of the channels through which it has passed.

Test one: substance

As cause-of-itself, the *perpetuum mobile* keeps going by virtue of its own self-contained, unlimited reservoir of energy. It is very close to what would later (but is 'later' relevant here?) be called an entirely closed system. By the late eighteenth century, however, the official search for the *perpetuum mobile* was at an end. In 1775, the French Academy withdrew the offer of prize money. By 1847, the German physiologist Hermann von Helmholtz mocked the efforts of the previous century thus:

> 'Perpetual motion was to create labour power inexhaustibly without corresponding consumption, that is to say, out of nothing. Work however is money. Here emerges the practical

problem which clever people of all centuries have pursued in the most diverse ways, namely to create money out of nothing. The comparison with the philosopher's stone sought by the ancient alchemists is complete.' (Helmholtz, 1892:140)

Helmholtz speaks from a position made possible by thermodynamics and the laws of energy conservation. It is no longer plausible to separate pure matter from energy. The whole basis of the timeless Newtonian universe is fundamentally altered. From now onwards motion will be seen not as a defining law but rather as a product bought through the appropriation of energy from the 'great general storehouse of nature'. It is this process of appropriation or energy conversion that will come to dominate the conception of 'work', now understood as *arbeitskraft*, labour-power. But if there is no longer a way to 'create money out of nothing', then this does not imply austerity. Quite the reverse: energy is ubiquitous, it lies in all things as a great untapped potential, awaiting release through the mediation of industry. This is the fundamental tenet of the Western Industrial Revolution, that great technological drive to seize upon nature as pure resource. Accompanying this revolution in technics comes a matching revolution in aesthetics. For artists such as Turner:

'Matter is no longer left in the prison of the diagram. Fire dissolves it, makes it vibrate, tremble, oscillate, makes it explode into *clouds* . . . No one can draw the edge of a cloud, the borderline of the aleatory where particles waver and melt, at least to our eyes. There is a new time being fired in the oven . . . The boiler's fire atomizes matter and gives it over to chance, which has always been its master . . . Turner enters full force into the swarming cage of Maxwell's demons . . . colour-matter triumphs over drawing with geometric edges.' (Serres, 1982:58)

What Serres here describes is a fundamental change in the classical conception of substance. The geometric method used by seventeenth century philosophers like Descartes in their attempts to theorize the movement of bodies through space is consumed by the fire of thermodynamics. With it is burned the whole aesthetic of precision and the epistemology build around formal cause. The doctrine of probability and an obsession with efficient cause take their place. Force and substance are united in the flames and furnaces of *arbeitskraft*, 'there is a new time being fired in the oven'.

But the 'new physics' of the nineteenth century did not completely break with its classical roots, nor have done entirely with the dream of perpetual motion. In his popular lectures on the laws of energy conservation, Helmholtz hit upon an arresting image—the 'true' *perpetuum mobile* is not a machine constructed by humans but rather the universe as a whole. It is the 'great general storehouse of nature' which goes on in perpetuity, the quantity of energy locked within inorganic nature being 'as eternal and unalterable as the quantity of matter' (Helmholtz, 1892: 141). In short, Helmholtz and his contemporaries dealt with questions of force and substance by turning nature into a kind of eternal manufacturing forge, set ablaze by the omnipresence of fire.

The flicker of these flames can be seen reflected in the sociology of translation. This in several ways. First, the way potential actants are instrumentally described as resources which stand ready for enrolment into putative networks bears more than a passing resemblance to the definition of nature as 'great general storehouse'. In a sense the radical symmetry of the actor-network approach actually completes the vision of nineteenth century thermodynamics by treating the natural and the social as equivalent fields of resources.[2]

Second, the concept of translation, which lies at the heart of the actor-network approach, has itself rested for a time in the furnace of thermodynamics. As Callon (1980) acknowledges, the term 'translation' is taken from the work of Michel Serres. In that early paper Callon gives the following gloss:

> 'Considered from a very general point of view, this notion [translation] postulates the existence of a single field of significations, concerns and interests, the expression of a shared desire to arrive at the same result . . . Translation involves creating convergences and homologies by relating things that were previously different.' (1980:211)

Here Callon explicitly makes translation a semiotic operation, part of what he describes as a 'socio-logic'. Translation is the manoeuvre whereby the logical relations between seemingly opposed sets of 'significations, concerns and interests' are displaced within a 'programmatic organization of both knowledge and social actors' (ibid:211). It's a matter of shifting interests by displacing the nature of a pivotal problem from one set of significations to another.

But if for Callon what is at stake in fundamentally a matter of semiotics, for Serres there is something else at work in translation. In his essay on Turner's aesthetic translation of Carnot's thermodynamics,[3] Serres seems to be hinting at a more radical operation taking place at the level of form. He writes of Turner's watercolour *An Iron Foundry*:

Perpetuum mobile

'There is no longer any representation in Turner's foundry. The painting is a furnace, the very furnace itself. It is a disordered black mass centered on the lighted hearths. We pass from geometry to matter or from representation to work . . . No more discourses, no more scenes, no more sculptures with clean, cold edges: the object directly. Without theoretical detours. Yes, we enter into incandescence. At random.' (Serres, 1982:62)

Turner's translation does not consist of a new 'discourse' on the nature of the world or a new 'theory' of painting. In this sense it has nothing to do with representation. It consists, to the contrary, in the attempt to make the object itself present by way of the painting, to bring the 'disordered black mass' of matter into the frame such that we, as viewers, can encounter the dissolution of matter in the fire of the furnace. Turner's painting, according to Serres, performs the furnace. Better, it 'is a furnace, the very furnace itself'. This performance is achieved by making the 'work' of thermodynamics act as a *figural* point of passage from foundry to canvas and back. The diffuse masses of colour billowing across the canvas act out the stochastic transitions of fire and metal, water and steam that are proper to the *arbeitskraft* of the foundry.

The very least we can say is that Callon's derivation of 'translation' still has a representational aspect to it which mislays the figural and non-discursive dimension to translation that Serres underscores in the Turner example.[4] One could describe these two different uses of 'translation' in the fashion of a double-faced janus, as in Latour (1987). One says: 'Translation is the semiotic ordering and organizing of significations, interests, and concerns'. The other: 'Translation is displacement of the object directly, no representation, no theory'. And, perhaps a little unfairly, we might also suppose that one looks back to Newtonian geometry whilst the other anticipates the 'swarming matter' of thermodynamics.

Third and finally, the most immediately philosophical of the works within the sociology of translation, Latour's *Irreductions* (1988), is in part a homage to the philosophers whose work bridges the classical and modern periods: Spinoza and Leibnitz. These materialist philosophies are involved in the massive transformation of the concept of substance from the *res extensio* of Newtonian physics to the 'new time' of thermodynamics. Put crudely, Spinoza's account of 'simple bodies', and Leibnitz's notion of the 'monad', both posit a basic formal unit of analysis, whose *relationships* and *combinations* come to serve as the basis for understanding the composition of the world. As Leibnitz has it:

'The monad, of which we shall speak here is but a simple substance which enters into compounds ... And these monads are the true atoms of nature, and, in a word, the elements of things.' (1973:179)

This formal concern with the combinatory possibilities of monads, an *ars combinatoria* or 'monadology' was seized upon by Norbert Wiener in his early formulations of information theory and the science of communication that he would go on to christen as 'cybernetics' (see Wiener, 1932). It also serves as the basis for Latour's own 'new materialism' (1988: 154), where the monad will henceforth be known as 'actant', its combinations the results of 'trials of force' (158). Thus the sociology of translation offers up an account of stability and change that would not be unfamiliar to the classical philosophers: we may conceive of only basic formal units of substance (actants) which enter into relationships (networks) by way of encounters (trials of force) wherein questions regarding the powers and identities of these selfsame units come to be temporarily settled by reference to the overall compound nexus of relationships within which they are now embedded (the translation and subsequent enrolment of actants). So when Latour (1987) describes the strength of a network in terms of its length, what we actually hear is a classical voice:

'According as the parts of an individual, or compound body, are in contact with each other on a greater or less surface so the greater is the difficulty or facility with which they can be forced to change their position, and, consequently, the greater the difficulty or facility with which it can be brought about that the individual assumes another shape. Hence bodies whose parts are in contact over a large surface I shall call hard, and those whose parts are in contact over a small surface I shall call soft' (Spinoza, 1993:51)

What Spinoza understands as the assembling of compound bodies out of masses of simple bodies is for Latour the building of networks from chains of facts and machines. Spinoza has it that the resulting compound bodies are 'hard', meaning they retain both their constituents and their overall general 'shape', when they extend their surfaces as far as possible. Latour similarly describes the ability of a network to generate 'hard' facts as a function of its ability to extend itself spatially.

This is not to say that the sociology of translation simply recuperates classical philosophy. Far from it. Although Latour (1988) adopts the methodological reliance on axioms and propositions found in both Spinoza and Leibnitz, the method itself is run the other way round. Whereas Spinoza begins by defining *substance* as it is ordered by God, and then eventually proceeds to a description of how this substance is modified, the *accidents* it befalls at the hands of finite beings, in actor-network everything is more or less reversed. First comes a *plane of pure action* out of which *networks* subsequently emerge. Take Cooper and Law's description of retrospection:

'Our view of action is that it is primitive. It *precedes* thought, ordering, or organization. Thus, in its most callow sense, an action is a *happening*; before anything else—before meaning, significance, before it's fitted into any schema—*it simply happens.*' (Cooper and Law, 1995:241)

Here 'simple happening' (*qua* accident) forms the ground against which 'thought, ordering, or organization' (*qua* ordered substance) takes place. Which is to say that first comes chance, disorder, hazard. Then comes necessity, order, organization. How is this possible? By repetition, Cooper and Law suggest. That which happens only once (the solitary accident) is properly nothing or 'no-thing' (ibid: 242). Yet when the accident occurs *again* repeatedly, and these repetitions are grasped as a series, then an ordering or organization seems possible. A single accident is simple fate, a series of accidents starts to look like a programme.

Before the accident, then, is 'no-thing', just an undifferentiated and indifferent happening which escapes signification or meaning. A situation rather like the state of total entropy envisaged as limit point by the second law of thermodynamics. No exchange, no connextion, no relations, just in-difference. The very end of the system. What the actor-network approach does is to take the end as its beginning and run counter to all chronology, moving 'backwards' to the flowering and blooming of networks. It makes the most curious of folds, where 'after' comes 'before' the 'beginning'. To be 'after actor-network' is then to be moving simultaneously away from and toward the end of things. In other words, to be going in circles, circulating around the fold.

Now this curious circulation is often submerged in the sociology of translation. So long as what is being explained is the extension of an already ordered network by repetition, the $(n + 1)th$ trial of the Apollo simulator, say, then the relation between the order of the network and the disorder on which it subsists seems relatively unimportant. There seems little need to explain the origins of order *per se*. But the approach nevertheless requires that this undifferentiated space—as distinct from 'real' or 'social' space (see Latour, 1997)—be at all times immanent to the apparent order of the network. For unless it is posited that there is some aspect of actants and their activities which is always fundamentally 'unpresentable' to the network, then the whole program of translation starts either to look totalitarian or to collapse into a realist account of scientific discovery. And this in turn makes it difficult to articulate how either innovation or betrayal is to be understood, other than as possibilities that are already inscribed within the space of calculation established by the network. Thus we find a deep ambivalence in the way disorder, or the 'outside' of the network is conceived. It is at once the 'great general storehouse of nature', where actants stand 'before', as resources to be enrolled, and at the same time a space which is constantly withdrawing, a space which the network must perpetually go 'after'.

All of which begs the question still more: how can the network secure itself in its ambivalent relationship to disorder? How does ordering happen at all? Consider again the notion of repetition. What is repeated becomes a basic element, a rhythm which is discernible as such and not as noise. Rhythm marks out time through a simple ordering achieved by a spacing between elements. In so doing it becomes located in a rudimentary space. Something like a 'territory' is formed. The rhythm then serves as the basis for more complex operations: signals, speech, music. We are close here to what Deleuze and Guattari call a 'refrain':

> 'A child in the dark, gripped with fear, comforts himself by singing under his breath. He walks and halts to his song . . . The song is like a rough sketch of a calming and stabilizing . . . Now we are at home. But home did not preexist: it was necessary to draw a circle around that uncertain and fragile center, to organize a limited space . . . Finally, one opens the circle a crack, opens it all the way, lets someone in, calls someone, or else goes out oneself . . . These are not three successive moments in an evolution. They are three aspects of a single thing, the Refrain.'
> (1988:311–12)

A refrain is here a rhythmic series—the child's song—that creates by its very repetition a sense of the familiar, a sense of place. Refrains circulate around this 'uncertain and fragile center', creating a limited pocket of organization. For Deleuze and Guattari, refrains such as this are intrinsically territorial, they are the basic means by which ordered space is marked out from disorder: 'the refrain is essentially territorial, territorializing, or reterritorializing' (1988:300). As the territory becomes secured, so the refrain is 'picked up' or reiterated by others who come to occupy the same space, much like bird-songs, or, they argue, cultural myths. Each time the refrain is picked up, it is articulated anew, yet it still remains recognizably the same repetitive series.

What this allows us to say is that the crucial movement from the 'before' to the 'after' and back is itself a refrain. Repetition is what holds together networks. And this is more fundamental to how a network secures itself than Latour's (1987) discussion of inscription and metrology suggests. Because the refrain, like Serres' version of 'translation' is not entirely semiotic, it is as much figural as discursive. It is about the repetition of certain forms as much as the repetition of particular significations. It skirts the borderline between what cannot be presented and what can be made familiar. It allows us to say that networks do not have to be conceived as massive programmes of world-ordering (although they can indeed resemble this), but can also, like the territories and 'songlines' of the Australian Aboriginals, be *sung into being*.[5] And for the sociology of translation the parts of the song are divided equally between the modern and the classical.

Test two: force

The appropriation of the *perpetuum mobile* by Helmholtz to describe the universe as colossal 'storehouse' had a further implication. It made it plausible to consider a form of politics based purely upon the stewardship of energy. A kind of social energetics.[6] From the late nineteenth century onwards, a discourse around energy starts to appear in economics, involving the reading of all transactions as, at base, the consumption of energy by one party in order to satisfy needs (Rabinbach, 1990). The population becomes conceived of in terms of collective *arbeitskraft*, and this itself is understood in thermodynamic terms as occurring within a bounded system. Inside and outside. Within, transactions must be calculated and administered such that gradually depleting resources are directed toward the most productive ends. Without, the relations between the state and other nations must be aligned according to 'scientific principles' governing the importing and exporting of energy.

Steven D. Brown and Rose Capdevila

The sociology of translation has a not unrelated concern with force. This is what Lee and Brown call its 'Nietzschean' basis (1994), a vision of the world as riven by opposing forces in perpetual struggle with one another. As Law (1991) makes clear, this vision comes by way of Foucault's account of power. It is easy to imagine that the status of this account is purely theoretical, that it is a model of how power *might* function in terms of the ordering and administration of the populace by a microphysical distribution of power-relations. But after reading Helmholtz and his contemporaries it becomes clear that what Foucault offers instead is a *straightforward description* of the political objectives which become plausible when discourses around *arbeitskraft* blur the division between organism, state and nature. Thus the much debated extension of the symmetry principle in the actor-network approach (Latour, 1992; Collins and Yearley, 1992; Callon and Latour, 1992), which levels the difference between humans and non-humans, can be seen as an appendix to nineteenth century social energetics. There is only labour-power and that which is engaged in its conversion. There are only actants and trials of force.

Now the point here is not to say that it is a mistake to rely on a conception of force to underpin networks. On the contrary, it is difficult to see how *not* to involve such a notion. It surely stands with family resemblance to ideas of instinct (Freud), drive/pulsion (Lacan), libidinality (Lyotard), desire (Deleuze and Guattari), the outside (Blanchot), the untimely (Nietzsche) and flesh (Merleau-Ponty). Indeed the more one struggles against one of these terms, the more they tend to combine and endlessly proliferate: the machinic unconscious, desiring machines, the force from the outside, a mobile army of metaphors and so on . . .

At the nub of the problem is the concern to have something outside the network itself, something which the network in some way completes or at least works by way of. This 'something' will then serve as medium, origin and destination. Networks are assemblages of forces, they emerge from and dissolve into the play of power. Power is what makes them what they are, and what—eventually—is responsible for their collapse. If power is left out of the approach then networks come fully to resemble the *perpetuum mobile*, curious structures which function endlessly without apparent reference to the world around them. Yet one cannot make power immanent to the network without making the network appear to be the model of power itself, much in the same way that Lacan cannot make discourse the medium of the psyche without simultaneously making the unconscious itself discursive (thereby abolishing what may be distinctive about the unconscious in the first place: the observation belongs to Lyotard, 1989). This, we take it, is roughly the kind of objection to the actor-network approach made by both Star (1991) and Pels (1996). If all power is networked-power then what is cut away is any space for *differing* with networks.[7]

Once again, there is not a little of nineteenth century materialism in this problem. Helmholtz's physiology ignored the soul.[8] This for necessary reasons. The slightest hint of subjectivism would have allowed Kant's famous objection to a 'science of the psyche' to stand. Human nature had to become entirely reduced to material substance. Only energy could be allowed as a transcendent quality, everything else would in principle be submitted to empirical demonstration. Surprisingly enough, this does not automatically mean a crude reductionism. Helmholtz's contemporary, Gustav Fechner, managed to work up a modest dualism of mind/body by positing that mental processes followed the same laws of energy conservation as physiological processes, thus availing them to empirical inspection (as pursued by subsequent Wundtian psychology). Theodule Ribot likewise managed to account for 'consciousness' and 'will' as emergent states produced by the actions of the twin physiological processes of perception and motor actions. Will is the re-representation, the reiteration of nervous activity, which is itself a transformation of labour-power. Will is energy folded back on itself. From 'I think: Myself thinking', to 'I labour: Myself labouring'.

This surely gives us some hope that the otherwise intractable debate around 'agency' and actor-networks (see Callon and Law, 1995) may likewise yield some novel resolutions. Agency becomes an issue for the actor-network approach when the 'missing' space for differing networks is assumed to be that occupied by the human subject. Yet in making this assumption a whole range of very different questions regarding, for example, consciousness, directedness, concern, understanding, willing, and deciding are mixed up together. The pragmatic approach would be to peel each of these away in turn for consideration (such as with Law and Mol's 1996 treatment of 'decisions'; Rachel's 1994 elucidation of 'action/passion'; Munro's 1997 discussion of 'will'). From this list, it is the issue of 'willing' that attracts us most, since, after Nietzche, will is inextricably linked to the question of force and its deployment.

Here we can take some bearings from Hetherington's (1997) discussion of the *will-to-connect*. Hetherington is concerned with how material artefacts may exercise something which resembles agency.

But this proves to be a peculiar form of agency, one entirely devoid of intentionality. It is characterized by an ability to generate strange topological effects or 'foldings' upon the ordering of space. This happens when an artefact, by virtue of its apparent 'blankness'— that is, its apparent lack of overt significations—disrupts the space into which it is placed:

'The agency of things does not come from within but from the "inscriptions" generated by a heterogeneous network upon . . . [its] blankness' (Hetherington, 1997:214)

Quite so. It is not the meaning of the artefact, what it has to say, which disrupts the network. It is rather the *lack of meaning*, or to be more precise what the object fails to say, what it does not and cannot present to the network which is so disturbing. Because this forces the network to fold itself around the object in innumerable different ways in order to accommodate its blankness. This 'functional blankness' is what Hetherington calls the 'agency of things. It expresses a will-to-connect inasmuch as the blankness provokes or incites the effort to connect and order.

This provides us with a novel way of reading will, one which is entirely devoid of subjective intentions or desires. Functional blankness is what enables relations to be formed, alliances to be made. Not on the basis of what *is* said or done, but on the basis of what *might* be possible, what *may be* subsequently presented. For are not all alliances at base *promises* about some future event? Do not all relations begin with an orientation towards *what may be granted* to the partners at some unspecified point(s) to follow? And in the spirit of actor-network symmetry, what we affirm of objects we can scarcely deny of those objects we call human. They too perform their own peculiar functional blankness (this is what psychologists often call 'personality', that unpresentable quality marking individuality), incite and form relations on the basis of what they do not present, do not say. Indeed it is precisely when we do not 'show our hand', so to speak, when we fail to speak or act according to the programmatic directions of the networks in which we are embedded that our 'agency' shines through most self-evidently. Which, of course, provokes the will-to-connect to ever greater excesses.

Fortuitously, there is nothing particularly new (scarcely modern) about this formulation. Spinoza's *Ethics* proposes that finite beings are driven by *conatus*, or the 'endeavour to persist in being'. This endeavour is expressed by way of making connections, ordering bodies and ideas. By way, then, of a will-to-connect. It relies upon discovering 'common notions' between beings during their encounters. A common notion is an attribute which is shared by two or more beings. Common notions are not immediately obvious. A relation between beings is only possible following a striving to make a common attribute presentable. Successful presentations enable relations, which in turn are described by Spinoza as increases in power. This labour is then integral to the endeavour to persist in being.[9]

But there is something else upon which Spinoza insists. Conatus is the *essence of the finite being*. Essence? Again the word shocks. But what Spinoza describes here is very different to what we would understand by the usual sense of that term. By defining conatus as 'endeavour to persist in being', Spinoza repositions essence as the manner in which a finite thing goes on or carries forth in its attempts to form relations. Essence is a kind of trajectory followed by the finite thing. All attempts to define the identity of the thing must then be indexed to this movement. In other words, the identity of the thing undergoes constant revisions according to the kinds of common notions it presents, the relations it forms. Or to put it still another way, what the thing is can only be discerned by following the way it moves through encounters, relations and networks. Being as preposition (beyond, before, toward, *after*). We are back with the sociology of translation: follow the actants beyond, before, toward, *after*.

This set of connections between the actor-network approach, classical philosophy and nineteenth century social energetics can be summarized in the following way. The identity of an actant must be formally indexed to the attributes it can present when it enters into relations. Forming relations and inciting connections is the expression of a will-to-connect. This will-to-connect is the actant's way of endeavouring to persist in being. That is, in one sense at least, 'agency'. It is also what drives networks to incorporate and fold around actants. In themselves, though, actants are 'functionally blank'. Their every presentation masks a more fundamental lack of presentation or failure immediately to signify. The unfolding of presentations, accompanied by this withdrawing from presentation, constitutes the essence of the actant. Such an essence is effectively a trajectory, a movement through successive presentations and relations.

To this we need simply add that this trajectory is not entirely random. Its movement—the before and the after, the toward and beyond—unfolds a territory. Here is why the word 'territory' is so apposite: because the order and security it provides are not static phenomena, but mobile. Much like the space marked out by a territorial animal, territory constantly shifts as it is continually re-marked and re-presented in different ways. And much as these territorial creature can only extend their territories at great cost, so we might also note the sheer difficulty of sustaining this process of re-marking. Perhaps, as Latour (this volume), seems to be suggesting, the problem was always with the technical inflection given to the word 'network'. From technology to ethology, what different kinds of space are disclosed by this alternative choice of root metaphor?

Test three: time

The *perpetuum mobile* is unlimited. It simply goes on (and on). No change in kind ever occurs, it never loses its own force. It just *is*. This observation provokes a question about just how the limitations of force are handled in the sociology of translation. Does it seem to be without end (as with the *perpetuum mobile*)? Or is it destined to exhaust itself in a gradual running down of all things (as in thermodynamics)? We have already made much of the operation whereby chronology is reversed, making the 'end' (*after*) swap places with the 'source' (*before*). To this we should add the overwhelming sense of disappointment in the actor-network texts, as though in spite of the shifting of heaven and earth (after and before), the swim upstream against the rush to equilibrium and exhaustion is always doomed. Certainly many of the best stories in the field are of failures (the electric car, the TSR2 aircraft, Aramis). In each case a labour to carve out a project in grand historical time (the TSR2 clipped out of the Cold War, the electric car cut into the global energy crisis) fails to sustain itself. The return of equilibrium, of undifferentiated matter, appears to be the destiny of all networks.

Of course it might reasonably be objected that the attention to failures is the result of narrative conventions, the need to tell a well-rounded story (Law, 1997). But this merely complicates the problem. If the failed projects are, for whatever reason, difficulties in reversing chronology, making the 'before' swap places with the 'after', then what further disrupts the narrative is the particular rhythms of storytelling. We have here a bouquet of times: the march of universal time (toward entropy), the beat of local time (cut out against the universal structure) and the roll of narrative time (as it tries to re-present the entire operation).

The relationship of actor-networks to the limits of force lies in this complex folding up of rhythms (the universal, the local, narrative). Posing the question in this way takes us away from the issue of representation. We have no burning interest in whether or not the 'mini-grand narratives' presented to us by such classic ANT studies as the story of the Pasteurisation of France (Latour, 1988) or of the UK Cervical Screening Programme (CSP) (Singleton and Michael, 1993) are essentially correct, or historically accurate. What matters for us is the way that narrating a 'single movement through a chain of argument, a chain of translations' (Law, 1997) establishes a rhythmic pattern that somehow *expresses* the manoeuvres and translations made in the networks under discussion.

The term 'expression' is used to underscore the way that actor-network studies attempt to become part of the networks of which they speak. To be able to trace a network means becoming interior to its activities (Latour, 1997), or mobilizing one's own texts in its service. This reworks the representational issue into one of relations of proximity and distance, a topology that has little to do with commonly accepted metrics. It is an 'imaginary geography' (Hinchliffe, 1996), one that is 'neither social nor "real" space, but associations' (Latour, 1997), and as such is no longer the sole domain of geographers. It is rather the mathematician, one skilled at defining 'problem space', who serves as the model for traversing this complex space of associations (see Latour's 1997 remarks on 'Lorenz transformations', Law and Callon, 1992, on 'negotiation space' and Serres, 1995, on 'shortcuts').

Expression is also the term used by Spinoza to refer to the explication of the relations between finite things and substance (that is, questions of property and essence). To express something is, with Spinoza, to reiterate an order or series of elements (such as orderings of bodies or of ideas). But it also means to join with another, to participate in their productions. Good expression is judged not by its accuracy but by its efficacy. It does or allows for something 'more' than previously existed. 'Expression' enables us to say that the essence of a thing—its way of going on—depends upon the relations of reiteration and production in which it is engaged. Which means exploring how rhythms (universal, local, narrative) become jointly articulated.

Another example. The 32 years of manoeuvres by GPs, patients, cervical cells and speculums, is a different matter to the thirty two year history of the Government initiative which expresses itself as the CSP. Any attempt to express a network in a single narrative rhythm, even that which 'concertinas the time frame' (Singleton and Michael, 1993), necessarily expands the territory. It does this by picking up the refrain which passes between local time and universal time. Perhaps this picking up of the refrains is all the more resonant when narrative and local time jar, forming counterpoints or unsettling changes in tempo. One might imagine a whole series of results akin to the peculiar acoustic effects produced by the arrival in the same space of a peak and trough in two different signals. The emergence of a 'dead space' (still recognizable as some-thing) that would be the temporal equivalent of what Michael (1996) describes as 'ambivalence' in the translation process (*there are optical errors in time as there are in space*). And as the actor-network approach informs us, errors and failures can often be sources of explication.

The shift from representation to participation in the expansion of territories necessarily changes how the analysis can present itself. The analytic question becomes 'what is the nature of the territory that is extended by my repetition of the refrain?'. Or more simply: 'at what kind of place have I arrived?'. One may arrive earlier or later. Law and Callon (1992) take their place 'after' the cancellation of the TSR2. Singleton and Michael (1993) find themselves at a point 'before' the GPs betray the CSP. Later or earlier (*after or before*) have nothing to do with grand historical time. They are positions made possible by the articulation of local and narrative rhythms (it is in the seizing upon of 'aircraft 3' as a moment of closure that Law and Callon place themselves later, and in the assumption of a deep ambivalence in the efficacy of the CSP that Singleton and Michael claim a place 'before'). Before and after are expressions. It is not a pull towards getting the history right that matters, but instead the ethical practice involved in choosing to arrive too soon or too late.

The same observations hold regarding the relation of local time to universal time. Local time is a manifold—properly a whole series of times involving many different actants—cut out from the universal. A reversal, a swim upstream. But there are always a number of ways of making this move, this gash. The 'negotiation space' of the TSR2, for example, is established in moves to catch up with US 'weapons system' designs, but also (and in contradictory fashion) in an attempt to maintain flexible naval force. There is simultaneously the impetus to maintain the UK aerospace industry, which itself flies in the face of moves to trim defence budgets to meet with post-war economic realities. Traversing all is the political concern with the historical shift in the status of the UK from Imperial power to Western alliance partner in the Cold War. These moves can be read less as expressions of 'interests', but rather as attempts to *shape time*, to impose a chronology that does a work of securing against some fate (the collapse of the industry, lagging behind in defence capability, maintaining the misplaced swagger of faded colonial power). Small wonder that the TSR2 is a piece of technology much like the car described by Serres (1995), standing at the intersection (the crumpled edge) of several very different times. The question then becomes, how does something that is made up of a manifold of times go on? In what way (*before, after, through, beyond*) could it proceed?

The goings on of the TSR2, of the sociology of translation itself, are unclear on this point (*there are optical errors in time as there are in space*). What, though, is discernible is that an investigation of how time is folded as territory, the manifold network, confronts at every point the question of universal time. Just what is it that territory is carved out from? Do we have to retain a unitary sense of history, some overarching time frame within which all these manoeuvres occur. A reterritorialization on a classical question. Yet in returning to this question the associations between the sociology of translation and classical philosophy (Spinoza and Leibnitz), between the concepts of translations, networks and actants and those of thermodynamics and nineteenth century social energetics (Helmholtz and Carnot), are made all the more active. And the more we ourselves try to pick up this refrain that circulates through all these points, folding them up in a most peculiar of territories, the more likely it becomes that the whole approach will start to extend itself across and between these lines—a movement of deterritorialization 'through', 'beyond', 'away'.

Helmholtz reterritorialized

Part of the impetus to question at such length this phrase 'actor-network and after' is that the actor-network approach is no longer the property of the sociology of translation alone. Actor-network terms and concepts have worked their way into organization theory, geography, medical anthropology and psychology.[10] It is the extension into psychology that bears directly upon us. Michael (1996) has worked up a case for actor-network as a means of examining the construction of identity in non-dualist terms. Kendall and Michael (1997) deploy ANT as a vehicle to create a passage through something they call 'postmodern social psychology'. Brown (1998) uses notions of translation and hybridity to understand the space for subjectivity and what is left of 'the human' within electronic networks.

Now we don't doubt that these moves are worth making. We are even somewhat convinced by the argument that now (after the discursive turn yet before social psychology becomes an adjunct to ethnomethodology) is the right time for the study of actants and translation processes within psychology. What we remain less convinced by is the idea that Actor Network *Theory* can be unproblematically translated across disciplines without something going astray. For what interests us most in actor-network is the problems that are most often submerged: those of territories, questions of how time gets folded into strange configurations. We do not doubt that in the appropriation of actor-network by psychologists, these issues will entirely fall away, replaced by an adherence to a novel methodological program. To state it simply: we want the sociology of translation to take us somewhere beyond (or before, or after) contemporary social psychology. We fear it will simply become another tool for the promulgation of more of same.

We can indicate something of this by momentarily gathering together our test signals. A case in point drawn in terms of social movements.[11] Consider Northern Ireland. Here different movements or organisations have been constructed around a number of issues, one of which is that of republicanism/loyalism. Each spring in Northern Ireland heralds the beginning of the Marching Season in which loyalists parade along specific routes which often pass through republican areas. Unsurprisingly, this almost invariably becomes a locus of conflict. The obvious question: why do the marchers choose to march through areas where they are not wanted? Or, reversed, what do the residents find objectionable in the marchers? Answer: two networks (at least) are performed in the dispute over space. One seeks to de-problematize 'Northern Ireland' through constituting points of passage, thereby enrolling the very ground, the soil itself. In response the attempt to re-problematize, to open out the seeming irreversibility of the Unionist network.

Perhaps. But there is also a strong element of repetition, a recalling of something old that makes a territory. A repetition with a difference: a refrain. The Irish marchers are clearly not simply out for a stroll, the marching is a performance and, hence, a making-present of an event that occurred hundreds of years ago. The marching is an act of ordering, a picking up the refrain. It territorializes in a very specific way. Time is folded so that the past becomes in-tensionally relevant, and repeatedly so. But the marching does not only fold time into the past but also toward the future, a goings-on that is intimately related to how the political situation will progress. So it territorializes both the past and the future. What differentiates the refrain, however, is that it does not necessarily do this in any chronological order. All instances can become proximate to all others. The individual actant becomes enrolled in these specific territorializations through the work of the refrain that folds time so that what occurred last week (ie, the Good Friday agreement) may become more distant than that which occurred hundreds of years ago, of 21 years ago or might occur in ten years time.

We recall that Helmholtz—one of the founders of the discipline in which we both work—became interested in the physiology of the nervous system in a peculiar way. He made an issue of the fact that there is an interval between the perception of an act and a response. A gap in time. It was this 'missing time' that he thematized with his original experiments on nervous transmission in frogs, what would later extend into the network of nineteenth century psychophysics. A defining moment, as later commentators felt impelled to note. Not quite the same problem, but good enough to make a fold by its repetition: how is it, then, that time goes missing? Because this is precisely what is going on in our social movements example. A problem with time. A problem with how time gets folded, how the 'before' switches places with the 'after'. A problem to do with the disappearance of the now. A gap being opened up, and one in which political destinies contest. How do these spaces and gaps appear in our metrics? Why are there as many optical errors in time as there are in space?

We don't know whether to say that Helmholtz and the *perpetuum mobile* circulate through (before, after) actor-network or that the sociology of translation enables us to pass through Helmholtz. We suspect that the issue is not decisive. Actor-network is itself a manifold, and one of the 'goings-on' folded up within it opens up a means for us to reterritorialize contemporary psychology to a place that is *before* the discipline became locked into its erroneous obsession with subjectivity and objectivity. A time when there *was no subject of psychology*. Simply a bundle of timings all crumpled up to form an object of study. A problem with missing time. It is this goings-on that leads us somewhere.

Acknowledgements

Revisions to this paper have benefited from encouragement and critique provided by Bob Cooper, Nick Lee and Annemarie Mol. To them, our thanks.

Notes

1 The same problem arises with the use of the term 'drift' in the work of Jean-François Lyotard, who is an influence on some of the more recent actor-network writing such as Law, 1996; Law and Benschop, 1997. On this see Bennington, 1991.
2 A move which is prefigured by Heidegger's account of Ge-stell (enframing or emplacement) in *The Question Concerning Technology* (Heidegger, 1977). This comparison is drawn at greater length by Lee and Brown, 1994; Brown and Lightfoot, 1998 and also by Cooper, 1993.
3 This essay originally appears in the volume by Serres which Callon cites as the source of the term 'translation' (*Hermes III: La Traduction*).
4 Our use of the difference between 'discourse' and 'figure' is itself derived from Lyotard, 1988; 1989.
5 Probably the most accessible account of 'Songlines' is that provided by Bruce Chatwin's travelogue of the same name (1987). Bill Readings (1992) provides valuable related discussion of translation and incommensurability as it relates to Aboriginal culture.
6 Rabinbach (1990) argues convincingly that this discourse of energy runs throughout Marx's texts and is particular overt in Engel's 'scientific Marxism'.
7 *Differing* rather than *opposing*, since this latter suggests, in a dialectical fashion, a commensurate yet opposed network-force.
8 The following examples are described in more detail by Rabinbach, 1992 and Danziger, 1990.
9 A more detailed reading of Spinoza, by way of Deleuze, is performed by Brown and Stenner, in press.
10 A list of relevant examples would take too much space—the actor-network resource at *http://www.keele.ac.uk/depts/stt/home.htm* provides ample evidence.
11 The example is drawn from a more substantive body of ongoing research by Capdevila.

References

Bennington, G. (1988), *Lyotard: Writing the Event*. Manchester: Manchester University Press.
Brown, S.D. (1998), 'Electronic Networks and Subjectivity', in A. Gordo-Lopez and I. Parker (eds), *Cyberpsychology*. London: Macmillan.
Brown, S.D. and Lightfoot, G. (1998), 'Insistent Emplacement: Heidegger on the Technologies of Informing', *Information Technology & People*.
Brown, S.D. and Stenner, P. (in press), 'Being Affected: Spinoza and the Psychology of Emotion', *World Psychology*.
Callon, M. (1980), 'Struggles and Negotiations to Define What is Problematic and What is Not: The Socio-Logic of Translation', in K.D. Knorr, R. Krohn and R. Whitley (eds), *The Social Process of Scientific Investigation: Sociology of Sciences, Vol IV*. Dordrecht: D. Reidel.
Callon, M. (1986), 'Some Elements of a Sociology of Translation: Domestification of the Scallops and Fishermen of St. Brieuc Bay', in J. Law (ed.), *Power, Action, Belief: A New Sociology of Knowledge?* London: Routledge and Kegan Paul.

Callon, M. and Latour, B. (1992), 'Don't Throw the Baby out with the Bath School! A Reply to Collins and Yearley', in A. Pickering (ed.), *Science as Practice and Culture*. Chicago: University of Chicago Press.
Callon, M. and Law, J. (1995), 'Agency and the Hybrid Collectif', *The South Atlantic Quarterly* 94(2): 481–507.
Callon, M., Law, J. and Rip, A. (eds) (1986), *Mapping the Dynamics of Science and Technology: Sociology of Science in the Real World*. London: Macmillan.
Collins, H. and Yearley, S. (1992), 'Epistemological Chicken', in A. Pickering (ed.), *Science as Practice and Culture*. Chicago: University of Chicago Press.
Cooper, R. (1993), 'Technologies of Representation', in P. Ahonen (ed.), *Tracing the Semiotic Boundaries of Politics*. Berlin: Mouton de Gruyter.
Cooper, R. and Law, J. (1995), 'Organization: Distal and Proximal Views', in S. Bacharach, P. Gagliardi and B. Mundell (eds), *Research in the Sociology of Organizations: Studies of Organizations With European Tradition* 13: 237–74.
Danziger, K. (1990), *Constructing the Subject: Historical Origins of Psychological Research*. Cambridge: Cambridge University Press.
Deleuze, G. and Guattari, F. (1984), *Anti-Oedipus: Capitalism and Schizophrenia*, trans. R. Hurley, M. Seem and H.R. Lane. London: The Athlone Press.
Deleuze, G. and Guattari, F. (1988), *A Thousand Plateaus: Capitalism and Schizophrenia*, trans. B. Massumi. London: The Athlone Press.
Helmholtz, H. (1892), *Popular Lectures on Scientific Subjects*. London: Longmans, Green and Co.
Hetherington, K. (1997), 'Museum Topology and the Will to Connect', *Journal of Material Culture* 2(2): 199–218.
Hinchliffe, S. (1996), 'Technology, Power and Space: The Means and Ends of Geographies of Technologies', *Environment and Planning D: Society and Space* 14: 659–82.
Jacob, F. (1973), *The Logic of Life: A History of Heredity*, trans. B.E. Spillman. Harmondsworth: Penguin.
Kendall, G. and Michael, M. (1997), 'Politicizing the Politics of Postmodern Social Psychology', *Theory and Psychology* 7(1): 7–29.
Latour, B. (1987), *Science in Action: How to Follow Scientists and Engineers Through Society*. Cambridge, Mass.: Harvard University Press.
Latour, B. (1988), *The Pasteurization of France* followed by *Irreductions*. (A. Sheridan and J. Law, Trans) Cambridge, Mass.: Harvard University Press.
Latour, B. (1992), 'Where are the Missing Masses? A Sociology of a Few Mundane Artifacts', in W.E. Bijker and J. Law (eds), *Shaping Technology/Building Society: Studies in Sociotechnical Change*. Cambridge, Mass.: The MIT Press.
Law, J. (1991), 'Power, Discretion and Strategy', in J. Law (ed.), *A Sociology of Monsters: Essays on Power, Technology and Domination*. London: Routledge.
Law, J. (1994), *Organising Modernity*. Blackwell: Oxford.
Law, J. (1996), 'Organizing Accountabilities: Ontology and the Mode of Accounting', in R. Munro and J. Kouritsen (eds), *Accountability: Power, Ethos and the Technologies of Managing*. London: Thomson Business Press.
Law, J. (1997), 'Traduction/Trahison: Notes on ANT', Internet document available at http://www.keele.ac.uk/depts/stt/home.htm
Law, J. and Callon, M. (1992), 'The Life and Death of an Aircraft: A Network Analysis of Technical Change', in W.E. Bijker and J. Law (eds), *Shaping Technology/Building Society: Studies in Sociotechnical Change*. Cambridge, Mass.: The MIT Press.

Law, J. and Benschop, R. (1997), 'Resisting Pictures: Representation, Distribution and Ontological Politics', in K. Hetherington and R. Munro (eds), *Ideas of Difference: Social Spaces and the Labour of Division*. Oxford: Blackwell.
Lee, N. and Brown, S.D. (1994), 'Otherness and the Actor Network: The Undiscovered Continent', *American Behavioral Scientist*, 37(6): 772–790.
Liebnitz, G.W. [1714] (1973), 'Monadology', in *Philosophical Writings*. London: J.M. Dent.
Lyotard, J-F. (1988), *The Differend: Phrases in Dispute*, trans. G. Van Den Abbeele. Manchester: Manchester University Press.
Lyotard, J-F. (1989), *Discourse, Figure*. Cambridge: Cambridge University Press.
Mayr, O. (1986), *Autonomy, Liberty and Automatic Machinery in Early Modern Europe*. Baltimore: Johns Hopkins.
Michael, M. (1996), *Constructing Identities: The Social, the Nonhuman and Change*. London: Sage.
Munro, R. (1997), 'Power, Conduct and Accountability: Re-Distributing Discretion and the New Technologies of Managing', Proceedings, 5th Interdisciplinary Perspectives on Accounting Conference, Manchester: Manchester University.
Pels, D. (1996), 'The politics of symmetry', *Social Studies of Science* 26(2): 277–304.
Proust, M. [1925] (1981), 'The Fugitive', in *Remembrance of Things Past*, Vol. 3. Harmondsworth: Penguin.
Rabinbach, A. (1990), *The Human Motor: Energy, Fatigue and the Origins of Modernity*. Berkeley: University of California Press.
Rabinbach, A. (1992), 'Neurasthenia and modernity', in J. Crary and S. Kwinter (eds), *Zone 6: Incorporations*. New York: Zone.
Rachel, J. (1994), 'Acting and passing, actants and passants, action and passion', *American Behavioral Scientist* 37(6): 809–823.
Serres, M. (1982), 'Turner Translates Carnot', in J.V. Harari and D.F. Bell (eds), *Hermes: Literature, Science, Philosophy*. Baltimore: Johns Hopkins.
Serres, M. with Latour, B. (1995), *Conversations on science, culture and time*, trans. R. Lapidus. Ann Arbor: University of Michigan Press.
Singleton, V. and Michael, M. (1993), 'Actor-Networks and Ambivalence: General Practitioners in the UK Cervical Screening Programme', *Social Studies of Science* 23: 227–264.
Spinoza, B. [1677] (1993), *Ethics* trans. A. Boyle and G.H.R. Parkinson. London: J.M. Dent.
Star, S.L. (1991), 'Power, Technologies and the Phenomenology of Conventions: On Being Allergic to Onions', in J. Law (ed.), *A Sociology of Monsters: Essays on Power, Technology and Domination*. London: Routledge.
Vonnegut, K. (1990), *Hocus Pocus*. New York: Berkley Books.
Wiener, N. (1932), 'Back to Leibnitz! Physics Reoccupies an Abandoned Position', *The Technology Review* 34: 201–25.

From Blindness to blindness: museums, heterogeneity and the subject

Kevin Hetherington

Abstract

This chapter critically engages with the idea of heterogeneity that has been important to actor-network theory. By looking at the history of the museum and of the kind of art associated with it at different points in time, the chapter shows how what we understand as heterogeneity has changed over time. The history of the ordering and displaying role of the museum reveals different responses to an idea of heterogeneity and to consequential conceptualizations not only of vision and agency but also of subject-object relations. The idea of heterogeneity is caught up with these changing relations between subject and object and with the spatial configuration through which they are constituted. The museum is an important historical site through which such changing relations and changing understandings of heterogeneity can be analysed.

Subjects, objects and the history of heterogeneity

In the case of both art galleries and object museums, the principle conserving and displaying roles of the museum both involve the arrangement and ordering of material heterogeneity. In attempting to achieve this, museums establish specific relations between viewing subjects and viewed objects. The museum has always been a distinctly visual space but it would be wrong to assume that the museum has historically constituted a space for seeing that has remained unchanged. What the museum tries to achieve is some form of homogeneous order. Such homogeneity may be organized through classificatory, aesthetic, narrative, and auratic means. In effect, the museum display performs some kind of a homogeneous relation between things on display through an ordering of material elements and their semiotic effects. How it has tried to achieve that order has changed over time, the main reason being that what we think of as 'heterogeneity' has changed. In looking at the history of the museum we see not only its changing mode of ordering the heterogeneous but also changing conceptualizations of heterogeneity as well.

We can think of the contemporary museum as an exhibitionary space in which heterogeneous effects and uncertainty are subject to controlling and ordering processes. In other words, heterogeneity should not be there. However, this is only the contemporary situation that museums find themselves in. In the past their role and their relation to the effects of heterogeneity were different. Taking elements of actor-network theory (ANT) out of the laboratory and putting them in the museum, then, might allow us a clear and unique perspective on the museum, not least on the relationship between heterogeneity and its agentic performance within such a network that constitutes the spaces that we call a museum (see Law, 1992: 1997; Law and Benschop, 1997). Seen through the lens of the museum as it has developed over time, however, we begin to realize that the importance of the idea of heterogeneity for ANT is problematic because we see that 'heterogeneity' is historically constituted and time has been something of a blind spot for ANT with its emphasis on spatial relationships and distributions such as in the metaphor of the network.

This chapter is, therefore, about the 'history' of material heterogeneity. It is about the complex and diverse relationships of things within which subjectivity and objectivity are constituted. It is told, in the main, through a story of the development of the spaces of the museum (and of the art objects associated with them) and their role in the constitution of the subject as a *point of view* associated with different ways of conceptualizing the externality of the object to the subject (see Mol and Law, 1994; Law and Benschop, 1997). It is about how the museum acts as an obligatory point of passage (Latour, 1987; 1988) for the constitution of the subject as a point of view in the West from the time of the Renaissance to the present. Heterogeneity is itself something heterogeneous (in the modern usage of this concept) and its effects in terms of subject-object relations will be seen to have varied at different point in time as well as space (see Foucault, 1989). In that sense this account of the development of the museum is also about the development of what we understand by the term heterogeneity and that has implications for actor-network theory.

Museums have become all about seeing clearly; of looking at

objects on display and being able to interpret them effectively with the help of the spatial regime and order of the museum. That was not always the case. Such a museum is a product of modernity, and so too is the homogeneous vision it tries to create. The 'history' of the museum is one that moves through a number of epistemic situations over a period of some six hundred years, from the princely palaces of the northern Italian Renaissance to the seventeenth century classical spaces of the cabinets of curiosity, to the modern, Kantian disciplinary museum. We are now, perhaps, beginning to see the emergence of new kinds of museum space, but it is too soon to tell for certain. This (effective) history of the museum is also a history of heterogeneity and the way that relations between subjects and objects are constituted (see Hooper-Greenhill, 1992; Bennett, 1995). By looking at the relationship that the museum has had with subject-object relations we see not only a social process in operation but at the level of metaphor, a space constituted by shifting patterns of redundancy and flux.

The history of the museum, then, has always been in some way defined by the relationship between subjects and objects. It constructs, at different moments, a 'point of view' through the constitution and arrangement of material 'heterogeneity' and in relation to it, the viewing subject. But this material heterogeneity is not something fixed. What counts as a subject and an object and the relationship between them is the effect of the field of possibilities and type of time-space that they occupy. I want to suggest in this chapter that what counted as heterogeneity for the Medici, for Francis Bacon and for Immanuel Kant and their (museum) interpreters was not the same thing and what happens to the museum in this century after Duchamp's intervention and his introduction of a new relation of heterogeneity remains to be seen.

What we can say now, however, is that the museum is a space that performs a geometry of seeing and ordering, associated with issues of materials, spaces, times and subjects. Rather than try to define the museum as a particular type of social space, I see it in more abstract terms as a space whose topology will alter within specific temporal, epistemological, cultural and material contexts. ANT can help us understand this—providing we first question its somewhat under-analysed use of the concept of heterogeneity. The museum, however, is not a space that exists in isolation. It can be compared with others at particular moments to other spatial arrangements that also have an exhibitionary role (see Altick, 1978; Markus, 1993; Bennett, 1995). The history of heterogeneity and the constitution of the subject in relation to that heterogeneity can be seen through the museum and the artistic and cultural modes of representation associated with the material objects that were put on display in those museums.

From Blindness to blindness. The shift from upper to lower case indicated in the title of this chapter is significant. The more we think we see in totality the less that is actually before our eyes. To see at all is to lose sight of the detail. The blind do not see, but they have the capacity of touch that can be highly sensitive to local detail, more so often that the eye. Touch is halting and cautious, it pauses as it goes on its way and opens up embodied forms of perception and knowledge (see Appelbaum, 1995). In moving in a linear way from the fifteenth century to the present what we see is not linearity and ordered Euclidean space but non-linear flows, jumps and starts. There is nothing linear and inevitable in moving from the eye to the hand. That is where we shall end up and that has implications for how we think about heterogeneity in the future.

The Medici and the display of the subject

The history of the museum is a history of the eye and how it sees (on the history of the gaze see Bryson, 1983). If we begin with the Renaissance and its invention of linear perspective and compare this with the types of object collections that emerged at that time (in the fifteenth century in particular) we begin to see something of the relationship between subjects and objects and the way that heterogeneity was constituted at that time.

Perspectival space and the development of linear perspective during the Renaissance, as Panofsky went to some length to point out, is quite different from perceived space and what is actually seen by the eye (1997: 27–36). We do not see with the eye in a linear way but in curves, largely because the retina is a curved surface. Linear perspective is a mathematical abstraction that simplifies perceived space and represents it without all of the actual distortions. It performs a certain kind of ordering that allows things to be seen clearly as if they were a representation of three dimensional reality as seen with the eye. A painting, a two dimensional surface, becomes the medium through which this three dimensional space is depicted. Above all, linear perspective interpellates the viewer as subject through a relation with the picture while leaving the actual embodied experience of viewing outside and apart (see Bryson, 1983; Krauss, 1994; Law and Benschop, 1997). The viewing subject becomes a disembodied monocular eye in which a geometrical relationship with the picture-object is established.

The topology of linear perspective is well known, indeed its mathematical principles were set down by Alberti as a guide to painters during the time of its invention. It consists in lining up orthogonals in a picture so that they all come together at one point, the vanishing point. Extending these lines outwards to the extent of the picture and then drawing a symmetrical mirror image of the lines extending outside the picture so that they too come together at another point, creates a viewing point that has a direct geometrical relationship with the vanishing point within the picture. Linear perspective locates the artist/viewer outside of the picture at the viewing point but looking it on it as if they were part of the scene and as if what they were seeing were the three dimensional relationship that would be seen with the eye. A plane is created between the lines that 'begin' in the vanishing point and in the viewing point. That plane where both sets of line are at their greatest extent apart is known as the picture plane and corresponds with the painted surface of the picture. This way of depicting in paint creates a spatial arrangement in which the picture plane acts like a window through which a viewing subject is able to see a three dimensional world of objects that come to be represented and ordered in a particular knowable geometry on a two-dimensional surface.

The invention of linear perspective occurred around a time at which the knowledge of classical antiquity had begun to receive a revival of interest. Ideas about space, such as those of Euclid and Vitruvius were a mainstay of Renaissance ideas about space, geometry and architecture (see Rykwert, 1980; Kruft, 1994). Above all, though, linear perspective relied on developments in mathematics, notably through an interest in the idea of infinity and its representation in the number zero (see Rotman, 1993). These developments had implications not only for painting and how people saw but also for their understanding of humans as subjects.

Originally a Hindu concept, zero found its way to Renaissance Europe by that well travelled route through the transmission of ideas to the west from the Muslim world. Its effect was to change the semiotics of number and their ordering as signs. As Rotman suggests, the most significant feature of the number zero is that it signifies the *presence* of nothing as non-presence (1993:4). By relating the presence of nothing to the ordering of integers (1,2,3,4 . . .)

zero is not only just another sign for a number in a sequence, 0, but a meta-sign for the ordering of numbers. As Rotman suggests,

> It is this double aspect of zero, as a sign inside the number system and as a meta-sign, a sign-about-signs outside it, that has allowed zero to serve as the site of an ambiguity between an empty character (who covert mysterious quality survives in the connection between 'cyphers' and secret code), and a character of emptiness, a symbol that signifies nothing. (1993:13)

Zero brings infinity to a point, a point represented as 0, in the same way that linear perspective brings infinity to a point in the vanishing point and then mirrors this in the viewing point within the picture-subject relation. The subject, a position that is interpellated by linear perspective at the viewing point, acts, as Rotman has argued, in the same way as the number zero (1993:19). The disembodied eye in linear perspective is located at the nowhere point of infinity. It too has this character of being both sign and meta-sign, part of the picture as well as that which stands outside the picture and gives it meaning. The construction of the viewing subject in linear perspective is one that is located as a point that represents nowhere as infinity. The subject (rather than God), perhaps for the first time, stands outside and separate from the material world, able to look in on it from this privileged position of infinity that formerly would have only been occupied by God. As Bryson suggests,

> The vanishing point is the anchor of a system which *incarnates* the viewer, renders him tangible and corporeal, a measurable, and above all a visible object in a world of absolute visibility. (1983:106)

This in turn echoes Panofsky's observations on the objectifying effects of linear perspective on the subject,

> Through this peculiar carrying over of artistic objectivity into the domain of the phenomenal, perspective seals off religious art from the realm of the magical, where the work of art itself works the miracle, and from the realm of the dogmatic and symbolic, where the work bears witness to, or foretells, the miraculous. But then it opens into something entirely new: the realm of the visionary, where the miraculous becomes a direct experience of the beholder, in that the supernatural events in a sense erupt into his own, apparently natural, visual space and so permit him really to 'internalise' their supernaturalness. (Panofsky, 1997:72)

Linear perspective establishes a unique relationship between the human subject as subject and the object world as something separate that is seen as if through a window. The subject, as Panofsky points out, is objectified (1997:66). *Ob-ject*, to throw out (see Serres, 1991). The subject is thrown out of the picture towards the point of infinity. Perspective constitutes 'the miraculous', the subject of many Renaissance paintings, as a world of objects separate from the objectified viewing subject and allows the subject, rather than God, the privileged role of being able to give that 'heterogeneity' a sense of order, just like zero does to the numbers one to nine. The subject, a Christian subject, is not simply a part of God's multiplicitous and miraculous world but a secular objectivized subject apart who can look in on that world, not from on high perhaps, but at least from a privileged position outside of the framing of things. All the same, the subject and object remain connected to one another, in some respects they are mirror images of each other connected through the picture plane.

Linear perspective establishes a spatiality and a materiality for viewing and in doing so creates a space for the subject to come into being. The way in which this subject sees, the constitution of its monocular gaze, and the relationship that this has with the world of things is something that we can look at in the case of the princely collection. There are distinct parallels between the operationalization of seeing in linear perspective and in the princely 'museum' collections of the Medici. It is important to note at this point, however, that when we talk about the gaze of the Renaissance subject this should not be interpreted through twentieth century ideas about the gaze put forward by Sartre, Lacan, Foucault and others. If we are to avoid essentializing the gaze we must recognize that it is constituted within a distinct epistemic field of possibilities and that that field of possibilities has a good deal to do with the way that the subject is understood in relation to the material world of objects and how they come to be represented. In other words, the character of the gaze and the character of what we now understand as heterogeneity have a direct relationship with one another. The modern gaze identified by writers such as Foucault is a part of this account but it is not to be found here in the fifteenth century 'museum' nor does that museum have a modern conception of heterogeneity.[1] A relationship between the Renaissance subject, material 'heterogeneity' and modes of ordering can be seen, therefore, in the 'museum' collections of the time. They served as obligatory points of passage in which the subject constituted by linear perspective was performed.

The Renaissance gaze was one that was constituted through a way of looking at the past through first hand observation (see Hooper-Greenhill, 1992:32ff). The discovering and re-evaluation of classical Greece and Rome from the fourteenth century led to a new way of seeing that had parallels with the subject position constituted by linear perspective and the mathematics of zero and infinity. Princes, scholars and merchants began to establish collections of artefacts, many of them from earlier classical times, and to display them in their ornate houses. The objects were located in a private space. They were only made visible to invited guests, other nobles, scholars and artists in particular. All the same, a sense that such a collection was an act of public patronage prevailed at the time.

Those objects were thought to be signs that could be deciphered and read as part of a wider cosmology. Their diversity did not represent heterogeneity in the sense of anomaly and difference but hidden and secret forms of connection that linked them as a totality. That cosmology was itself performed through distinct modes of ordering. In what Hooper-Greenhill has described as the 'calculating and measuring look' of the Renaissance subject, we find an example of the Renaissance gaze (1992:43). She argues, following Foucault (1989), that the key features of the Renaissance episteme were a belief in correspondences between things that could be understood through relationships of similitude that were themselves informed by: a belief in the animate nature of the universe; powers of the supernatural; a quickening sense of the present; a sense of history in which the present could be compared with the (classical) past and the constitution of a calculating and evaluative gaze (1992: 23–46).

In other words, the Renaissance outlook does not have a strong sense of the heterogeneous as something different, disordered or Other (Bataille, 1985). Order is established by the gaze of the subject through forms of similitude: *convenientia*; *aemulatio*; *analogy* and *sympathy* (see Foucault, 1989:17–25; Hooper-Greenhill, 1992:14). The Renaissance world is a world of resemblances and circular relationships in which a diverse array of things is brought together rather than separated out and classified as distinct. In Levi-Strauss's terms, in a world where similitude is part of a magical cosmology, the bricolage of things is brought together as heterogeneous and ordered through their (secret or hidden) correspondence into the form of an homology (1966). There is no sense at this time of heterogeneity as a form of difference. Everything is similitude and that similitude is represented through a *hidden mimesis*, often in allegorical form, through the spaces of paintings based on the principles of linear perspective as well as in the 'museum' collections of the great and wealthy.

There is no narrative or fixity of meaning in the Renaissance collections. They perform, as Hooper-Greenhill argues, similitude and the ability to marshall abundance as a form of merchant power and patronage. Begun as treasure houses in which the value of rare items could be realized in money terms when needed, these collections became conspicuous displays of wealth, taste and status. They came to reflect the glory of the prince who owned the collection. Filled with objects from classical antiquity, carved gems and other items inscribed with magical powers, the order of contemporary paintings and art objects was not established through any form of classification but through correspondence and through these principles of similitude. Chains of resemblance, an endless and multiple ordering was constituted in the space of these collections (Hooper-Greenhill, 1992). What allowed this to happen and what made similitude meaningful as a mode of ordering was the objectivized subject (of the prince and later the connoisseur, artist and scholar) who stood outside as an appreciative eye located at the point of infinity. The Renaissance collection is constituted as a deictic space in which the subjects can say that they see the multiplicity of their power and influence in their multiplicitous collection. In its totality it resembles the totality and unity of the prince as subject.

The Renaissance gaze identifies directly with the principle that we would now describe as heterogeneity. It does not seek to produce a classificatory representation of heterogeneity or to banish it from sight but rather uses it as a way of understanding the subject through the multiplicity of things as signs. Sign and meta-sign, the subject as zero, the Medici is mediated through the similitude of signs. As Rotman puts it,

> In short, where medieval painted images make God's invisible prior world manifest through 'natural' icons, Renaissance images represent an anterior visual world through a convention of signs, artificially produced by a humanly imposed system of perspective. (1993:22)

Just as the artist comes to be represented as a subject by the vanishing point, so too the prince comes to be represented in the same way by his collection. In actor-network terms the heterogeneous materiality of a network, in this case the collection of artefacts, the artists who produced them, the scholars who come to study them, the

Kevin Hetherington

buildings in which the collection is housed, is embodied in the Prince who is mirrored by his collection. And yet they were not seen as heterogeneous in the way that ANT uses this term. It relies on a more recent conceptualization of heterogeneity and is in danger, because of its a-historicism, of essentializing it. The prince acts as a network of artefacts and the semiotics that they generate and that is seen as entirely natural. The idea of a distinct subject position is discernible but not in the modern sense because it corresponds, is identical with, the 'heterogeneous' material world. There can be no sense of the heterogeneous as difference here because there is a correspondence between all things and between subjects and objects. Like the number zero and the vanishing point, the Prince occupies the omnipotent (meta-signifying) point of infinity and heterogeneity is simply the picture plane through which this is projected back from the world of things.

The classifying table and the cabinet of curiosities

While the word heterogeneity and its derivations has its origins in medieval Latin, it is only from the seventeenth century that it begins to be used to signify difference, incongruous relations and anomaly.[2] Such an idea corresponds with the emergence of the idea that the subject is separate from the material object and this can be seen in the seventeenth century museum as well as in the art of that period. We move on then two centuries to the middle of the seventeenth century, to what Foucault has called the classical age (1989) or what might more conventionally be described as the Baroque, and witness a direct challenge to linear perspective by Dutch art, and also witness the emergence of a new type of museum in Europe—the cabinet of curiosities (see Alpers, 1983; Bryson, 1983; Impey and McGreggor, 1985; Saumarez Smith, 1989; Hooper-Greenhill, 1992; Law and Benschop, 1997). Both Dutch art and the 'cabinets of curiosity' have something in common, they are both engaged in the constitution of heterogeneity as a world of objects separate and distinct from the viewing subject. The 'heterogeneous' world is identifiable with the position of the objectivized subject during the Renaissance and that identification is organized through similitude into an homology between a viewing subject and a multifarious object world. If the classical age can be said to be about anything it is, as Foucault has shown, about the move away from ways of knowing through similitude to ways of knowing through mathesis and representation (1989). While we might take issue with the speed and degree of completion of this epistemic shift, representation as a way of knowing, as a form of gaze, comes to be constituted through the separation of the subject from the world and the development of an idea of material heterogeneity as something Other to that subject. The work of Francis Bacon perhaps best exemplifies this sense of the discovery of heterogeneity as something that cannot be absorbed by the order of things (1974). It comes into being, rather, in their ordering in non-homologous ways,

> For I find no sufficient or competent collection of the works of nature which have a digression and deflexion from the ordinary course of generations, productions, and motions; whether they be singularities of place and region, or the strange events of time and chance, or the effects of yet unknown proprieties, or the instances of exception to general kinds. It is true, I find a number of books of fabulous experiments and secrets, and frivolous impostures for pleasure and strangeness; but a substantial and severe collection of the heteroclites of irregulars of nature, well examined and described, I find not: specially not with due rejection of fables and popular errors. For as things now are, if an untruth in nature be once on foot, what by reason of the neglect of examination, and countenance of antiquity, and what by reason of the use of the opinion in similitudes and ornaments of speech, it is never called down. (Bacon, 1974:69)

Here, in Bacon's *The Advancement of Learning*, we find a new conception of heterogeneity. Only by understanding the anomalous and monstrous, the heteroclites, he argues, will we be able to discern the true natural history of the world. The heteroclite, as Foucault points out, is a major concern of the scientific community in the classical age of which Bacon was a prominent and influential member (1989). Heteroclites also fascinated the 'museum' collectors of the time, such as Elias Ashmole, and oddities and exotic items were a prominent part of their collections. It was through a recognition of the anomalous and freakish that the space of knowing constituted by the classical age, the two dimensional classificatory table, came into being. The grammar of nature as a series of connected resemblances was seen to be broken by the heteroclite, and that grammar was revealed as a mode of ordering in its breach (Foucault, 1989: xvii–xviii). Heterogeneity can no longer disappear into similitude and secret connection as it was during the Renaissance, instead it has to be laid out on a table and scrutinised by a subject who is not heterogeneous nor linked with the world of things. Such scrutiny presupposes a different sort of gaze and indeed a different sort of subject doing the gazing.

During the Renaissance we might say that the subject, the one able to occupy the viewing point was synonymous with the 'heterogeneity' of infinity. One saw the 'heterogeneity' of God in the picture plane from a privileged and yet still attached vantage point. With Bacon, as indeed with artists like Velasquez and Vermeer who were his contemporaries (Alpers, 1983) and with those scientific collectors who followed Bacon's lead in establishing classificatory 'museum' spaces in which to observe the heteroclites (Hooper-Greenhill, 1992), heterogeneity became something that was no longer synonymous with the eye but something separate that was seen by the eye and indeed helped to constitute that eye as distinct. The infinite variety of the world was laid out on a table to be viewed and classified by the viewer in the hope of attaining the position of God by viewing that world as a picture (see Heidegger, 1977).

For Foucault, the classical eye seeks to be able to speak and in speaking to be able to describe all that is in the world in a single table (on seeing and saying see Deleuze, 1988). Describing consists of a classificatory mode of ordering heterogeneity (1989). If, during the Renaissance, the subject, represented through linear perspective in painting, and the Medici collection, remained an object of the world, in the paintings of the Dutch artists of the seventeenth century, the subject ceases to be seen as objectivized but as a subject separate from the world who sees it from outside but not from a fixed point defined by the geometry of the object-painting (see Bryson, 1983; Alpers, 1983; Rotman, 1993).

Separating the world as an heterogeneous material stratum from the subject, locates that subject outside of the picture altogether. The viewing subject is no longer constituted through Euclidean geometrical relations with the picture/collection but through a more complex and fluid topology (see Law and Benschop, 1997). Foucault's well known discussion of Velasquez's *Las Meninas* tells us this (1989). The subject is not established in a viewing point as in linear perspective, and what is pictured is not to be understood through similitude but through forms of representation. What this picture shows, and indeed is also shown in much of seventeenth century Dutch art (see Alpers, 1983; Bryson, 1983), is the constitution of the subject at this time as something separate from and defined in relation to the heterogeneity of the world. The gaze of the subject is separate from the picture. Such a subject looks in from outside, into

From Blindness to blindness

a picture that is laid out as a spectacle for the gaze of the detached subject. Whereas the relationship between the subject and object in linear perspective is a Euclidean one that allows for nothing but connection and correspondence, in the art of the seventeenth century, Vermeer as much as Velasquez (see Alpers, 1983; Bryson, 1993), the relationship between subject and object is topologically more complex, even crumpled and folded (see Law and Benschop, 1997). Rather than being defined as a subject through a correspondence with the heterogeneity of the world in all its infinity, now the subject becomes irrevocably separate from the object and the array of objects come to be seen as heterogeneous and apart and in need of classification. One can stand in a multitude of different places and look in on a picture that has no distinct vanishing point. The assertion of the picture plane as an opaque surface for representing the multiplicity of the world allows for many particular subject positions but also a positioning of the subject as something apart from the world.

Such was also the case in the museums of the time. Many large houses had 'secret' rooms used to house collections of exotic items, both natural and artistic. These cabinets of curiosities as they were called, took up Bacon's charge that the scientist, a type of collector, the person interested in the world, should pay special attention to the heteroclites, or anomalies. The aim of the cabinet of curiosities was encyclopaedic, it sought to bring together in one space all of the artefacts of the world and to order them so that the total order of the world might be revealed (see Hooper-Greenhill, 1992:90). In doing so, it began by still relying on the principles of similitude from the Renaissance, notably through constructing the cabinet of curiosities as a memory temple in line with contemporary thinking about the art of memory. But it very soon undermined the principle of similitude it drew upon by universalizing it in an idea of universal order and representation (see Hooper-Greenhill, 1992; Yates, 1992).

The ancient art of memory was a mnemonic device used in classical times by political orators as part of the skill of rhetoric. A speaker, living in a time before printing, had to devise a method of remembering a speech and delivering it in such a way as to try and convince the audience of the validity of the argument. This was done by associating parts of the speech with parts of a remembered building and the objects contained within it. Speakers learned the skill of being able to travel through the building in their minds' eye, in their memory, looking at its architectural features and the objects within it—its materiality—associating each of those features with a part of their speech. A distinct route was followed and in so doing speakers were able to remember each part of their speech faultlessly and in some cases was able to deliver an oration fluently for hours without the need for any other prompt. This art of memory was rediscovered during the classical age and given a new meaning. Philosophers like Giordino Bruno adapted this memory skill into a hermetic skill used in the attempted discovery of secret and lost knowledge that was believed to be encoded in the symbolism of the architectural features of buildings (see Rykwert, 1980; Yates, 1992). Buildings, architectural features and gardens were believed to contain symbols and cyphers; if the similitude of their correspondences could be correctly interpreted, it was hoped that they would reveal secret or forgotten knowledge, known only to the ancients and to the skilled interpreter.

Places were constituted as memory temples that had an inscription of a secret social memory that could be revealed to those initiates with the knowledge of how to read that code. The cabinet of curiosities was one such memory temple (see Hooper-Greenhill, 1992). It relied on the resemblances constituted in similitude to provide a way of deciphering the hermetic and allegorical use of symbols encoded in the heteroclite items on display. In doing so, however, it did not replicate that Renaissance way of knowing. By giving a prominent place to the heteroclite or anomalous—by singling it out as different—it adapted the principles of similitude into a new system in which there was no correspondence between subject and object. From within, it undermined the project of similitude through a process of universalizing its main principle of resemblance (see Foucault, 1989:52). The main principle of the classical form of representation is that of comparison. Comparison, Foucault argues, takes two forms: that of measurement and of order, which Foucault calls mathesis (1989:53ff). For something to resemble something else there has to be some form by which comparisons can be made to see if something does indeed resemble something else or not. To perform an act of comparison, one has to be able to see and to see one has to be detached from what one sees. In other words, one must have a relationship to what one sees that is not performed by the homology of direct geometrical relationship. Rather there has to be topological complexity that allows the eye to be not only detached from the space of the constituent objects that it views, but also to be able to move freely over the range of objects that it sees and to be able to discriminate between them. For Foucault, this means that the world comes to be perceived as if it is laid out on a two dimensional table, a principle that lay behind the cabinet of curiosities, so that comparisons could be made through the vision of the detached eye that hovered above the objects on display. The table/cabinet of curiosities comes to represent order, the array of normal objects as heteroclites on display in the museum. What started out as secret cyphers that are connected through similitude, became in their totality as a classificatory mode of ordering a cipher for the idea of order itself.

Modernity and the disappearance of heterogeneity

If, during the seventeenth century, heterogeneity became of great interest and was put on display, heterogeneity—or ambivalence—by contrast became a worry to modern forms of understanding. It became something that has to be ordered and disposed of (see Bauman, 1987; Hetherington, 1997a). The idea of eradicating rather than studying heterogeneity and disorder is an important part of the project around which the idea of modernity is founded. To order the world and make it knowable only makes sense, however, if the already detached subject that views that world is also seen to be ordered. When talking about the seeing subject within modern society and its anxieties about heterogeneity we have to recognize that such a subjectivity is more than just separated from the object world. During the Renaissance, subjectivity was objectified, during the Baroque it became separated from the world of the objective, in modernity subjectivity becomes subjectivized. It recognizing this last point it is hard to avoid speaking about panopticism.

The story of panopticism that Foucault presents us with is now well known (1977). Bentham's blueprint for the prison consisted of a circular space with a series of backlit cells around the perimeter that the prisoners were to be housed in and a watch tower for the (unseen guard) at the centre. The form of surveillance established by this technological apparatus was one where the unseen gaze of the guard (the representation of society's authority over its deviants) was internalized as a form of self-discipline, bringing the authority of society into the subject itself. The panopticon tries to banish our vision of heterogeneity in the material world, something that becomes a source of anxiety, by internalizing it in a subjectivized subject. As an effect, modern subjects are constituted as controllers of the heterogeneous object world who act by controlling heterogeneity (or passions) within themselves.

Seen in terms of issues of subject-object relations, the panoptical apparatus bears some passing resemblance to the geometry of linear perspective although it does diverge from it in important ways. In the panopticon, the position of the subject and the object are reversed. In linear perspective, the heterogeneity of things is brought to a point in the vanishing point within the picture. This is mirrored through the picture plane in the viewing point that becomes the location for the eye of the subject. In the panopticon it is the object, the watch tower, that is located at the 'viewing point' and the subject, the prisoner, in the 'vanishing point'. In Renaissance linear perspective, the subject is synonymous with material heterogeneity, in the tables of the classical age, heterogeneity is put on display for a viewing eye that is able to survey it from above from no particular location. The classical subject defines itself in relation to, yet at the same time as separate from, the world of material heterogeneity. In modern times, heterogeneity disappears from view. The object has no place, the subject is all (see Latour, 1993). The object comes to be seen as something external to the individual but it loses its heterogeneous character, it becomes unimportant. The watchtower represents the ordering of the material world. Heterogeneity does not disappear altogether though, it is absorbed into the interior of the subject and is dealt with there by a process that substitutes uncertainty for certainty within the world of things, nature and society by expecting individual subjects to affirm this sense of external order by ordering themselves. It is the subject itself, therefore, that now becomes heterogeneous and looking at that heterogeneity means looking within. Gazing at the outside world becomes only a means to inner reflection. This is nowhere better illustrated than in the modern museum and the type of gaze that it helps to establish: the Kantian gaze of the connoisseur.

For Kant, aesthetic judgement is the product of a disinterested eye (1957). The object before our eyes is of no real interest to Kant, what is of interest is a person's reaction to that object and their ability to make claims about the beauty of that object that can be taken as universal and communicated to an aesthetic community. Heterogeneity takes the form of sense perceptions and the process of ordering them thereby becomes a way of making sense of that heterogeneity. This process is one that is internal to the subject and is not revealed in the object itself (Kant, 1957). The Kantian gaze is akin to an autistic gaze, it is unable to make sense of the world of objects in themselves so it projects their heterogeneity inwards and seeks to make sense of itself instead. To be a Kantian inspired aesthete is to be highly disciplined in one's artistic tastes and aesthetic judgements. The process of ordering the sense impressions that things create is internalized and subjectivized. Doing this allows one to see from a position of order and look for order in the external world of things. Such an aesthetic gaze exhibits an affinity with the gaze of the prisoner in the panopticon. While the viewing subject sees the watchtower as an external object, its gaze as a separate thing that has the powers of surveillance, creates a disciplinary effect of internal reflection. In the panopticon, the watching object makes the subject aware of their internal heterogeneity, their 'crimes' or 'deviances' (artistic tastes based in personal, interested judgements) and disciplines them through an internal process of ordering that heterogeneity and making sense of it in terms of oneself as an orderly human being. Heterogeneity is banished from the world and internalized in the subject where it has then to be ordered and classified. In the gaze of the connoisseur, a prisoner in the panopticism of a modern sense of beauty, the sense impressions generated by an object are chaotic and heterogeneous but their heterogeneity is ordered within the mind of the subject by categories of beauty and taste.

The modern museum, a Kantian space, facilitates this ordering just as the carceral institution does for the deviant subject. The modern museum was established from the latter half of the eighteenth century as a public site for the conservation and display of artefacts. Its role became that of conserving and representing high cultural forms and of educating the public into an appreciation of their aesthetic and moral worth as individuals (see Bennett, 1995). The ordering of objects and their spatial arrangement were generally Euclidean in character, allowing the relationships between objects, their grouping and their order to make sense and form a narrative (often a narrative about improvements or later, in the nineteenth century, about national progress and human evolution) to be performed. All attempts were made at removing heterogeneity (what Bennett describes as the carnivalesque, 1995) from the display itself. The objects on display were then to be viewed with a Kantian eye by training the public to appreciate the beauty of improvement/ civilization/the nation as it was represented through a narrative about beautiful objects. This kind of museum allowed a disciplined and disinterested aesthetic judgement to be presented to the public who were in turn constituted as an appreciative aesthetic community or alternatively as deviants if they chose not to belong to this community.

Kevin Hetherington

Hidden heterogeneity and the reassertion of similitude

One of the first challenges to the Kantian gaze and indeed to the modern project and its internalization of heterogeneity begins with a urinal. Some might argue that Freud's making visible the inner heterogeneity of the subject under the name of the unconscious is a more important event. However, Freud's project is still very much a part of the disciplinary project of modernity. Marcel Duchamp's project and indeed that of the other Dadaists and later Surrealists was not. As proto-actor-network theory, the Dadaist project is fundamentally about restoring heterogeneity to the object world by challenging bourgeois conceptions of art and art's taming within the disciplined exhibitionary spaces of the gallery and the museum and their associated positioning of the viewing subject (see Motherwell, 1979; Nadau, 1987; Lewis, 1990; Krauss, 1994). By placing his famous urinal in an art gallery and through the use of ready-mades and collages of everyday objects, Duchamp made apparent the heterogeneity of the world of things that could not be assimilated at the time within a Kantian gaze. He celebrated the heterogeneous nature of objects and attributed the power of agency to objects through this process. That agency was performed as heterogeneity and the object was 'subjectivized'. The ready-mades escaped the Kantian gaze and its internalization and disciplining of heterogeneity by creating a rupture in its geometry of seeing. They undermined the project of the modern subject as defined by processes of ordering heterogeneity. The space remained the same, the galleries and museums in which objects like the R. Mutt urinal and the other ready-mades were put on display, was one that was unaltered. What changed was the character of the object on view and the way that it unsettled the connoisseur ideals of the Kantian eye. A piece of porcelain that one urinated in, when displayed in a museum, mocks the idea of formal and disinterested judgement; one can only be shocked or laugh at the idea established by the spatial location of such an item and the idea that such an object can have beauty. Such an object is heterogeneous and one can only behave in an undisciplined way before it. It does more than mock, however, it is accredited with the power to act and with a kind of subjectivity.

The real challenge that the Dadaists established, however, was not to mock bourgeois ideas about art and beauty as has often been stated but more fundamentally to challenge modern ideas about heterogeneity and subjectivity. The object is made heterogeneous through its incongruous location in a space in which it does not belong. It creates a fold in the Euclidean space of the modern museum or gallery (on folds in museums see Hetherington, 1997b), it introduces a trickster element into the object (see Serres, 1993), a functional blankness that has agency written all over it (see Hetherington and Lee, forthcoming) and in so doing it performs a blind spot before the eye. The ready-made cannot be seen by the modern Kantian eye without that eye being revealed to itself as an artifice. One is hardly encouraged to discipline one's inner heterogeneity in the face of such unassimilable heterogeneity in the object world.

It was the Surrealists, of course, who first realized, in the face of the Dadaist object, the heterogeneous character of the modern subject and they sought to celebrate that and represent it in their art objects. Krauss has described this process as one in which an optical unconscious (heterogeneity) is revealed in the object world of art (1994). She argues that while modernist art, with its pre-occupation with the surface of the painting and with form, replicates the erasure of heterogeneity within modernity, heterogeneity in Surrealism has a tendency to spill out into the object world and reveal itself as attaining the powers formerly attributed to the subject. This optical unconscious can take a number of 'forms': time, eroticism, informe (form as formlessness and resistance to form), all of which celebrate the heterogeneity of the subject in the visual world of the object and in so doing allow that heterogeneity to be made subjective in the object world.

Returning heterogeneity into the world of objects outside of the eye rather than seeking its eradication has been one of the major preoccupations of contemporary philosophy too. The contemporary interest in: desire, the decentring of subjectivity, discourse and intertextuality, the techniques of deconstruction, difference as a source of resistance, nomad thought and the construction of rhizomes, partially connected networks and indeed the attempt by actor-network theory to reveal agency as an effect of material heterogeneity, all rely on the agentic capacity of the heterogeneous appearing in the world of things/texts rather than within the subject alone. Louis Bunuel and Salvador Dali were perhaps the first to realize this as a 'post-modern' exercise, when they slit open the Kantian eye with a razor and allowed all the heterogeneity to spill from within the subject into the material world of things.[3] They hoped, as others have hoped since, that as a consequence, the subject might free itself from disciplinary constraints and mirror itself instead in that free-flow of material heterogeneity. We know that it is now difficult to sustain a view of the modern subject in the face of such heterogeneity. No doubt the next issue will be to reveal the unbounded and fluid character of the object, dissolved into a similitude of signification with no attachment to a subject at all (see Law, 1999). That is perhaps the project for the next type of museum. Perhaps that museum is already here but we have yet to be able fully to see it and identify its location. It is unlikely to be found in the social space of the modern museum but somewhere else.

Conclusion

In this chapter I have tried to provide a sketch outline of the effective history of heterogeneity and the changing character of subject-object relations that is constituted in relation to it. I have looked at this through examples of museums (as well as the art they have been associated with) located in different epistemic points of time-space. As a useful summary, Rotman has suggested that there are four moments in the constitution of the subject (1993). We might attach to these the moments in the constitution of heterogeneity. The character of the subject, Rotman argues, can be seen to correspond to a relationship between things and signs that are illustrated by the history of the number zero and the concept of nothing. These moments (not stages) in the history of the subject Rotman defines as: 1) the gothic, a pre-perspectival, medieval subject that corresponds to the absence of zero and therefore to any notion of a meta-sign; 2) the perspectival subject, located in a geometrical relationship with the object at a viewing point outside of the picture, a point that exists nowhere but acts as a meta-sign; 3) the looker, the classical subject, in which the meta-sign has been internalized in the subject who is able to look out of the world from the position of God; and finally 4) meta-subject, in which the subject becomes synonymous with the punctum (1993:40). Heterogeneity starts off with the recognition of the principle of infinity in connection and it orders it as a point: in linear perspective and its reading in similitude, the subject and object are synonymous and there is no sense of the heterogeneous in either but in the relation between the two as a principle for their ordering. In the classical age, heterogeneity is made visible by laying it on a table. Ordered and measured it becomes something separate from the subject and representable in the material world. In the modern world, heterogeneity becomes something of a problem, it can no longer be ordered in the world of things but has to be neutralized and made invisible by internalizing it and then disciplining it within the subject who is seen as master of the world of nature and things. Finally, in this century, we see modern artists cut open that eye, blinding it, and let the heterogeneity out. What is heterogeneous within the subject flows out from the eye into the material world of things and is celebrated as a source of agency.

Afterword: a fifth subject position

Now the fluid of heterogeneity that was once inside the eye is placed outside, the eye no longer attains the privileged position of being able to represent the subject (see Haraway, 1991). Where once we were Blind to our subjectivity, now blindness is the character of our subjectivity. The object itself begins to see. Our response to the 'seeing' object becomes increasingly blind. Our knowledge becomes situated (Haraway, 1991) and partially connected (Strathern, 1991). Perhaps we have to rely on senses other than sight to explore this new space,

> The theme of the drawings of the blind is, before all else, the hand. For the hand ventures forth, it precipitates, rushes ahead, certainly, but this time in place of the head, as to precede, prepare and protect it. (Derrida, 1993:4)

A Scene in a Museum

First person (enquiring): 'What are you doing?'
Second person (annoyed, kneeling and pat-pat-patting the ground before them): 'I've dropped my fucking contact lens.'

Notes

1 One of the problems with Panofsky's account (1997) is that he sees the development of linear perspective as part of a modern way of seeing and does not make the distinction over changes in ways of seeing that have occurred since that time (on the history of vision see Lindberg, 1976; Stafford, 1997).
2 Oxford English Dictionary.
3 The reference is of course to the famous eye slitting scene in the film *Un Chien Andalou*.

Bibliography

Alpers, S. (1983), *The Art of Describing: Dutch Art in the Seventeenth Century*, Harmondsworth: Penguin.
Altick, R. (1978), *The Shows of London*, Cambridge, Mass.: Belknap Press.
Appelbaum, D. (1995), *The Stop*, New York: SUNY.
Bacon, F. (1974), *The Advancement of Learning*, Oxford: Clarendon Press.
Bataille, G. (1985), *Visions in Excess*, Minneapolis: University of Minnesota Press.
Bauman, Z. (1987), *Legislators and Interpreters*. Cambridge: Polity Press.
Bennett, T. (1995), *The Birth of the Museum*, London: Routledge.
Bryson, N. (1983), *Vision and Painting: The Logic of the Gaze*, Basingstoke: Macmillan.
Deleuze, G. (1988), *Foucault*, London: Athlone.
Derrida, J. (1993), *Memoirs of the Blind*, Chicago: University of Chicago Press.
Foucault, M. (1977), *Discipline and Punish*, Harmondsworth: Penguin.
Foucault, M. (1989), *The Order of Things*, London: Tavistock/Routledge.
Haraway, D. (1991), 'Situated Knowledges: The Science Question in Feminism and the Privilege of Partial Perspective', pp. 183–202 in *Simians, Cyborgs, and Women*, New York: Free Association Books.
Heidegger, M. (1977), 'The Age of the World Picture', pp. 115–154 in *The Question Concerning Technology and Other Essays*, New York: Harper.
Hetherington, K. (1997a), *The Badlands of Modernity: Heterotopia and Social Ordering*, London: Routledge.
Hetherington, K. (1997b), 'Museum topology and the will to connect', *Journal of Material Culture*, Vol. 2(2): 199–220.
Hetherington, K. and Lee, N. (forthcoming), *Social Order and the Blank Figure*.
Hooper-Greenhill, E. (1992), *Museums and the Construction of Knowledge*, Leicester: Leicester University Press.
Impey, O. and McGregor, A. (eds) (1985), *The Origins of Museums: The Cabinet of Curiosities in Sixteenth and Seventeenth Century Europe*, Oxford: Oxford University Press.
Kant, I. (1957), *Critique of Judgement*, Oxford: Clarendon Press.
Krauss, R. (1994), *The Optical Unconscious*, Cambridge, Mass.: MIT Press.
Kruft, H. (1994), *A History of Architectural Theory*, London and New York: Zwemmer/Princeton Architectural Press.
Latour, B. (1987), *Science in Action*, Cambridge, Mass.: Harvard University Press.
Latour, B. (1988), *The Pasteurization of France*, Cambridge, Mass.: Harvard University Press.
Latour, B. (1993), *We Have Never Been Modern*, New York: Harvester Wheatsheaf.
Law, J. (1999), *Aircraft Stories: Decentering the Object in Technoscience*. Forthcoming.
Law, J. and R. Benschop (1997), 'Resisting pictures: representation, distribution and ontological politics' pp. 158–182 in K. Hetherington and R. Munro (eds), *Ideas of Difference*, Oxford: Blackwell.
Levi-Strauss, C. (1966), *The Savage Mind*, London: Weidenfeld and Nicholson.
Lewis, H. (1990), *Dada Turns Red: The Politics of Surrealism*, Edinburgh: Edinburgh University Press.
Lindberg, D. (1976), *Theories of Vision: From Al-Kindi to Kepler*, Chicago: University of Chicago Press.

Markus, T. (1993), *Buildings and Power*, London: Routledge.
Mol, A. and J. Law (1994), 'Regions, Networks and Fluids: Anaemia and Social Topology', *Social Studies of Science*, Vol. 26: 641–671.
Motherwell, R. (ed.) (1979), *The Dada Painters and Poets*, Cambridge, Mass.: Belknap.
Nadeau, M. (1987), *History of Surrealism*, London: Plantin.
Panofsky, E. (1997), *Perspective as Symbolic Form*, New York: Zone Books.
Rotman, B. (1993), *Signifying Nothing: the Semiotics of Zero*, Stanford: Stanford University Press.
Saumarez Smith, C. (1989), 'Museums, Artefacts and Meanings', pp. 6–21 in P. Vergo (ed.), *The New Museology*, London: Reaktion Books.
Serres, M. (1991), *Rome: the Book of Foundations*, Stanford: Stanford University Press.
Stafford, B. (1997), *Good Looking: Essays on the Virtue of Images*, Cambridge, Mass.: MIT Press.
Strathern, M. (1991), *Partial Connections*, Savage: Rowman and Littlefield.
Yates, F. (1992), *The Art of Memory*, London: Pimlico.

Ontological politics. A word and some questions

Annemarie Mol

Abstract

This is a chapter that asks questions about where we are with *politics* now that actor network theory and its semiotic relatives have reshaped *ontology*. They have reshaped it by underlining that the reality we live with is one performed in a variety of practices. The radical consequence of this is that reality itself is multiple. An implication of this might be that there are *options* between the various versions of an object: which one to perform? But if this were the case then we would need to ask *where* such options might be situated and *what* was at stake when a decision between alternative performances was made. We would also need to ask to what extent are there options between different versions of reality if these are not exclusive, but, if they clash in some places, depend on each other elsewhere. The notion of choice also presupposes an actor who actively chooses, while potential actors may be inextricably linked up with how they are *enacted*. These various questions are not answered, but illustrated with the example of anaemia, a common deviance that comes in (at least) clinical, statistical and pathophysiological forms.

In this chapter I would like to ask a few questions. These have to do with *ontological politics*.[1] They have to do with the way in which 'the real' is implicated in the 'political' and *vice versa*. For even if the traditional divisions between the two have been pulled down iconoclastically, by actor network theory and by its many relatives, it is as yet by no means clear what this might mean for further action. What it might imply for going about life in various sites and situations—state politics, social movements, and technoscience formation. And what it might suggest for handling the interferences between these. For interfering.

Ontological politics is a composite term. It talks of *ontology*—which in standard philosophical parlance defines what belongs to

Ontological politics

the real, the conditions of possibility we live with. If the term 'ontology' is combined with that of 'politics' then this suggests that the conditions of possibility are not given. That reality does not precede the mundane practices in which we interact with it, but is rather shaped within these practices. So the term *politics* works to underline this active mode, this process of shaping, and the fact that its character is both open and contested.

To be sure, it has always been assumed that 'reality' is not entirely immutable. Such was the point of technology—and indeed politics. These worked on the assumption that the world might be mastered, changed, controlled. So within the conventions of technology and politics the question of how to shape reality was open: at some point in the future it might be otherwise. But along with this it was assumed that the building blocks of reality were permanent: they could be uncovered by means of sound scientific investigation.

Over the last two decades, however, they have been undermined, these neat divisions between the present and the future; between that which is well-set and that which is still-to-be-formed; between the building blocks that are given and the modes by which they might be differently adjusted. This work—of which actor network theory did quite a bit but that it by no means did alone—has robbed the *elements* that make up reality—reality in its *ontological dimension*—of its alleged stable, given, universal character.[2] It has argued, instead, that reality is historically, culturally and materially located.[3]

Located where? The answer depends on the field in which it is given. In social studies of science it was the laboratory that was redescribed as a sociomaterial practice where reality is transformed and where new ways of *doing* reality are crafted.[4] From there they are exported, not so much in the form of 'theory' but rather—or at least as much—in the shape of vaccinations, microchips, valves, combustion engines, telephones, genetically manipulated mice and other objects—objects that carry new realities, new ontologies, with them.[5]

Ontologies: note that. Now the word needs to go in the plural. For, and this is a crucial move, if reality is *done*, if it is historically, culturally and materially *located*, then it is also *multiple*. Realities have become multiple.

Not plural: multiple. A clarification is required here, a differentiation. For ontological politics is informed by, but does not directly follow from or easily coexist with either perspectivalism or constructivism. Its pivotal term is slightly different: it is performance.

Perspectivalism. As against the singularity of the single truth voiced by the anonymous, objective 'expert', it has been argued that there are *many experts* with different professional and social backgrounds, or indeed with no specific *professional* background at all: the word 'lay expert' was invented. And since each of these experts is a different person and comes on the scene from somewhere different, none of them is objective. They are instead specific social subjects, each. They bring with them their own particular skills, habits, histories, preoccupations which means that their *eyes* are different. They look at the world from different *standpoints*. This means that they see things differently and represent what they have seen in a diversity of ways. Much of the subsequent discussion has turned around the question of how this diversity must—or might—be valued.[6]

Perspectivalism broke away from a monopolistic version of truth. But it didn't multiply *reality*. It multiplied the eyes of the beholders. It turned each pair of eyes looking from its own perspective into an alternative to other eyes.[7] And this in turn brought *pluralism* in its wake. For there they are: mutually exclusive perspectives, discrete, existing side by side, in a transparent space. While in the centre the object of the many gazes and glances remains singular, intangible, untouched.

A second kind of pluralism took the form of *construction* stories. These show how a specific version of the truth got crafted, what supported it, what was against it, and how its likely alternatives got discredited. Many stories about the support facts-to-be and artefacts-being-shaped require in order to survive, tell about relevant groups of researchers and/or others who are involved (and here constructivism links up with perspectivalism). But in other constructivist stories material rather than social support is foregrounded: the lenses in which the wave theory of light is made durable, or the dissection room with its knives and skills that anchor the *fact* that diseases carve structural changes in the body.[8]

The sting of construction stories is that the alternatives for any currently accepted fact or well diffused artefact were not doomed to lose from the beginning. They got lost somewhere along the way, as a matter of contingency. We might have had another kind of bicycle, keyboard or video system. It just happens that we've come to stick with the ones we've got. And with facts it is the same. The secret of their success lies not in the laws of nature but in the intricacies of history. Thus constructivist stories suggest that alternative 'constructions of reality' might have been possible. They have been possible in the past, but vanished before they ever fully blossomed. So there is *plurality* again. But this time it is a plurality projected back

Ontological politics

into the past. There have been might-have-beens, but now they have gone. The losers have lost.

Talking about reality as *multiple* depends on another set of metaphors. Not those of perspective and construction, but rather those of intervention and performance.[9] These suggest a reality that is *done* and *enacted* rather than observed. Rather than being seen by a diversity of watching eyes while itself remaining untouched in the centre, reality is manipulated by means of various tools in the course of a diversity of practices. Here it is being cut into with a scalpel; there it is being bombarded with ultrasound; and somewhere else, a little further along the way, it is being put on a scale in order to be weighed. But as a part of such different activities, the object in question varies from one stage to the next. Here it is a fleshy object, there one that is thick and opaque and in the next place it is heavy. In performance stories fleshiness, opacity and weight are not attributes of a single object with an essence which hides. Nor is it the role of tools to lay them bare as if they were so many *aspects* of a single reality. Instead of attributes or aspects, they are different *versions* of the object, versions that the tools help to enact. They are different and yet related objects. They are multiple forms of reality. Itself.

Let me give an example. It is a story about *anaemia*.[10]

Anaemia is no longer at the centre of heated controversies in front line science. And yet the question 'what is anaemia?' has not been answered in a single or stabilized way. Or, whatever answer one may hear if one asks about it, when one observes what is done in practice, anaemia appears to be *performed* in several different ways. Here I'll separate out three (or rather three genres) of these.

> One: in a consulting room a patient tells the doctor that he gets dizzy. Too tired. The doctor asks some more, about when these symptoms come and how they do. And then she approaches the patient and lowers an eyelid, maybe the other one too, to check its colour. How white, or rather red do these eyelids look? What general impression does the skin give? The patient's talk, the doctor's further questions and the observations made on the outside of the body all relate to anaemia. How do they stage it? The answer is: as a set of visible symptoms. As complaints that may be articulated by a patient. This is the *clinical* performance of anaemia.
>
> Two: however in the *laboratory* routines of any hospital other things are being done. Here anaemia equals a low haemoglobin

level in a person's blood. For here blood is tapped from veins and fed to machines which pour out number for each blood sample they receive. (Beware, this is only one of the laboratory techniques used to measure haemoglobin levels. There are others that I won't go into here.) The number generated is then compared with a standard: a normal haemoglobin level. So that is a laboratory way of performing anaemia. But it comes in different versions. For there are different ways of setting the standard for a normal haemoglobin level. Most common is the *statistical* method. This depends on assembling data for a population, the norm being set at, say, two standard deviations from the mean figure of the population. The people whose blood tests reveal a haemoglobin level below this norm are then diagnosed as having anaemia.

Three: the other method is *pathophysiological*. This depends on finding, for every single individual again, the dividing line between the haemoglobin level that is enough to transport oxygen through the body properly, and the abnormal level which, by contrast, is too low.

So there are at least these three performances of anaemia: clinical, statistical and pathophysiological. How do they relate? In textbooks they tend to be described as being linked, as being, indeed, aspects of a single deviance. A haemoglobin level too low to carry oxygen from lungs to organs in sufficient amounts to supply an individual's organs (pathophysiological) is supposed to fall outside the normal range established by calculations based on population data (statistical), and then to surface in the form of symptoms that give the patient so much trouble that he will seek medical help (clinical). But that is not necessarily the way things work out in practice. For in practice sometimes people don't get dizzy or have white eyelids and nevertheless have a haemoglobin level that (if it were measured) would appear to be deviant. Or people's organs lack oxygen because their haemoglobin level has just dropped but it still lies within the normal statistical range. And so on. In practice the three ways to diagnose 'anaemia' each diagnose something different. The objects of each of the various diagnostic techniques do not necessarily overlap with those of the others.

This does not lead to big debates, to attempts to seek consensus or even concern. It is simply how it is. Once in a while a discussion may flare up about which method of diagnosis to use in some specific context. But by and large these three ways of handling anaemia

Ontological politics

or, rather, these three different anaemias, have co-existed for decades now. And there is no sign that this situation is changing.

The reality of anaemia takes various forms. These are not perspectives seen by different people—a single person may slide in her work from one performance to another. Neither are they alternative, bygone constructions of which only one has emerged from the past—they emerged at different points in history, but none of them has vanished. So they are different versions, different performances, different realities, that co-exist in the present. This is our situation, one that actor network theory and related semiotic sociologies have articulated for us. And I'll take this situation as an occasion for asking my questions. Questions about the kind of politics that might fit this ontological multiplicity. Four of them:

- *Where* are the options?
- *What* is at stake?
- *Are* there really options?
- *How* should we choose?

Where are the options? On political topoi

If there are various ways to perform a deviance, it might seem that there is, or should be, a *choice* between them. But where, at which *site*, where might this be located?[11] For we should not accept the illusion that most decisive moments are explicit. Take the question of how to organize the *detection* of anaemia. Roughly, there are two alternative models: one is to have a system of professionals available for people who actively seek help. The other is to organize a screening system and try to mobilize the entire population to come for regular check-ups. The first performs anaemia clinically, the second statistically. The outcomes differ: if the detection of anaemia is organized in a clinical manner there will be some people with statistically low haemoglobin levels who go undetected for they either have no complaints or do not take these to be sufficient reason to go and see a doctor.

In most countries the detection of most diseases is organized in a clinical manner. Screening programs have been established in only a very few exceptional cases. Where was this decided? It is important first to recognize that this situation emerged historically. It grew out of a great number of contingencies and forces, but there was never a moment or a place where it was decided. Most current cure and care provisions are an historical product of the patient-seeking-help model. The other model, that of the state taking its population under control, got embedded in other contexts—for instance in public regulations, water provision, vaccination programmes and other preventive measures.

If there *were* a site, here and now, where this situation was to be reconsidered, or if it were created, there would be arguments available as to why—at least in anaemia—clinical medicine should indeed prevail over the detection of statistical deviance. For screening would yield more false positives than real deviance since (at least in populations that are well fed and not chronically infected) anaemia is very rare. And, different argument: if people have no complaints because of their anaemia, then there is no reason to treat it. Or, different argument yet again: it is not cost-effective— indeed far too expensive—to screen properly for every deviance people may have. I do not here seek to either agree or disagree with these arguments. I want to point to something else. What they do, each of them, is shift the *site* of the decision elsewhere: to move it along. So they displace the decisive moment to places where, seen from here, it seems no decision, but a fact. These places are, respectively: the intricacies of measurement techniques; considerations about good and bad reasons for treatment; and health care budgets.

I hope that this helps to illustrate why the question about *where* the options are is so relevant to the shaping of ontological politics. For as it is, many conditions of possibility are not structured as the outcomes of 'decisions' at all.[12] They happen to be the way they are—or they derive from facts imported from elsewhere. So the question becomes: should they be restructured? Is this what ontological politics must imply, that we make the 'options' more *explicit*? I doubt it. For it would imply an extension of the argumentative format that tends to follow when everything is recast into an option. We need to better investigate what this would imply, intellectually and practically. What it is to live things as *options*.[13] What the goods and bad of this way of living are. And what its practical limits might be. For it might happen that arguments that are mobilized in decision making shift the 'real' options to other sites, and then on again to further and more distant locations. That there *is* no last resort but instead there are 'options' *everywhere*. So that at any given site, they always end up seeming *elsewhere*.

What is at stake? On interference

What is at stake in ontological politics? The organization of the detection of a deviance like anaemia is not a 'merely practical' matter. It also has reality effects. It makes a difference to the way anaemia 'itself' is performed. But it is not only the reality of anaemia that is at stake. Many other realities are involved too. For objects that are performed do not come alone: they carry modes and modulations of other objects with them. Thus: with clinical anaemia comes the reality of conversational interaction, this well investigated ritual of two people trying to insert each other into their own highly specific agendas.[14] With laboratory anaemia comes the needle, the ex-corporation of blood, the controlled infliction of pain. And so on. There's one example I would like to expand upon briefly. It is well suited to present *interference* here, for it shows the linkage between two ways of performing *anaemia* and the performance of a phenomenon that is far more extensively politicised: that of *sex difference*.

The *normal haemoglobin level* can be established in two ways: either statistically or pathophysiologically. Since Hb-levels vary between individuals these two ways of setting norms do not necessarily give overlapping answers. If someone has a high Hb that suddenly drops it may be pathophysiologically abnormal while still lying within the statistically normal range. A statistically deviant Hb, on the other hand, may be pathophysiologically normal since it provides a specific individual with adequate oxygen-carrying capacity. So there is a tension. In current medical text-books there is a preference for the pathophysiological way of setting norms, since this does more justice to the individual. By contrast, in current health care practice the dominant method for setting norms is statistical. There are, again, historical reasons and 'good arguments' for this. And it is not my aim to argue about these. Instead I want to point to a 'side-effect' of the difference between pathophysiology and statistics.

The epidemiologists who make statistical norms differentiate between populations. If statistical norms were made for 'the population' as a whole they would systematically be too high or too low for various groups of people.[15] Therefore different norms are usually set for different groups: for children (of different age groups), men, women and pregnant women. This implies that the members of these groups are compared with better standards than would be the case if there were no differentiation between populations. But it also implies that 'children' are separated out as a group that differs from 'adults'. And it implies—and it is this I want to consider here—that 'women' are separated out from 'men'. This turns 'women' into a group of people who have more in common with each other than with 'men', however much the two curves happen to overlap. It also performs the category 'women' as one that is biological. For it implies that one of the ways of differentiating it from that other category of 'men' is by comparing this bodily characteristic: the haemoglobin level.

Pathophysiology knows only individuals. Thus it does not require differentiation between the sexes in order to distinguish between normal and abnormal haemoglobin levels. Rather, it involves comparing an individual's Hb-values at a moment of possible deviance with those of the same person at a healthy moment. This provides individuals with a bodily history, a persistent physicality that is a part of their identity. There is a lot to be said about the goods and bads of that. But one of its consequences is that it *doesn't* contribute to dividing humans into *men* and *women*. If medicine were to perform all deviances in individualized ways, a lot of 'undeniable' biological sex differences would simply disappear.[16] Thus the 'decision' about whether it is practically feasible or hopelessly cumbersome to work with individualized norms in medicine not only involves the reality of 'anaemia', but also that of 'women' and 'men'.

The separation of 'pregnant women' is also interesting. From the point of view of treating pregnant women this is sensible: since the blood volume increases when a body gets pregnant, its haemoglobin level tends to decrease. But what I want to point at here, is that this sensible distinction means that laboratory forms differentiate 'pregnant women' from both 'men' *and* 'women'. Thus the very statistical practice that performs the sexes as biologically separate groups, also intriguingly undermines a simple dichotomous categorization of the sexes. For it suggests that 'pregnant women'—of all people—are *not* in fact 'women'.[17]

So this is the phenomenon of interference.[18] Once we start to look carefully at the variety of the objects performed in a practice, we come across complex interferences between those objects. In the ontological politics around *anaemia* it is not just the reality of anaemia that is at stake, but that of the *sexes*, too. And no doubt there is more. If we recognize and analyse these interferences then the question of evaluating performances becomes more and more complex. For while it might just be possible to think of aligning the

Ontological politics

arguments around the goods and bads involved in performing any specific single object (for instance anaemia) things become more and more complicated if the arguments around other objects, the sexes, individual identity and so on, must also be balanced simultaneously. Indeed, such balancing will never find a stable end point, there are too many elements. Which implies that *ontological politics* is unlikely to come at rest once the accounts are closed—because they won't be closed. Tolerating open-endedness, facing tragic dilemmas, and living-in-tension sound more like it.[19]

Are there options? On inclusion

I've said that clinical, statistical and pathophysiological ways of handling anaemia do not entirely overlap with one another. And I've argued that rather than simply revealing different *aspects* of anaemia they perform different *versions* of it. Might it be possible to choose between such versions? The notion of ontological politics seems to imply the possibility of 'choice'. But is this the only way of implementing it? So far we've gone into the questions of *where* options might be located and *what* is at stake in the 'decision' between different versions of anaemia. But now we take a step back to ask: but is it the case that there *are* options? The answer is not necessarily, for if realities-performed are multiple this is not a matter of pluralism. What 'multiplicity' entails instead is that, while realities may clash at some points, elsewhere the various performances of an object may *collaborate* and even *depend on* one another.

Let us concentrate on two of the performances of anaemia: the clinical and the statistical.[20] Anaemia may be diagnosed by clinical means or by a laboratory test whose result is assessed against a statistical standard. If the question is how to *detect* anaemia, then the two are in conflict. Clinical rationality demands that doctors be available to all those who have complaints, while if the laboratory and its statistical norm setting were given priority, then the entire population would have to be regularly screened. But this clash about detecting anaemia doesn't mean that there is a *general* clash between clinic and lab.

For instance, in the surgeries of Dutch general practitioners, clinical and laboratory ways of working calmly coexist. First a patient comes to the surgery. There he is interviewed and physically examined. If these two activities suggest anaemia, the patient's blood is tested—using laboratory techniques. There is no clash. Instead the two performances are put in *sequence*. The clinical performance comes first, but unless the laboratory supports it, no therapy for anaemia results. And there is no clash for a tropical doctor working in a poor region of Africa. She sees a patient, lowers an eyelid, and if this looks too white she prescribes iron tablets. Clinical diagnosis is enough to act on by itself. The lab is expected to agree, but it isn't actually called upon. If there is a lab at all, it is better for it to concentrate on more difficult tasks. Thus, in this situation the clinic *stands in for* the lab.

The relation between clinical and laboratory practices becomes even more entangled at the moment the standards by which the normal and pathological will subsequently be distinguished are established. These standards are not given with clinical and laboratory practice: they are a *part* of these practices. How does this work? Take a statistical norm. In order to set this so called *normative data* are assembled. These are the haemoglobin levels of, say, a hundred men, women, pregnant women and children of different age groups, drawn from the region where the laboratory will recruit its patients. But who should be picked out of each of these populations? Usually laboratories try to assess *healthy* people. But since they are in the process of establishing their normal values, they have no laboratory norm in order to differentiate between healthy and deviant haemoglobin levels. They have, and use, clinical means to differentiate normal and deviant people. They ask people to participate only if they feel well. Thus: when laboratory standards are established, clinical diagnosis is *included*.

But the clinical means mobilized in one context are in turn contested and adapted elsewhere. There are occasions when clinical signs are reopened for investigation. For instance, some Dutch general practice researchers started to doubt the usefulness of the many (negative) Hb-tests done by general practitioners. They wondered whether all these tests were really indicated. What were the clinical signs that prompted general practitioners to have their patients' Hb tested?[21] The researchers discovered that 'tiredness' was a frequent reason for ordering an Hb test. But was this a good reason? To assess this, the researchers compared the Hbs of a hundred patients who had come to their doctor with complaints of 'tiredness' with the Hbs of the hundred random patients coming after them in the doctors' schedule of ten minute visits. And it turned out that there was no difference. The conclusion was that 'isolated tiredness' is not a clinical sign of anaemia. Which reveals that laboratory measurements are in turn *included* in the process of establishing clinical orientation.

Studying the performances of anaemia reveals their multiplicity. But this multiplicity does not come in the form of pluralism. It is not as if there were separate entities each standing apart in a homogeneous field. So anaemia is multiple, but it is not plural. The various anaemias that are performed in medicine have many relations between them. They are not simply opposed to, or outside, one another. One may follow the other, stand in for the other, and, the most surprising image, one may include the other. This means that what is 'other' is also within.[22] Alternative realities don't simply coexist side by side, but are also found inside one another. But this is a situation that does not easily fit our traditional notions of politics. Which means that new conceptions of politics need to be crafted. But which ones? What kind of politics is implied here—or required?

How to choose? On styles of politics

In health care there has recently been a lot of noise to do with *choice*. The idea is that if medical interventions do not necessarily follow from nature, if there are choices to be made, then patients should make these. There are various ways for shaping such choosing. Roughly they may be divided into two models: a market model and a state model. The market model takes health care to be divisible into discrete activities, discrete *goods* that may be bought and sold on the market. It configures the patient into the role of customer who represents his or her desires in the act of buying. In the state model the patient is configured as a citizen. Health care becomes something to be governed. This time there are no discrete goods, but an *organization* with appropriate rules and regulations. This means that patient-citizens should represent themselves in the places where health care organizations are managed, and rules and regulations get their shape. There is a lot to explore here, a lot to ask about the advantages and disadvantages of these two different ways to model self-representation in the complex context of health care.[23] An urgent task.

But there is more to do. For both these models assume that *information* is available and may be provided to the patient. It should be provided willingly and fully by the professionals who have it, to lay people who need it in order to make good decisions. However, if we think in terms of *ontological politics*, then information is no longer given—to anyone. The stories professionals might tell have

Annemarie Mol

lost their self-evidence. And what is more, it is not only the representations of reality in information circulating as words and images that have become contestable, but also the very material shaping of reality in diagnosis, interventions and research practices. So if it is important to attend to the way patients *represent* themselves (as customer or as citizen), it is at least as important to ask how they *are represented* in knowledge practices. Which parameters replace and denote our troubles? What are the endpoints marking an 'improvement' or a 'deterioration' of one's condition through the course of time? A clinical trial in which the *effectiveness* of various interventions is assessed, can no longer be taken at face value. For another question must come first: what are the *effects* that we should be seeking? Answers to that question are incorporated in the information, but also in the techniques, we currently live with. They tend to be implicit, entangled and inextricably linked up with the various performances of any one disease. Thus it is a fairly superficial matter to choose 'after the facts', given the information and the techniques that have helped to generate these. But what if we seek to be less superficial? Who, then, might *do* ontological politics, how to handle *choice incorporated*?

Afterword

The word 'ontological politics' suggests a link between the real, the conditions of possibility we live with, and the political. But how to conceive of this? In this text I've not laid out a response to this question, but rather articulated some of the problems that come with a specific interpretation of politics, one that is posed in terms of deliberation or choice. We may list these. One: if we think in such terms then we risk the ramification of options everywhere—with the consequence that they end up always seeming to be elsewhere. Two: the interference between various political tensions is such that each time one thing seems to be at stake (say: anaemia) an unquantifiable number of other issues and realities are involved as well (say: sex difference). And three: the various performances of reality in medicine have all kinds of tensions between them, but to separate them out as if they were a plurality of options is to skip over the complex interconnections between them. And then there is a fourth problem. Who is the actor who might decide between the options? Might, or should, this be a patient-customer making choices between discrete goods available on a market; or should it be a patient-citizen trying to organize the health care system for the benefit of all? Or, again, are the crucial moments not those where 'patients' act as an agent, but rather those where they (we) are defined, measured, observed, listened to, or otherwise *enacted*?

These, then, are my questions. I have noted them down here, for while they may be mine, they are not mine alone. These are questions that follow from a semiotic analysis of the way reality is done, from studying performances, from making a turn to practice. They come with and therefore *after ANT*. And what comes after *them*? Answers, maybe. Or perhaps practical explorations of the political styles that seem to be called for. But it is also possible that these questions will evaporate and we'll enact and undergo, yet again, a shift in our theoretical repertoire, finding other ways of diagnosing the present.

Notes

1 The term 'ontological politics' is an invention of John Law. I thank him for pushing me to develop, as well as question it. See also: John Law, *Aircraft Stories: Decentering the Object in Technoscience*. Mimeo, Keele, 1998.
2 Crucial in the ancestries of many of the intellectual articulations of ontological politics is the work of Michel Foucault. See in English, eg, P. Rabinow, ed. (1984), *The Foucault Reader*, New York: Pantheon Books. Foucault is also present in the analysis made here: terms such as 'conditions of possibility' or 'diagnosis of the present' come straight out of his work, while my concern with the articulation of 'politics' is clearly informed by what he has written about the topic.
3 With this trope of 'locatedness' metaphors in which to articulate spatiality gain in importance. See on this the work of Michel Serres, eg, M. Serres (1979), *Le Passage du Nord-Ouest*, Paris: Les Éditions du Minuit; and M. Serres (1994), *Atlas*, Paris: Julliard. And for an example in an actor-network theory (or after?) mode, see: A. Mol and J. Law (1994), 'Regions, Networks and Fluids. Anaemia and Social Topology', in: *Social Studies of Science*, 24, 641–671.
4 But in, eg, Queer Theory other places (such as gay and lesbian subcultures) were pointed to as sites where new realities are being made. See: J. Butler (1990), *Gender Trouble*, New York: Routledge; M. Warner, ed. (1993), *Rear of a queer planet? Queer politics and social theory*, Minneapolis: University of Minneapolis Press; S. Dudink (1994), 'Het privilege van de democratische grensoverschreiding. Radicale seksuele politiek en grensoverschreiding, in: *Krisis*, 14, 50–64, 1994.
5 See for the vaccinations: B. Latour (1984), *Les Microbes*, Paris: Métaillié, 1984; and for the mice: Donna Haraway (1997), *Modest_witness@Second Millenium.FemaleMan©_Meets_OncoMouse*^{TM}, New York: Routledge.
6 A huge pile of literature, again, alluded to in just a few lines. But see for the social studies of science version of this line the classical: B. Barnes (1977), *Interests and the Growth of Knowledge*, London: Routledge and Kegan Paul; and for the text where the visual imaginary reaches its 'logical end point': M. Ashmore (1989), *The Reflexive Thesis. Wrighting Sociology of Scientific Knowledge*, The University of Chicago Press. For some good examples of perspectivalism in the sociology of

medicine, see: S. Lindenbaum and M. Lock (eds) (1993) *The Anthropology of Medicine and Everyday Life*, Berkeley: University of California Press. And for a version in which perspectives are linked up with belonging to one sex or rather the other: S. Harding (1992), *Whose Science? Whose Knowledge? Thinking from Women's Lives*, Ithaca: New York University Press.

7 For an astute situation of perspectivalism in the way kinship is done in late twentieth century western/english culture, see: M. Strathern (1992), *After Nature. English kinship in the late twentieth century*, Cambridge University Press.

8 Another library to refer to. But see the book that made its title shift between the first, social, and the second, sociomaterial, version of constructivism: B. Latour and S. Woolgar, *Laboratory Life. The Social Construction of Scientific Facts*, London: Sage, 1979; which became in its second edition: B. Latour and S. Woolgar, *Laboratory Life, The Construction of Scientific Facts*, Princeton University Press, 1986. And for another classic: K. Knorr-Cetina (1981), *The Manufacture of Knowledge. An Essay on the Constructivist and Contextual Nature of Science*, Oxford: Pergamon Press.

9 Performance stories link up with literatures as diverse as I. Hacking (1983), *Representing and Intervening*, Cambridge University Press; and E. Goffman (1971, or 1959), *The Presentation of Self in Everyday Life*, London: Pelican. They radicalize the notions of the former by spreading them out to other sites than experimental research alone and rob the latter of any notion of a 'back stage'. See, eg, C. Cussins, 'Ontological Choreography: Agency for Women Patients in an Infertility Clinic', in: M. Berg and A. Mol, *Differences in Medicine. Unravelling Practices, Techniques and Bodies*, Duke University Press, 1998, 166–201; or A. Mol, 'Missing Links, Making Links: The Performance of some Atherosclerosis', in the same volume, pp. 144–165.

10 There is nothing specific about anaemia that turns it into a better example of a multiple identity than any other object. Its advantage is simply that I've taken time to study it. I have reported on this study in various articles. For more background the reader may turn to these, I have made footnotes to all of them. Here I do not pretend to do justice to the material: my only aim is to articulate some wide questions that, I think, we face—or should face.

11 For the trope of locating performances of a deviance, with details on anaemia, see: A. Mol, 'Sekse, rijkdom en bloedarmoede. Over lokaliseren als strategie' in: *Tijdschrift voor Vrouwenstudies*, 42, 1990, pp. 142–157; and A. Mol, 'Topografie als methode van kennisonderzoek. Over het naast elkaar bestaan van enkele bloedarmoedes' in: *Kennis en Methode*, 1991, pp. 314–329, the last one translated as: A. Mol, 'La topographie comme méthode d'investigation des savoirs. De la co-existence de diverses anémies' in: *Culture Technique*, 25/26, 1995, 285–305.

12 This may be compared to Bruno Latour's quest after the moment where the 'decision' was made to stop Aramis, where Aramis failed, or was killed. This moment/site remains elusive, despite all the efforts to capture it. See: B. Latour, *Aramis ou l'amour des techniques*, Paris: Éditions de Découverte, 1992.

13 Michel Callon asks a related question when wondering how a market is practically made, see 'Actor-Network Theory—The Market Test', this volume.

14 For an example, see: D. Silverman, *Communication and Medical Practice. Social Relations in the Clinic*, London: Sage, 1987.

15 For the question how to separate out populations and how to delineate the region from which they are taken, see: A. Mol and R. Hendriks, 'De hele wereld één Hb? Universaliteit, lokaliteit en bloedarmoede' in: *Krisis*, 58, 1995, 56–73.

16 Epidemiology doesn't necessarily produce 'sexes'. It might also separate out populations in other ways, as to the percentage of their fat mass, their height, the time they spend doing sports, or some other parameter. Such classifications might coincide better or less well with measured haemoglobin levels. Historically, however, two sexes have been epidemiology's favourite way of splitting up the world. Most forms around have M/V boxes and thus allow for making this division.

17 See for the complexity of 'making the difference' also: I. Costera Meijer, 'Which difference makes the difference? On the conceptualization of sexual difference' in: J. Hermsen and A. van Lenning, *Sharing the Difference. Feminist debates in Holland*, London: Routledge, 1991.

18 For a technical philosophical version of the notion of interference, see: M. Serres, *Interférence*, Paris, Les Éditions de Minuit, 172. For a more political mobilization of this metaphor, and others related to is, see Donna Haraway, *Simians, Cyborgs, and Women. The Reinvention of Nature*, London: Free Association Books, 1991.

19 For the related notion of knowing in tension see J. Law, 'After Meta-Narrative: on Knowing in Tension', in Robert Chia (ed.), *Into the Realm of Organisation: Essays for Robert Cooper*, London: Routledge, 1998, pp. 88–108.

20 For the co-existence of the various performances of anaemia, see: A. Mol and M. Berg, 'Principles and Practices of Medicine. The co-existence of various anaemias' in: *Culture, Medicine and Psychiatry*, 1994, 18, 247–265.

21 This was complicated by the fact that patients do not only have deviances, but theories about these as well. When we interviewed them, general practitioners told us they often measure in response to these, and not because they presume a low haemoglobin level to be present. See: A. Mol, 'Van wie is de theorie? Bloedarmoede en de meta-positie' in: *Gezondheid. Theorie en Praktijk*, 1, 1993, pp. 5–16.

22 Images such as that of mutual inclusion are being developed in sites where spatiality is a persistent concern. A good case in point is Soja's depiction of Los Angeles as a city that has spread out its image everywhere—so Los Angeles is everywhere—while it also assembled pieces of the rest of the world inside it—so that everywhere is also in Los Angeles. See: E. Soja, *Postmodern Geographies. The reassertion of space in critical social theory*, London: Verso Books, 1989. See for a thoroughly theorized handling of complex spatial images also: M. Strathern, *Partial Connections*, Savage, Md.: Rowman and Littlefield, 1991.

23 Such questions are currently being explored in a variety of ways in political theory. See for a good recent collection of essays, that take up the (state oriented) political question par excellence, that of handling difference: Seyla Benhabib, ed., *Democracy and Difference. Contesting the Boundaries of the Political*, Princeton: Princeton University Press, 1996. For an attempt to relate issues in economy to the shaping of 'good lives' see: M. Nussbaum and A. Sen, eds, *The Quality of Life*, Oxford: Clarendon Press, 1993.

Who pays? Can we pay them back?

Nick Lee and Paul Stenner

Abstract

This chapter is about a very old question that is thrown up again in discussion related to ANT. Do orders have necessary limits to what can belong to them? It is possible to read ANT as containing or demanding a moral commitment to the inclusion of the disenfranchised. It can often seem to be in the business of giving credit where credit is due, spreading recognition to even the most unexpected quarters. To sustain itself such a morality would depend on the possibility of infinite inclusion. By identifying this picture of 'belonging-by-assemblage' and its traditional counterpart 'belonging-by-banishment' and by finding both at play within ANT, the paper argues that ANT is an ethical rather than a moral enterprise, bringing the unanswered question of the nature of belonging to bear across domains, rather than approaching each domain with a 'cookie-cutter' moral formula. The disturbing 'unsecuring' of belonging that ANT involves continues within the philosophical tradition ANT trades on and contributes to in the form of an abiding controversy over the place of the natural world.

Introduction

'The Delphic priests were guardians not only of the logos but also the doctrine of sacrifice. When the Athenians consulted the oracle after Sopatrus's cruel gesture, the Pythia answered with the brutal words that would make it possible to found the city, to found any city, because cities can only be founded on guilt. Eat the victim's flesh and don't be squeamish: with these words civilization was born. All the rest is honey and acorns, the Orphic life, nostalgia for a pure beginning.' (Roberto Calasso, 1994:312)

Who pays? Can we pay them back?

An account of foundation, order and belonging, then, that is based on a sacrificial exclusion and a cannibalistic inclusion. Without the burden of guilt, carried in the belly of every citizen, but always disowned in false nostalgia for a blameless past, no city, no civilization to belong to. Perhaps this return to antiquity sits awkwardly in a volume that is 'after' Actor Network Theory (ANT)? We chose this beginning, however, in the light of Serres' (1995) debt to Girard (1977), the theorist of sacrifice and order, and in the light of ANT's debt to Serres.

ANT can be viewed as a moralistic project of the peaceable enfranchisement of the 'missing masses' (Latour, 1992) and of 'hybrids' (Latour, 1993). Lee and Brown (1994) adopt this reading in order to raise critical questions about ANT. What fascinates us is that this moralistic reading is at odds with Serres' recent portrayal of a potentially vengeful nature, going by the name of the 'worldwide world' (1995). There seems to be a contrast between an understanding of order as necessarily involving certain key exclusions and an understanding of order as involving only contingent exclusions. For example, 'belonging' on the ANT account seems to have no necessary limit, while on the Pythias' view in the quotation above, the possibility of belonging to the order of the city is entirely dependent on a radical exclusion of the 'victim' from the benefits of membership. If an order is fuelled by the consumption of the excluded, then no recognition recompense or inclusion of the victim can occur without the collapse of that order, signified for Serres by ecological collapse, the revenge of the 'worldwide world'. How far then are we able to repay those who have paid for the orders we enjoy?

As we hope to make clear, this question keys into an issue that is fundamental for any social scientific approach and in any domain of research in which questions of justice, of paying back debt in words of acknowledgement, in money or in kind arise: is a just and final settling of accounts possible?

This chapter takes the following pattern. First we will clarify the grounds on which ANT is able to launch its calls for inclusion and thus be read as providing a 'moral'. We then distinguish between a general sacrificial/exclusionary account of order (belonging-by-banishment), and a general inclusionary account of order (belonging-by-assemblage). To illustrate the significance of this distinction across specific domains and to bring to light the ethical play that takes place between accounts as they are taken up as principles of justice, we examine; the position of child witnesses in UK legal proceedings; a debate over what inclusion means in the context of gender; and majority world debt. Turning finally to a discussion of debate between Serres and Latour (1995) concerning the powers of the 'worldwide world', we conclude by noting that it is the persistence of the difference between our two accounts of belonging and order *within* ANT that qualifies its inclusionary calls as *ethical* rather than moralistic.

I. Making a start

Decentering, dependency and belonging

Actor Network Theory de-centres. Some understand post-structuralist 'de-centring' as a slogan, commitment or ultimate goal of analysis, and then, depending on their persuasion, either as a moral good or as an empty gesture of those more interested in radical chic than in the serious business of describing the world we live in. But, as is evident from studies influenced by ANT, de-centring is better understood as a method of analysis, which, given the observation 'something was done', systematically avoids the form of 'explanation', provided by grammar (which is at once fundamental and beside the point) that runs; 'some one must have done it.' Rather than simply rejecting the notion of centres of control, ANT gives account of how control may, temporarily, become centred. If this is no 'better' than accounts based on taken-for-granted centres of control, it is certainly a form of inquiry that is more sensitive to the conditions of centredness than is to be found in traditional, centred, distal (Cooper and Law, 1995) social theory. If we wanted to tease 'centred' theory, we might say that the analytic paths it follows (if, in fact, it is to be found anywhere in operation without its own tacit de-centring strategies) owe more to its observance of grammatical convention, than to thought:

'Something was done? Well then, some one must have done it!'

Of course, it should be recognized that the requirement to discern a 'centre' is here inseparable from the question 'who [or what] is responsible'? Responsibility in this sense is to do with who gets the credit or who the blame, and hence also to do with the control or steering of the state of affairs in question. The centred or grammatical modes of explanation which answer that 'he did it' or 'economics did it' or 'genetics did it' are ways of finding clear centres of responsibility amongst otherwise confusing states of affairs. To identify the responsible figure is to identify the 'owner' of a state of affairs, the one who is properly answerable for its effects and who is charged with its maintenance. Centres of responsibility are simplifying short-cuts through complexity which afford coordination.

ANT, by contrast, is a way of asking empirically how centredness, order and difference arise and are maintained, a way that is based on a methodological caution against the employment of narratal/ grammatical origins of action, such as the human agent. The themes of responsibility, dependency and ownership are set in play by ANT as questions that have no predictable answer. The being of an actant is contingent upon its capacity to act, and its capacity to act is dependent on its relations to other actants. The centredness of agentic responsibility is distributed into a dispersed network of interdependencies and co-responsibilities.

An actor-network clearly does not depend on or belong to a centre, because what passes for a centre is an effect of, and hence depends upon or belongs to the network. Where, on the distal view, the centre transcends the periphery in the sense that it is responsible for the periphery, while the periphery is not responsible for it, on the proximal view, the 'centre' is immanent with the 'periphery'. The similarity of ANT's proximal view to Derrida's arguments concerning the indifference of 'event' and 'context' (Derrida, 1995) makes it tempting to place 'centre' and 'periphery' under erasure.

ANT allows that the concepts of dependency and belonging can be applied recursively. So, in any study we may ask what elements provide for those elements that provide for a given capacity to act. Further, there is no necessary limit to this recursion. For ANT then, there is no final instance of analysis because there is no first instance in the formation of states of affairs. ANT, then, has allowed a poststructuralist rejection, not just of centre, but also—if indeed they can be separated—of 'origin' to inhabit empirical study. This is no mean achievement. Thus, for ANT, there is no final word, no line to draw under an analysis to bring it to a close, no necessary completion of accounts. Thus there is no necessary end to the elements that may contribute to a network, no general criterion by which ANT may bring an end to the list of what belongs and what is responsible. This feature of ANT has been noted by Strathern (1996).

But to what extent can ANT's methodological subtlety be employed in circumstances where the foundation of an orderly state of affairs, say a city or an institution, rather than the performance of an action, say, a 'decision', is at issue? If ANT is suspicious of 'origins' of action, does this suspicion extend to questions of the foundation of institutions, to those areas of life in which, arguably, the exclusion of some provides for the membership of others?

As we proceed we will suggest that just as ANT has helped to make sense of 'de-centring' as something that is more than a slogan, so it could help us make sense of being 'anti-foundational' as something more than oppositional wishful thinking. This would mean doing for origin-as-moment-of-foundation what ANT has done so far for origin-as-source-of-action. Just as 'de-centring' means a return to the question of how centres are possible, making account of them as immanent rather than transcendent, so 'anti-foundational' would mean a return to the question of how institutions, or any organization or state of affairs, 'start'. The notion of immanent 'starts' can be approached through Lee (1998a), or by analogy, through Strathern's 'cuts' (Strathern, 1996), or, as we shall see Serres' (1995) notion of 'departures'.

Foundations and departures

'These things never happened, but are always.'
Sallust, *Of Gods and of the World*

This line of enquiry was party provoked by the title 'We Have Never Been Modern' (Latour, 1993). Although social theory has long been performed by people under the impression that they belonged to an institution called 'modernity', that this institution, by posing certain problems, set the parameters of social theoretical enquiry, and that this institution had an, admittedly difficult to pinpoint, inception date, Latour suggested that we had never belonged to such an institution. But, beyond the title, his argument was more ambivalent with regard to this question of our 'belonging' to modernity. We have been involved in a constitution. But what we had mistaken for modernity was in fact the systematic refusal to pay a debt of respect to the hybrid (neither subject nor object) forms of organization whose labour allowed us to conceive of ourselves as pure and autonomous in our humanity (subjects as distinct from objects). Rather than simply denying our membership of modernity, rather than simply suggesting that we do not, in reality, have the purity and autonomy necessary to make us 'clubbable', and rather than making the question of modernity as simple as one of whether we belong to it or not, Latour laid out a view of what an institution is.

Taking Latour's approach to modernity as our model, an institution is a form of belonging where the possibility of belonging is guaranteed by the exclusion and silencing of certain characters, in the case of modernity and Latour's argument those excluded are the hybrids. The excluded ones do the work that pays for our belonging, and this injustice is the condition on which that belonging depends.

Despite Latour's insistence that we have never been modern, he gives us a model of modernity as an institution. This model calls for us to identify the moment at which the exclusion of hybrids began and at which the institution of modernity was founded. This 'call-of-institution' may of course be ignored as little calculable cost. But if we attend to that call, we find that Latour has written into ANT the possibility of thinking 'starts', decisive points at which institutions begin. What, after all, is a 'constitution' if not something that can be introduced and observed, something with at least the ambition of marking a decisive moment of change? As we have seen, this notion of 'starts' is quite at odds with a more obvious feature of ANT—the refusal to identify origins, causes or centres as points-of-spaces or point-moments at which states of affairs under analysis can be said to have begun—the feature which has made it possible to read ANT as moralistic.

But to show how Latour gives an account of the start of modernity which nevertheless allows that modernity has never really begun and hence that we have never really belonged to it, we will have to go into a little more detail. Precisely, then, it is not quite right to say that, for Latour, the modern world 'starts' with the exclusion of hybrids. It is more by their inclusion. While they are present in the making of the modern world, like the flesh of the victim in the belly of the citizen, their presence is effaced. This effacement involves a mode of thought which insists that the relations between the natural and cultural are subject to a law of excluded middle. This effective exclusion of hybridity from thought and from credit is the condition of possibility for their inclusion in action and their proliferation in actuality.

Modernity, in this account, is founded upon a moment of systematic misrecognition: we must speak as if nature and culture are clear and distinct realms but act as if they were not. We produce the modern world by mixing natural and cultural things into productive hybrids who can then promptly be ignored thanks to the purifying tendencies of modern thought.

Above the surface, the pure voice of clarity, below the surface, the monstrous rumble of hybrid activity. Being modern, for Latour, means adopting this relationship to the world, and adopting this relationship to the world creates the contemporary world of proliferating hybrids. Yet Latour argues that he is *not* engaging in an unveiling of false consciousness or illusion—such a denunciatory move would be, of course, archetypically modern. The difference between purity and hybridity, then, is rather like the contrast Deleuze's Foucault (Deleuze, 1988) draws between the 'visible' and the 'articulable', where the relation between them is not a determined one of reflection or representation and they are related by a certain flexible and changeable 'non-relation'. Latour is very clear on this point, saying, for example:

> 'But the relation between purification and that of mediation is not that of conscious and unconscious, formal and informal, language and practice, illusion and reality. I am not claiming that the moderns are unaware of what they do, I an simply saying that what they do—innovate on a large scale in the production of hybrids—is possible only because they steadfastly hold to the absolute dichotomy between the order of nature and that of society, a dichotomy which is itself only possible because they never consider the work of purification and that of mediation together.' (Latour, 1993:40)

But, even if we accept this conscious claim that the argument is not to do with illusion and reality, language and practice, conscious and unconscious, it is clear that we are dealing with an argument about the distribution of visibilities and articulabilities, and about a differential pattern of activities that occurs within spaces that are well lit and spaces that are shadowy and dark. Hence under the title 'what the constitution clarifies and what it obscures' (ibid: 39) we are indeed told that anthropologists have found that pre-moderns remain pre-moderns because they keep their hybrids in check by thinking continuously about hybrid connections between the social and the natural.

> 'To put it crudely,' says Latour 'those who think the most about hybrids circumscribe them as much as possible, whereas those who choose to ignore them . . . develop them to the utmost.' (Ibid: 41)

So, in the shadows, hybrids grow—hybrids that are not recognized for what they do by the official constitution of modernity . . .

> 'The link between the work of purification and the work of mediation has given birth to the moderns, but they credit only the former with their success'.

Who pays? Can we pay them back?

We stop being modern when we think the top and the bottom of Latour's diagram together. But in 'adding the bottom half to the top half' (Latour, 1993:41) light streams into previously darkened spaces and the hybrids can be recognized and given names. With recognition and a name comes the credit and blame of centred responsibility, and hence a tractability which permits a degree of control.

This is why Latour is not unveiling a secret plot. Secret plots are planned, alternative visibilities which make themselves invisible for strategic reasons by hiding. Really they are visible, if only we can unmask them. It is not just that the world in fact exists in such and such a way which we, as moderns, are either unable to see or recognize, or are concealing. Rather, the positive production of the modern world as modern depends on—and has historically depended upon—our adopting a stance of avoidance or ignorance—Latour even calls it obfuscation (Latour, 1993:46)—concerning the relation of the natural order to the social order. A refusal to give credit where credit is due is a necessary feature of modernity as an institution. The avoidance, the not saying and not seeing, is productive. The obfuscation itself is an actor in the network. So we have a start that is not really a start. Modernity starts when hybrids proliferate because we exclude them, but modernity has never started because we never actually excluded anything. The purifying thought of modernity made a clean break with the 'premoderns' which created a sense of a radical rupture in history (allowing premoderns to be just that). Premoderns thought monstrously, moderns think purely. This radical rupture is transformed when, added to this, is the observation that premoderns kept their monsters in check, whilst moderns allowed them to proliferate. But even whilst demonstrating that modernity had never started, Latour has given us a start, a model for the foundation of an institution.

Following Serres (1995:51) we may find it helpful to think of this kind of start in terms of the concept of departure—which means not just beginning, but also partition; a parting that allows a start; a parting that remains in play as long as the institution persists; a thing that never happened, but always is. The concept of departure may not trap us so quickly into the paradoxical or contradictory position of describing a start whilst simultaneously denying that it ever started, and of evoking a metaphorics of visibility whilst denying any connection to the unconscious, the unthought, the unreal and the unofficial. A departure is a beginning grounded in a division, a decision if you like—a cut or a furrow in the ground that permits a seed to grow. The division between nature and culture would hence be a decisive incision which defines, encloses and protects a fertile space wherein hybrids can develop and thrive.

So far we have argued that ANT can be read as containing a view of order that treats exclusions from the benefits of order as accidental *and* a view of order that treats certain exclusions as necessary to each form of order. ANT oscillates between these views. We have been working toward a characterization of ANT as an ethical practice of description rather than a moral one. This distinction and its applicability to ANT rests on an acknowledgement of ANT's inability to decide between our two accounts of order. ANT's ethical character lies in the way it sets the difference between our two accounts of order in play rather than seeing any clear duty for itself to decide between these two accounts of order. ANT leaves the question of whether we can 'pay them back' open.

II. Drawing the contrast: belonging by assemblage, belonging by banishment

Much of our discussion rests on an ability, temporarily, to discriminate between two accounts of belonging. One such account derives from a reading of Girard (1977) and his problem of the moment of division between human and animal in terms of cultural membership. It lends itself easily to describing forms of organization such as identity, convention and institution. The second derives from a reading of certain concepts that belong to ANT—obligatory passage point, *interessment, hybrid collectif*. We are separating these accounts as a way of teasing ANT into asking itself how it makes relationships between them. So let us work toward the clearest separation we can make.

Order—a definition!

If there is to be an order, then those elements that compose that order *must be* organized. Some elements, at least, must belong in a place or set of places and they must abide in their place or places for some length of time—in other words, the order must be relatively stable—at least to an infinitesimal degree. With proper places established, with elements established in those places and with the proviso that these arrangements endure for some time, it is possible to

Who pays? Can we pay them back?

mark off our arrangement as an order, as against disorder. Order, belonging, difference and relative stability arrive together.

'Must be'?

This most general and abstract definition of organization is surely uncontroversial. But let us attend to that 'must be' which we marked out. Is it a command? If we follow this reading we find a situation in which the one who 'must' should not expect to be able to question the command. The worker is banished from communication. We (Lee and Stenner) would seem to be saying 'Here is your task. Perform it well and without complaint and we will hear no more about the matter.' This worker would be alienated from its labour. In the moment when it is told 'Here is your task' it is separated from the run-up to the moment of organization and from that moment's aftermath. It is through being set to the task that our worker is silenced, and it is through the worker's silence that it is established that the task does not really belong to the worker. Since the task belongs to the commanders (Lee and Stenner), we will reap all the benefits of its performance, all the benefits of order, while the silenced worker, through its labours, ensures that order is produced—that there is something to be had. So it is our order, even though someone else made it.

On the other hand, could that phrase 'must be' be read as a piece of axiom-setting, an invitation to look at things in a certain way? Is it like the mathematical propositional use of the word 'Let', as in 'Let $X = 3$' (Rotman, 1993)? On this reading, we would be saying 'Colleagues, join us in this shared effort'. We would include others in our communication, hoping that they had something to contribute. We would enrol them into our effort, letting them belong if they wanted to. And the more people that belong to our discussion, the more it is worth belonging to. Though the discussion would be shared, and all might profit from it, if we were canny, we could contrive to have the discussion known as the 'Lee-Stenner conjecture', or something of that kind. All would be equal in belonging, all would benefit to some extent, but some would be more equal than others. 'Lee and Stenner' would become an obligatory passage point into the shared discussion.

So who pays for order and who pays for the existence of discrete and identifiable arrangements to which we may belong? How is order founded and what informs the possession of and belonging to order? There would seem to be (at least) two sorts of answer:

A. Belonging by banishment (BBB)

Order is produced and belonging and possession are established by the banishment of those who pay from the circle of communication. In this case, the one who pays is the one who is banished, the one who does not belong, and Lee and Stenner get to dine for free. Order is produced suddenly and the moment of foundation is identifiable. There is an absolute and necessary boundary between those who belong and those who do not.

B. Belonging by assemblage (BBA)

Order is produced by a Spinozian 'joyful encounter' (Deleuze, 1988, b) in which Lee and Stenner meet and become 'assembled' with others in a manner which increases the power of all concerned. This assemblage yields a new entity, which is more powerful or profitable than Lee and Stenner or any of the other participants alone. This assemblage or *hybrid collectif* or actor network relies on an open flow of communication (in the form of speech and the circulation of profits) between its elements. This does not prevent Lee and Stenner from collecting greater benefits from the belonging than others. Order is produced over time, it makes no sense to talk about a moment of foundation. Boundaries are not 'real', but may be performed.[1]

For Latour, using our terms, we belong to modernity by banishing the thought of the hybrid, but this can be put right and we can belong, although no longer to modernity, by assemblage. In other words, the story goes, empirically, via ANT, we can trace a network of dependencies which clearly indicates that we are dependent for our modern world upon hybrids, yet we do not credit them for their role. We humans belong, but only because we have banished those who do the work for us. Having empirically recognized the banishment situation, we can set about giving rights and recognition to the disenfranchised hybrids, who can then belong-by-assemblage with the rest of us.

> 'By deploying both dimensions at once, we may be able to accommodate the hybrids and give them a place, a name, a home, a philosophy, an ontology and, I hope, a new constitution.'
> (Latour, 1993:51)

The force of this argument comes from the partition or space opened up between belonging by banishment and belonging by assemblage. We are morally enraged by banishment—by the idea of sacrificing someone or something else for the sake of the maintenance of our own order, and by the idea of parasitism: that we live, like vampires, only because we kill and eat the flesh, plant or animal, of those we kill. If we're good people, we set about exposing such banishments—giving names to those involved and reimbursing the abused. The following examples should bring our contrast home and emphasise how vital it is to the question of just reimbursement and recognition.

Childhood and legality

Although, so far, these issues may seem unpalatably abstract, they call for our attention in the most everyday and practical settings. The legal system of England and Wales can be quite uncontroversially described as an institution. In this institution, speaking rights, in the form of the ability to testify and to have one's testimony heard are distributed according to the assumption that normal people are at least capable of delivering a true and full account of past events. Unsurprisingly, this institution has proved itself impermeable to the findings of psycho-analysis and deconstruction that lead us to doubt the existence of such psychological and memorial coherence amongst normal people. To protect the possibility of courtroom sense-making by normal people, certain categories of potential testifiers have, traditionally, been excluded and silenced—children, especially the very young, are amongst these. There is a sense in which normal people's belonging to the institution of legality is guaranteed by the exclusion of others, that adults are deemed sensible only in opposition to those excluded children. By being childlike, children do the work that allows us to see ourselves as adult, with all that implies for psychological and memorial coherence. But though this institution would seem to be founded on precisely the exclusion that Latour identifies in the foundation of modernity, in recent years, interview practices and video-recording techniques have made it possible for children to be heard as good witnesses (Lee, 1998b). An absolute exclusion, a firm division, instituted at some moment in legal history is approached by the gradual and creeping boundary dissolution of an actor network. Does the institution really change? Should it not crumble if its exclusionary support is removed? Do children now belong in court as much as adults do?

We might shrug off this meeting of BBA and BBB as nothing remarkable. Indeed the stated purpose of this subsection has been to demonstrate that it is indeed unremarkable. But let us not abandon the duty of curiosity too quickly. We know that our two forms of belonging co-exist, but we have yet to imagine what that co-existence is like.

The following is another attempt to imagine that co-existence and to give some sense of how crucial BBA and BBB, in their distinctiveness and their co-existence, are to ethico-political matters, to decisions over how to do the right thing.

Gender and labour

PAID IN FULL
(apologies to David Mamet, Martin Amis and Elmore Leonard)

'Okay, so the situation we've got here is like this, this is the way you put it: You've been doing all this work . . . what did you call it "emotional labour" and such? . . . and er you've not been getting credit for it. You're talking about some debt about which we, on our side, for our part, we've not been doing anything about it? Am I okay so far?'

'Uhuh'

'So your thinking is "Look at these guys . . . riding high . . . and we've been cut out of the loop?"'

'Yeah, that's what we're saying'

'Alright then. This I can understand. You see, we've been wondering, we're businessmen (we think about these things don't worry) . . . we're thinking, like, why didn't you come to us earlier? You want a piece of the action? Sure, we understand that . . . what you got there is "legitimate grievance". But what do you want from us, that we should be mind-readers?'

'Okay. What are you putting on the table?'

'Our thinking is we *can* come to an understanding. It's a big thing to you, this thing, huh? Its got your nose out of joint. We can see that. To us . . . some arrangement . . . its nothing. So . . . what have we got . . . we're talking about some dollar amount, some figure.'

Who pays? Can we pay them back?

'Hey, just hang on a minute!'

'Simmer down lady. We want to make you happy on this. That's why we're talking here, yeah? We didn't have to come.'

'You want us to be grateful? I can't believe this shit!'

'We want you to be happy . . . you're happy . . . we're happy . . . a payment for services rendered. This is no kiss-off we're talking here. Now listen. This is in perpetuity. What we're saying is you keep your end up with the "emotional labour" and shit? and we . . . are going . . . to see you right. We wanna make this thing right.'

'You wanna make it right?'

'That's what the man said.'

'Okay. Get this, mister man. You think we just want your money, like we come here for some handout? It's not the money, it's the whole setup's gotta change. Its like always. You come here waving your money around and expect everyone to get in line. What kind of a human being are you, treat people like that?'

'You're starting to question my ethics now lady, you should just back off from that hostility right now!'

'I'm not hostile, it's just you don't get it. You say you pay us for services rendered? It'll be the same. We just get some crumbs off the cake, you're still living large at the trough with your tails in the air. Or, say out of just ethical goodness you give us a pitch. You feel good, sure. And what if the marks don't wanna play the numbers no more? Who's back indoors? You? We're saying that you're established, fine. It's just we've got to get established too.'

'You mean you wanna do a man's job? Wait a minute . . . who's gonna clean up around the place? I can't be running around after the kids the whole time . . . how's a guy supposed to run a business with these terms?'

'That's your problem, sweetheart.'

'But what you're saying it's just . . . I'll tell you what it is, it's an attack on the foundations of good business practice!'

In order words, and to leave these amateur dramatics behind, there are at least two reimbursement schemes at work here. The difference between them is that one understands all debts as repayable, and the other is aware of a limit to the repayment of debt. What our plaintiff is calling for, and what 'the man' cannot comprehend is one of Serres' 'departures', or one of our 'starts'—a decisive change in arrangements which is based on recognition that an unpayable debt has accumulated.

Hunger and debt

'... the smooth functioning of such a society, the monotonous complacency of its discourses on morality, politics and the law, and the exercise of its rights (whether public, private, national or international), are in no way impaired by the fact that, because of the structure of the laws of the market that society has instituted and controls, because of the mechanisms of external debt and other similar inequities, that same 'society' puts to death or ... allows to die of hunger and disease tens of millions of children (those neighbours or fellow humans that ethics or the discourse of the rights of man refer to) without any moral or legal tribunal ever being considered competent to judge such a sacrifice, the sacrifice of others to avoid being sacrificed oneself. Not only is it true that such a society participates in this incalculable sacrifice, it actually organizes it. The smooth functioning of its economic, political, and legal affairs, the smooth functioning of its moral discourse and good conscience presupposes the permanent operation of this sacrifice.' Derrida (1995: 86)

Do they mean us?

In the quotation above Derrida gives a sacrificial/exclusionary account of how those of us in the minority world come to belong to wealth, good-conscience and responsibility for the provision of human rights and how those properties come to belong to us. In a few phrases ('the market', 'the smooth functioning of society', 'morality, politics and the law') he gathers together these aspects of the global state of affairs which we, in the 'minority world', are able to enjoy. We profit materially and spiritually (in the form of positive self regard) from the circulation of goods, finance and discourse. We are able to profit from this circulation because we have been enrolled in the networks this circulation follows and sustains. Though few of us are multi-billionaires like Bill Gates, we are in a position to give him a little money so that we can make a little money. So money appears to us to make money, and this alchemy seems to take place for free. Derrida asks to what we owe the relative stability and order that allows us to benefit from circulation. He asks whether the 'expansion of the market' with all that this entails for the generation and enjoyment of profit is a free lunch. He asks questions that are as thermodynamic as they are ethico-political—where does the energy come from to maintain order? His conclusion is that whatever variable shapes 'the network' may take, the energy required to maintain those shapes is taken, indirectly to be sure, from those who are excluded from the networks. BBA and BBB co-exist as a matter of necessity in the global 'free trade' economy, and coexist in such a way that the global economy must always break its own law of reciprocity; for free trade and fair exchange to be possible, there must be those who are stolen from. This issue comes up when we discuss the question of what to do about third-world debt. Clearly, we, humanity, have got ourselves into an unfair situation. How can we expect the majority world to achieve low child-mortality rates and political stability when as soon as they make a buck they have to give it up to their creditors? What we should do is cancel all that debt. But if we cancel the debt we lost an enormous source of income. Without the majority world servicing its debt, there will be no circulation and our networks will collapse. Our wealth depends on their poverty.

BBA/BBB: Other/others: infinitist/finitist ethics

'The Other'—a phrase which can be used to generate an impression of moral seriousness. That capital 'O', with its fat, hieratical, sententious promise. What does this singular capitalized 'Other' bring to our discourse about belonging, exclusion and the possibility of order that we cannot get from a multitude of plain old empirical 'others' (apart from ecclesiastical gloom, litanies and incense)?

If some of those many ordinary 'others' have been excluded, cut out of the loop, then it is only by some accident or oversight. Restitution can be made. They can be repaid. They can be invited into belonging, and we can satisfy ourselves that the state of affairs is now fair. But 'the Other', marked off from temporal affairs by a passage into the supernatural, by death in the case of a mortal, by inherent qualities in the case of a deity, makes an inexhaustible call upon us. In God's eye no state of affairs is fair. We can never repay those we have put to death. The Other brings a limit to calculability of restitution and to moral sense-making. The infinitude of the debt makes our finitude obvious. This is the condition of the ethical. The incalculability makes our moral calculations seem tawdry. The difference between 'Other' and 'others' marks a difference between two orders. And it is this difference that differentiates the moral and the ethical. The 'other' can always be brought back into communion, into the fold of responsibility, communicate dependency and mutual recognition (belonging), and it is our duty to bring the 'other' back. The Other marks a limit to this open, communicating network of mutuality. Together, those others and the Other tell us that sometimes there is a circulation, sometimes it does make sense to think in terms of a law of reciprocity or *interessement*, but that this circulation has its limit. 'Global capitalism' with all its free trade, has its limit in those who have died willingly or unwillingly in its service. Who pays? They pay. Though the order may be described as a network, that network depends on those excluded from it.

As we saw in the case of Latour, ANT does not forget 'the Other' in its bid to cross ontological boundaries by recognizing the 'rights' of non-human empirical others. It is through an oscillation between BBA and BBB that Latour's argument makes itself pertinent. BBB crops up in two shapes in Latour (1993). First among moderns in the strange start of a modern constitution. Second in the way that pre-moderns circumscribe hybrids. Strathern's 'cuts' and our 'starts' or 'departures' are already at work in ANT. If any further argument is needed, consider how whenever a new agent joins a network, the network and all within it change. It seems that exotics like starts, cuts and departures are the most workaday features of networks.

And what allowed us to articulate this problem of finding relations between apparently contradictory ethics and modes of ordering? On what does this ANT insight concerning the actuality of hybrids depend? On a combination, says Latour, of the boundary forsaking tendencies of ANT to ask the question of centredness and organization in an empirical way and the fact that the hybrids have become so prevalent that it is impossible to ignore them. Here we see that ANT, in Latour's version at least, is a lot more than just another social scientific moral fable. ANT allows, or is part of, the sketching of a new constitution for a new, yet already occurring, amodern world. Just as the modern constitution was not just an account of reality, but an integral actant in the production of the state of affairs we called modernity, so ANT is presented as a point of departure for an amodern world. The point of departure is the refusal to disavow our dependencies. A commitment to belonging by assemblage. If empirically what we have is a network of interdependencies with each actant playing its part in the production of reality, then our constitution too should take the form of an inclusive network. No longer will obfuscating and exclusion be key actants in the network. But upon what does that network depend? What are the limitations of this network? Are there no limits to inclusiveness? Are we amoderns unlimited in our capacity for acting? Are we not in danger of introducing a further productive obfuscation into our account, the obfuscation of our limitations? Is the source of our powers so infinite that we can all continue drawing upon it forever? Is not the dream of inclusive network itself dependent upon something else for its power and sustenance? Can we all get cut into the loop? On what does the loop depend? It is at this point—as we imagine, with Latour, how better to live—that the Other reintroduces itself.

The natural contract

> 'BL But we still inhabit the same world of necessity. How can we escape from it?
> MS Does your sweet youth prevent you from seeing the recent change?' (Serres and Latour, 1995:169)

Michael Serres, in *The Natural Contract* (1995) puts together an argument superficially very similar to Bruno Latour's, but in important ways quite different. For Serres the natural or worldwide world and the human or worldly world of culture and politics, far from being part of the same network, have always had a violent and antagonistic relationship 'a combat that has lasted since prehistory' (Serres, 1995:35). He defines traditional wisdom as that which helped us bear inevitable pains which were the result of confrontations with a potentially cruel and devastating natural world independent of us, which nevertheless provides us with the gift of life. In an interview with Latour (Serres and Latour, 1995), he says that 'from our beginnings we had regulated our actions on the distinction between things that depended on us and those that in no way depended on us' (Serres and Latour, 1995:169).

For Serres, although this antagonism did not start with modernity, modernity gave us, and was given to us through such ideas as the social contract which, in principle, or virtually, united all men in the collectivity of society as against the state of nature; a philosophy of mastery and possession; and a declaration of the rights of men which proposed, in the name of human nature, to include, again in principle or virtually, all those people who had been excluded. All people are united in that they can be subjects of a social contract.

But as Serres points out, nature had no part in all this. Nature was the old enemy that mankind could defeat more effectively by ganging up. Our relationship to nature became increasingly defined in the Cartesian terms of mastery and possession, ownership and domination. Through science and technology, he argues, we have indeed come to dominate and possess the worldwide world, and to push back and back the degree to which it limits our activities and capacities. Most of us, for instance, live in cities where we can function in blissful ignorance of the very existence of an external nature—we can have light, heat, comfort, food and drink on call 24 hours a day everyday. Having 'almost eliminated what does not depend on us' we have also eliminated the grounds for any wisdom which orients itself in terms of these old objective dependencies and limits. This wisdom is replaced by scientific knowledge which is itself concerned with the mastery and possession of nature.

The worldwide world or external nature has no rights in the social contract—all law is on the side of the worldly world. It is fair game to exploit the worldwide world to the maximum, to control it, appropriate it and manipulate it until, far from us depending on it, it comes to depend on us. So where previously we depended upon the necessity of an independent world, now that world depends on us, and on a global scale: we have the capacity to destroy the planet. Yet what would we be without our planet? Perhaps by the time we destroy it we will have invented the technology necessary for inhabiting other planets, or for living in space, who knows! But save that, we are nothing without our planet. For Serres, this realization should lead us to want to invent another contract, a natural contract which recognizes nature's capacity as a subject to act against us or for us and hence gives it rights and prevents it from being mastered and possessed and hence abused. Those that master and possess take everything and give nothing: they are parasites, but parasites which destroy their hosts destroy themselves. Our mastery—our quest for an independence that makes everything depend on us—brings us face to face with our dependencies and limitations after all. Serres takes us to the crushing or freeing realization that just at the point where everything seems now to depend on us we are confronted with the fact that 'it does not depend on us that everything depends on us.' The pressing question becomes 'how to master our mastery'? The natural contract would hence be a new departure made possible by the linking together, the contracting, of two worlds which had been decisively separated through the conflict between people and nature. The contract is an affirmation of our symbiotic connection or mutual dependency. We hence cast off under a new definition of our nature or Being.

For Latour, as we saw, the problem seems to be one of formally recognizing the role that objects play in human networks. These hybrids are so called because, being implicated in these networks they can not properly be called 'natural' objects. For Serres, a very similar set of themes is developed, but certainly not with the intention of more knowingly and controllingly incorporating objects into the increasingly powerful human network. For Serres the Otherness of nature screams out on its own terms, from its own world, and the issue, on pain of life and death, concerns balance and reciprocity—the maintenance of an order not dictated solely by our terms. This would be a new contract, not the emendation by filling in the productive blanks of the old social contract. Modernity as a departure sent us on a way—destined us—cast us off to dominate nature. With the gift of life given us by nature, we determined, under modernity, to challenge nature and to strive to force it into compliance with our requirements. That is what we did with the gift: taking nature into our mastery we strove to make ourselves independent of it, and it dependent on us. We succeeded, it seems, but at the great cost of a self-imposed detachment from and perhaps even destruction of the nature that is the source of our life.

> 'From the nature we used to speak about, an archaic world in which our lives were plunged, modernity casts off, in its growing movement of derealization. Having become abstract and inexperienced, developed humanity takes off towards signs, frequents images and codes, and, flying in their midst, no longer has any relation, in cities, either to life or to the things of the world'.

So thorough has become this derealization of modernity, so alien to most of us the old natural world of necessity, that any talk of a nature independent of human interests is met with incredulity, as if it is the height of naivety not to realize that everything in the world, including nature and human nature, is a human construct which has been given birth to by human words. Everything, we are told, depends on us. God, for instance, was simply invented by people before we realized that we are, in fact, Gods. How foolish to listen to God when we, as God, are the only thing worth listening to. We look, and we see ourselves, we listen and we hear our own booming voices:

> 'Meanwhile man, precisely as the one so threatened, exalts himself to the posture of lord of the earth. In this way the

impression comes to prevail that everything man encounters exists only insofar as it is his construct. This illusion gives rise in turn to one final delusion: It seems as though man everywhere and always encounters only himself. . . . In truth, however, precisely nowhere does man today any longer encounter himself.' (Heidegger, 1977:27)

Conclusion

In sum, what we are suggesting is that as we break ontological boundaries and render everything 'networky', we will become insensitive to complexity and heterogeneity if we forget that there is an heterogeneity between Other and others. Unless we find some way of recognizing debts that cannot be paid as well as debts that can be paid, we risk seeing in every other nothing but our own reflection. In the case of childhood and representation, it is neither analytically, ethically nor strategically satisfactory to simply declare that they have the same competences as adults. In the case of feminisms, it makes little sense to map gender relations as a network unless we are aware that such a network may be open to fundamental and decisive change—a stop, a start, a departure. In the case of Serres and amodernity, Nature recomposes itself as an Other, calling for a departure, after a period of relative quiescence and just at the point where our powers reach their maximum through the accumulation of an unrepayable debt.

We have argued that ANT does not and cannot decide between two forms of belonging—between the call of institution and moments of foundation and the call of flexibility, transgression and an analytic disregard of moments of foundation. The point has not been to force ANT to make that decision, nor to inspire it to turn its back on the 'undecidable' as an unpromising research project, but to make the relation between being and becoming, form and change articulable as a question for theoretical and empirical study within ANT. We offer our immanent 'starts' and Serres' 'departure' as elements of a vocabulary designed to preserve ANT's ethical rather than moral character.

Notes

1 These contrasting schemes—BBB having a pre-incorporated but necessarily exteriorised term, BBA having a boundless genuine exterior ready for blameless

incorporation—and their equipotent persuasiveness have long provided the resources for monotheistic theological dispute concerning the transcendence or immanence of God. Compare, for example, the differing characters accorded to God by Descartes and Spinoza. More recently our contrast has informed Deleuze's rejection of Hegelian dialectic (Hardt, 1993) and his preference for 'becoming' without end and plurality rather than unity as the starting point for the problem of the one and the multiple. A reading of the later Guattari (1995) suggests to us that the currently highly mobile terms 'complexity' and 'self-organization', while busy on their variously, and often indistinguishably scientific and ideological tasks, trade quite univocally on BBA. This makes the indecision between BBB and BBA that attends ANT particularly timely.

References

Calasso, R. (1994), *The Marriage of Cadmus and Harmony*, Vintage: London.
Cooper, R. and Law, J. (1995), 'Organisation: Distal and Proximal Views' in Bachrach, S., Gagliardi, P. and Mundell, B. (eds), *Research in the Sociology of Organisations: Studies of Organisation in the European Tradition*. Greenwich, Conn.: JAI Press.
Girard, R. (1977), *Violence and the Sacred*. Baltimore: John Hopkins University Press.
Deleuze, G. (1988, A), *Foucault* (trans. Hand, S.), Minneapolis: University of Minnesota Press.
Deleuze, G. (1988, B), *Spinoza*: Practical Philosophy. San Francisco: City Lights Books.
Derrida, J. (1995), *The Gift of Death*. Chicago: University of Chicago Press.
Guattari, F. (1995), *Chaosmosis: An Ethico-Aesthetic Paradigm*. Sydney: Power Publications.
Hardt, M. (1993), *Gilles Deleuze: An Apprenticeship in Philosophy*. London: UCL Press.
Heidegger, M. (1977), *The Question Concerning Technology*, trans. Lovitt, New York: W. Harper Torchbooks
Latour, B. (1992), 'Where are the missing masses? A sociology of a few mundane artifacts'. In W.E. Bijker and J. Law (eds), *Shaping Technology/Building Society*. Cambridge, MA: Harvard University Press.
Latour, B. (1993), *We Have Never Been Modern*, trans. Porter, C. Hemel Hempstead: Harvester Wheatsheaf.
Law, J. (1997), *Aircraft Stories: Decentering the Object in Technoscience*.
Lee, N. M. (1998a), 'Two Speeds: How are Stabilities Possible?' in Chia, R. (ed.), *Organized Worlds: Explorations in Technology and organization with Robert Cooper*. London: Routledge.
Lee, N. M. (1998b), 'Faith in the Body: Childhood, Subjecthood and Sociological Enquiry' in Prout, A. (ed.), *Childhood Bodies*. London: Macmillan.
Lee, N. M. and Brown, S. (1994), 'Otherness and the Actor Network: The Undiscovered Continent'. *American Behavioral Scientist*. 37. 6. 772–790.
Rotman, B. (1993), *Ad Infinitum: The Ghost in Turing's Machine*. Stanford: Stanford University Press.
Serres, M. (1995), *The Natural Contract*, trans. MacArthur, E. and E. Paulson. The University of Michigan Press.

Serres, M., Latour, B. (1995), *Conversations of Science, Culture and Time*, trans. Lapidus, R. The University of Michigan Press.
Strathern, M. (1996), 'Cutting the Network'. *Journal of the Royal Anthropological Institute*, 2, 517–535.

Materiality: juggling sameness and difference

Anni Dugdale

Abstract

Many studies of controversy tell stories of convergence, of movement from difference to sameness, of a narrowing from many competing versions to a single stabilised 'reality'. This paper explores a case of science policymaking about IUDs in Australia. What begins in controversy ends with a single view of the IUD—a view presented in a consumer information leaflet. But surprisingly, what is found is that this stabilisation of a singularity depends on multiplicity. The negotiation of a compromise involves the making of a centred knowing position, an object—the IUD, and a consumer choice. But this is only made possible by the proliferation of difference: the decentring of the knowing subject, the 'doing' of many different IUDs, and the dispersion of choice from the head of the consumer across time and space. Closure then becomes a very different story, a story of oscillation between sameness and difference, of doing singularity and multiplicity together.

A parable

Odo is the security officer of the space station Deep Space 9, a Star Trek TV series. Odo is a shape shifter. His 'people' are the founders. Sent into space as an infant, a changeling, Odo is picked up as a shapeless blob of goo. Gradually, he learns to hold various shapes—a cube, a sphere, a cylinder, eventually that of a humanoid, and to shift between them. There are times when Odo appears as a solid (usually a humanoid). But for some hours each day we see him as fluid, as he regenerates in a special bucket. Sometimes Odo is clearly both solid and fluid, oscillating between liquid and solid, his centred identity as Deep Space 9's security officer trembling as his decentred state threatens. At these times Odo is both solid and

Anni Dugdale

liquid, simultaneously a singular object and a multiplicity of objects. And when Odo revisits his home planet he becomes part of the great link, poured into the ocean that is the continuum, in which all founders on the planet are merged, having at one and the same time both different individual identities and the same collective identity. Shape shifting is science fiction, or is it?[1]

Introduction

This chapter is about policy-making. Specifically, it is about a committee which was set up in Australia to advise on the health dangers in using intrauterine contraceptive devices (IUDs). The committee was composed of experts—a gynaecologist, a representative of industry, a government scientist, a family planning physician, a public servant, and a consumer representative. One of its major policy recommendations and tasks undertaken was the drafting of a leaflet for women which was to be given to them by their physicians as they considered whether or not it was safe to use the IUD.

There is a way of talking about science policy-making, and so the deliberation of committees such as this, which treats their debates and, more particularly, their outcomes, as effects of different interests and the power of those different interests to influence both what counts as knowledge and the policies such knowledge claims are taken to authorize. This approach is not far from that of the sociology of scientific knowledge (SSK). Truths—or in this case compromises—are hammered out in (more or less concealed) controversy, and the consequence is closure (Jasanoff, 1990; Richards, 1991; Martin, 1991).

There is some evidence that when the Australian government set up the committee it was being guided by some such model of the politics of scientific policy making. Thus the Labor Party (which was in power at the time) sought to broaden the representation on expert committees to include consumer representatives. (This was, indeed, the reason why I know about this committee: I was the chosen consumer representative). In good social-democratic mode, its thinking appears to have been that the biases inevitably brought to policy-making by professionals and representatives of industry might be undone, at least in part, if other stake-holders, and especially consumers, were included in discussion.

No doubt the government was in some measure right. I am sure that my presence on the committee made a difference in certain ways, both to its deliberations and to its conclusions. The outcome was probably marginally more 'consumer-friendly' than would otherwise have been the case. But in this chapter I want to explore the adequacy of the model of closure—and interest politics—on which such thinking is based. Or, more particularly, I want to consider how it is that 'compromises' such as that embodied in the text of the leaflet, are created. As I've mentioned above, the model appears to look like a version of social constructivism in SSK and SCOT (social construction of technology). Certainly this is a more adequate model than the linear model of science/technology development in which scientific and technical 'facts' are quarantined from social forces. In the SSK/SCOT model the process is imagined as one of negotiation, where bargaining positions are backed up by various forms of power (MacKenzie, 1990; Bijker, 1995). My argument is that whilst this isn't exactly wrong, it begs a number of questions:

- First, it assumes that various interest groups *have* power that is somehow constituted through the social arrangements in which they have participated prior to and outside of the science policy context. That there *is* power is no doubt right. But referring back to such an externalized power distribution as explanatory tends to let the analyst off the hook. This is because it uses as explanatory something that should be explained: *how is power mobilized? How does it show itself? How is it reproduced and organized in the proceedings at hand?* If power is to work, then it has, as Foucault points out, to appear in and be constantly reorganized in the course of negotiations (Foucault, 1979, 1980).
- Second, it implies a particular model of the subject as a centred decision-maker and knower who is, in addition, probably rational. The *representatives* involved in such negotiations, for instance, stand for particular and specific (though possibly moveable) points of view. I don't want to say that representatives are irrational. Neither, do I simply want to say that they are de-centred. But I *do* want to say that they are constituted in part in the course of negotiation. In short, I want to introduce some of the arguments about the decentering of knowing subjects common in post-structuralism to the case of bargaining behaviour in policy-making.
- Third, it makes an analogous series of assumptions about the *objects* being considered in policy-making. Objects, such as the IUD, are generally considered in social constructivist science and

technology studies to be embedded in various heterogeneous systems and thus to generate competing knowledges and technologies (Shapin and Schaffer, 1985; Hughes, 1983). But the object itself is in some senses singular, and in particular the technological system or scientific knowledge claim that is the outcome of negotiation is said to stabilize a particular object. But if the subject is 'decentred', then it may be—and this is what I argue here—that the object is also *and always* decentred (Mol, 1998a; Law, 1998a).

- Finally, and in order to explore how power is mobilized and subjects and objects constituted, I want to explore a further feature of negotiation which is most often conspicuous by its absence: *practical materiality*. For committees of all sorts sit in rooms, drink coffee, and shuffle through paperwork. And it is in and through such material arrangements that decisions are made possible. This, of course, is one of the lessons of actor-network theory (Callon, 1986a, 1986b; Latour, 1987, 1988, 1996; Law, 1987, 1994).

Context

It was the Australian Government's Therapeutic Goods Administration (TGA), as it's now known, which established the subcommittee on IUDs. It met from 1989 to 1991, and then its function was subsumed into a new and more general committee on reproductive medicine.[2] The IUD subcommittee was formed partly in response to publicity about a U.S. court finding that the manufacturer of the Copper-7 IUD, Searle, had been negligent (ABC TV, 1988). The court awarded $7 million in punitive damages (Ellis, 1988). The court accepted that Searle was in possession of information about the higher risks of infection for young women using IUDs, and given this and its sales campaign stressing the particular suitability of the Copper-7 for young women who had never been pregnant (because of its smaller size and ease of insertion), it should have issued a warning and tested its product more fully (Federal Supplement, 1989). Prior to this finding Searle had withdrawn the Copper-7 from sale in the U.S. (due, Searle insisted, to insurance problems and not to a product defect), but not in Australia. This led to much lobbying for its withdrawal in Australia by individual women and consumer organizations. During the time the committee met, the Copper-7 was indeed withdrawn and other copper IUDs were subjected to an extended premarket approval process under new therapeutic device legislation.

Materiality; juggling, sameness and difference

The committee itself had various tasks but one of them—which followed one of its recommendations—was the production of the consumer information leaflet mentioned above. I will talk more about this leaflet below. But first I want to explore the material workings of the committee itself.

Scene 1

I am still bleary eyed from a 5 am start to catch the Sydney to Melbourne flight booked for me by the TDEC (Therapeutic Devices Evaluation Committee) secretariat. It is the first time I have been flown first-class, been admitted to 'flight-deck' (the international hotel standard business coffee lounge), or used taxi vouchers. I am standing in front of a nondescript building which the taxi-driver had trouble finding. There is only some small writing on the glass door to identify it. It is in a light industrial inner suburb of Melbourne. Inside there is a very small foyer and I wait for someone from behind the counter to take me through to the meeting room. I am clutching a green folder of agenda papers and documents sent to me that will be considered at the IUD subcommittee. The only exit except the door to the street is blocked by a locked door. I get the impression that this is not a place often visited by members of the public. We proceed along corridors, past small laboratories in one of which I am later proudly shown the condom testing machine. We must negotiate several locked doors. Secret codes are deftly punched in to open them. The meeting room is large but unremarkable. It is a working space with neither pictures on the walls nor views from the windows. The cement floor has been hastily covered with dark coloured, nylon carpet squares which seem to have run out before quite reaching one corner. I take my place around the tables pushed together on one side. I take off the jacket carefully purchased for the occasion and roll-up my sleeves blending in with the men in suits and the women in neat doctor garb; power-dressing is conspicuous by its absence. As others arrive we help ourselves to coffee, later sandwiches are brought in and we stand around balancing plates and orange juice.

By then I have been introduced to each of the people listed on one of the documents in my green folder headed 'membership'. Alongside each name the organization of which they are a representative is listed: the Commonwealth of Australia's Health Department, the Family Planning Association (FPA), the Royal Australian College of Obstetricians and Gynaecologists (RACOG), the Women's

Anni Dugdale

Committee of the National Health and Medical Research Council (NHMRC), the MDDPB (Medical Devices and Dental Products Branch), the Consumers' Health Forum of Australia (CHF), and TDEC. The FPA representative, experienced on government committees, kindly checks that I know that I am entitled to travel allowance for being away from home, and discusses how to fill out the expenses form with the Commonwealth of Australia logo in the corner. A young man employed by the MDDPB who has been quietly taking minutes during the morning, tells me that I should be paid a sitting-fee for the day at 'category 2' professional rates. Before the meeting ends we are encouraged to leave our green folders behind and reminded that if we keep them then we must ensure they are secured in a place where their confidentiality is assured. I think of my university office and its filing cabinets shared between several postgraduate students, the door rarely locked, and take my folder with me; I need it to write a report. I am obliged as a consumer representative to report to the CHF, to justify my actions to consumers through a process of public reporting. We have finished early, and whilst the Melbourne people return to their regular jobs, those of us from Sydney and Canberra eagerly depart for a spot of shopping in this retail and clothing capital of Australia.

This scene contains a multitude of *materials*: air tickets, cab charge vouchers, buildings, letterheads, claim forms, arrangements of locked doors, rooms, schedules of reimbursements, the list of subcommittee members. We are prone to treat such materials as background, as essentially unimportant to an analysis of the business of making science policy. But here, in conformity with much work in actor-network theory, and also with feminist work analysing the materiality of the body (Haraway, 1991, 1997; Oudshoorn, 1994; Keller, 1992; Grosz, 1994; Bordo, 1993; Diprose, 1994; Gatens 1996; Franklin, 1997) I want to suggest that such materials are crucial in producing the bodies that are assembled together *as subjects*. It is the mixing together of such materials with bodies that constitutes subjects of a particular kind. For the subjectivities of the participants are already being produced in these material arrangements, even before any verbal performances have occurred.

All of the members of the committee are translated by arrangements of these materials from their identities in other contexts—parent, student, doctor, administrator, shopper—into TGA committee members. All are present as part of a *bureaucratic performance* that constitutes them as subjects of a certain kind. They are

Materiality; juggling, sameness and difference

subjects with a set of relationships and trajectories that pertain to government—the government of objects (therapeutic goods), of companies that manufacture those goods, of health professionals who recommend and use them, of consumers whose bodies bear their effects. Before entering the building I am already part of a web of relationships with people and things that constitute me as a government bureaucrat: pre-booked flights, cab-charge vouchers, letter-headed expense claim forms, the knowledge that I will be paid for my time by the Health Department, all catapult me into a particular mode of bureaucratic subjectivity.

And then there is the building. Its architecture encodes a very particular set of relations. This is the Australian Government Health Department—small and weak in relation to the Medicare scheme and the State Health Departments that administer public hospitals. Even the medical profession is strong compared to the Australian Government Health Department, having resisted many attempts to bring the practice of medicine under government organization (Gillespie, 1991). The TGA may be strong in relation to manufacturers who are bound by law to subject certain products for approval, but many pharmaceutical companies resist by simply failing to pursue what is quite a small market for their products.

These relations can be read in the building. In the back streets of a light industrial suburb, it is not the kind of place that is easily found by the general public or by business leaders. This is a work building. It looks unimpressive, barely announces itself to the infrequent passers-by, its foyer is featureless and without a waiting area—no brightly coloured walls or flash receptionist or anything designed to impress such as the vaulted ceilings of Cathedrals and Shopping Malls. It reminds me of the chest-clinic I had been sent to following a positive TB test. There the paint was peeling from the walls and one followed signs along damp and cold corridors to the makeshift reception area. Visitors entered as part of a gulag, there by compulsion. This was a government that worked in the shadows, protecting the health of its citizens, but unused to dealing directly with them as such. It was only later that the TGA would rewrite its architecture, reinventing the public and manufacturers as its 'customers', and itself as a professional and modern service provider.

So my first point is that subjects do not come to the subcommittee ready-made. Instead, bureaucratic subjects are being constituted in such material arrangements. But there are other subjectivities being produced too. For instance, I also find myself being performed as part of a hierarchical system of surveillance, a chain of command arranged to prevent leaks, a set of arrangements designed to ensure privacy. Here participants are being produced not only as agents of the state, but also as commercial agents. Thus to enter the building was to encounter not the security arrangements of a prison, but rather those of industry—designed to prevent sabotage. Overlooking a back-lane and far from the public eye, we eat in. There is no danger of careless conversations being overheard. One of the papers in my green folder declares that 'in respect of commercial matters' papers are to be 'held in a secure place, or returned to the secretariat for disposal' and that discussions are 'not to be revealed to other persons without the consent of the chairperson'. Such technologies of secrecy are crucial to the contract between government and industry. Public scrutiny designed to prevent another thalidomide or heart-valve tragedy is to be done behind closed doors. In fact very little testing is done by the government regulator of therapeutic devices. The regulator relies on company-supplied documents. The companies only comply when they have ensured that the TGA space is an extension of their manufacturing plants, with the same security arrangements to stop the stealing of secrets. We become embedded in a security apparatus that constitutes us as commercial agents.

So we are carefully inserted into *bureaucratic* and *commercial* performative arrangements which confer certain limited agencies on us. These agencies neither precede their 'doing' in such arrangements (a mind inside a body), nor do the materials provide a substrate which determines them (Butler, 1990; Law, 1994; Mol, 1998a, 1998b). Indeed the story is more complicated. For we are also being constituted as *scientific 'experts'* and *democratic 'representatives'*. I have been flown to the meeting first-class, accompanied by consulting professionals, senior public servants and high-ranking business people. The subcommittee has been established under the TDEC terms of reference which are in my green folder and tell me that our task is to make 'medical and scientific evaluations of such devices for therapeutic use as the Minister refers' to us. Payment is set at 'Professional Rate' and the 'flight-deck' lounge whilst simply being the icing on the cake, marks our status and rank as experts through material markers of prestige and exclusion.

The building constitutes us as experts somewhat differently. It is fitted out as a scientific place. As I have noted, priority is given to laboratory space and fittings, rather than to the kind of fittings that generate a sense of importance and occasion in other settings, such as board rooms, courts and university senates. Here the TGA is competing with medicine's claims to scientific expertise, and a past marked in Australia by the vigorous defence of the autonomy of the medical practitioner. So we are to meet in a building where the claims to professionalism by the MDDPB are writ large in the design of its laboratories, in devices like the condom testing machine, and in the 'experts' recruited to committees. And while less attention is lavished on its conference rooms than on its laboratories, these are also important because they work to insert us into a specific *scientific* professional order in which openness and lack of deferral to rank are markers. Hence the unadorned room hails us as equals. A shared training in the scientific method and thus a privileged access to objectivity are performed as levellers. Rank, occupational positions, or years of experience are irrelevant. The very drabness of the room underlines the openness of science that is the basis for its bid as a privileged place of knowing.

So we are bureaucrats, commercial agents, experts, but alongside these 'modes of ordering' (Law, 1994) we are also being pulled into a political (small p) performative arrangement operating with a democratic logic. The list of subcommittee members orders our names under the heading 'representatives'. The organizations that have nominated us are listed alongside our names. Inside the green folder are the agenda and related papers for the meeting, carefully separated by coloured dividers. Next to each divider is a sheet of paper nominating the agenda item together with 'Recommendations' and a 'Draft Resolution'. We rarely vote, but the consensus decision making procedure by which we progress through the agenda is no less a marker of a political process. Disagreements over knowledge of IUD effectiveness and safety are expected. This democratic ordering performs a different logic of knowing than that performing us as experts, a logic of sharing perspectives and accommodating difference.

Perhaps, then, we are dealing with pluralism? Bureaucrat, industrial employee, scientific expert, and democratic representative. Some 'postmodern stories' might celebrate this multiplicity. Others might link it to stories of negotiation and compromise, ideally as a function of the legitimacy of the power of each position. But I'm suggesting that something more complicated is going on:

- First I'm saying that *the subject positions are being constituted in the committee in its material arrangements*. They are put into play by those arrangements. This, to be sure, is a lesson that we learn from actor-network theory.

- Second I'm saying that *all the members of the committee are being constituted in all of these logics*. That, for instance, I am (nearly) as much an industrial employee as the representative of industry. Which means that we have much more in common than might otherwise appear to be the case.
- Third, as a result of this, I'm saying that the struggles between the different positions *reproduce themselves in our individual, and multiple, subjectivities*. This is not a retreat to the 'micro'. Nor is it to deny the 'macro'. It is, however, to raise questions about the nature of this division. It is to follow how the 'macro' flows because of the 'micro', and to explore how the 'micro' reproduces itself and thus becomes the 'macro'. (See Latour, 1998) Note that the 'macro' is not merely *expressed* in the 'micro'; there is movement for *all* of us between different subject-positions and this is performed through local and very specific arrangements.
- Finally, I want to suggest that despite the movements and the multiple subject-positions, we are also, both as individuals and as a committee, being *constituted as a single body*. Meeting in one room, we will make one decision, one set of recommendations, draft a single leaflet. Bureaucratic, commercial, scientific and democratic orders will work together to produce the subcommittee and each member of the subcommittee as a single subject, as speaking with one voice.

So something interesting is happening. It is that the material arrangements of the process of bargaining co-produce both multiplicity and singularity. As with Odo, there is something like an oscillation between centred and decentred subjects (Law, 1998a, 1998b). It turns out to be necessary to hold both difference (multiplicity) and sameness (singularity) together if a compromise is to be reached. But what is the compromise about? And what form does it take?

Scene 2

Here is a conversation of the kind that occurred early in the history of the IUD-Advisory Panel. The discussion went something like this:[3]

Garth *(government scientist): We cannot recall a device without positive proof that it is dangerous!*

Me *(consumer representative): We have received over 300 letters telling the government of troubles with this device. 300 consumers,*

Materiality; juggling, sameness and difference

many more than ever before, have taken the trouble to write to you. TDEC needs to take action to restore people's faith in the Health Department's ability to maintain public health and prevent unscrupulous manufacturers from dumping devices, condemned in other countries, on the Australian market.

Gretal *(gynaecologist): But there is no evidence that this IUD is harmful. Just because the manufacturer has had to pay-out punitive damages does not mean a thing. You'll always get lawyers conspiring with people who might even genuinely believe that they have been injured if there is the possibility of making so much money—especially in the U.S. where medical litigation is out of control. There is nothing wrong with any of the IUDs currently available here. Read the medical literature.*

Bob *(bioengineer employed in industry): We all represent different agencies that must work together if we want to ensure best practice across the whole system. We have to make sure that doctors get it right but maybe this should come from the profession, not from the health department. Perhaps it would be useful to have the various companies prepare an information pamphlet for women, to ensure that women decide carefully. It is the companies who should provide the information specific to their products. The government's role is to approve this. But the important thing is to work together—to get it right across the whole system.*

Fiona *(Family Planning physician): There are many women who prefer IUDs to other contraceptives. As long as doctors advise women carefully and ensure that only women not at risk from STDs (sexually transmitted diseases) get them there is no problem. The NHMRC (National Health and Medical Research Council) have just issued new guidelines that will help ensure this.*

Me *(Consumer representative): These guidelines are for doctors. Surely one thing TDEC could do is ensure that a consumer information pamphlet was given to every woman thinking of using this or any IUD that informed her of the real risks involved.*

Gretal: *For once I would agree with you there. We need to counter all this ill-informed media coverage with the facts.*

Cal *(Chairperson, Senior employee of the Health Department): OK let's see if we can draw things to a close here. Do we have a consensus that we should produce a consumer information leaflet? Yes.*

Anni Dugdale

There are many things going on here, including the performance of the various subject logics discussed above. But I want to switch tack and attend to the way in which the talk constitutes the IUD as an object. For everybody is telling stories about IUDs. These stories, like the things in Scene 1, participate in multiple arrangements that perform different realities which contain different subjects and objects. But how is this done in practice? My (ANT) suggestion is that we need to attend to each snippet of talk as an arrangement of words and silences which performs an IUD as a particular kind of object. And, if we do this, we begin to notice difference. We discover that the IUD is being performed as multiple objects, just as 'I' was 'being done' as multiple subjects.

Bob's talk is enacting the IUD as a 'system' that can be analysed in terms of its parts, human and non-human, to ensure that all parts are working efficiently. The talk of the government scientist performs the IUD as just one of many devices that have to be managed through a series of processes—listing on a register, calling for premarketing approval applications to be lodged, responding to complaints about adverse reactions, or issuing product recalls. And for all of these there are procedures to be followed. Gretal's talk presents the committee with an IUD that is an array of expert knowledge to be read 'in the medical literature'. This is an IUD with calculable risks and benefits—'The facts'. Fiona's talk embeds an IUD in a range of contraceptives, each of which offers a unique combination of risks and benefits that need to be matched with the varying desires, life-styles, values and practices of patients. In my talk the IUD is different yet again, one that is linked to '300 letters' of complaint and a negligent manufacturer.

Are these performances of a single IUD? One tends to want to say: of course. But I want to dissent from this. If we attend seriously to the *specificities* of the talk, then it turns out that we are dealing not simply with one, but also with half-a-dozen different IUDs. This is a semiotic move implicit, and sometimes explicit, in the ANT programme. It is a semiotic move because semiotics insists that entities are created relationally. That, for instance, subjects are made in relations (which is what I was exploring in the section above, and is generally conceded in post-structuralism). But also, and this is more novel, that *objects are made in relations* too. That they are, as Law and Mol point out in this volume, performed into being. This can be done in talk, as I have shown in Scene 2, but it is also done in other material orderings. What I am suggesting is that rather than thinking of this 'talk' as describing different perspec-

Materiality; juggling, sameness and difference

tives on the same object, we approach it as 'ontological politics', as 'doing' different IUDs. (Mol, 1998b) In which case, we need to say that the talk, in just a few minutes, constitutes not just a series of subject-positions (which are embedded, no doubt, in the different logics that I discussed above) but also a series of *different IUDs*.

But perhaps, in dissolving the identity of the object into multiplicity, we have done away with singularity too quickly. Because the talk *is also predicated on the assumption that all its participants are talking about a single IUD*. Indeed the same IUD. This shows itself in a series of specificities. Bob talks of *a* device (singular) being either dangerous or not. And he assumes that we recognize that it is manufactured to a certain standard and design, specified on a patent, and that its trial data is summed together. I also talk of *this device* as a single object. Fiona presupposes a single IUD by differentiating between it as an object on the one hand, and the way that object is used on the other. This makes her IUD that has sometimes been unsafe (for women at risk of STDs) and requires new practices to ensure that injuries are minimized, the same as Gretal's IUD—*this* IUD—of known properties (effectiveness and safety measures) from clinical trials.

To summarize, I am saying that the conversation performs a kind of oscillation, an oscillation between the (presupposition) that there is a single object on the one hand, and the performance of different objects on the other. Indeed, though I will stick with it since I lack a better term, perhaps the term 'oscillation' gives too much away, for *both*, I am saying, are being performed simultaneously. Indeed, more strongly, I want to say that the conversation and the agreement that is struck by Cal, is only possible at all because of this oscillation. For it is something like this: at least in this conversation, the enactment of a single IUD demands or depends on the mobilization of several different IUDs. If we all had to agree on the nature of the IUD, then the conversation would come to an abrupt halt.

This, then, suggests something about negotiation and compromise. *That it is oscillatory in character rather than being convergent* and that the objects mobilized and then secured in negotiation are *always* both singular and multiple, rather than converging from multiplicity to singularity. I am saying, then, that compromise is a continued oscillation between singularity and multiplicity rather than a movement from oscillation to a resting-place. This, however, is something that I would now like to test by attending to the materialities of the leaflet drafted by the committee.

Anni Dugdale

Scene 3

After a long process of drafting, the IUD consumer information leaflet was finally approved on 27 July, 1992—and it is still issued to all women in Australia who are contemplating the implantation of an IUD. Here are some excerpts from it (Commonwealth Department of Human Services and Health, 1992):

What about Pelvic Infection?

If you use an IUD you have a small increase in risk of developing a serious infection called pelvic inflammatory disease (PID). PID is an infection of the womb, fallopian tubes and ovaries, most often caused by an organism (bug) that is transmitted through sexual intercourse.

However, the latest evidence suggests that the main increase in risk of PID with an IUD is in the first three weeks following insertion. If you only have one sexual partner and he also has no other sexual partner, your chance of getting PID following this first three-week period is low.

PID is a serious infection which can cause infertility (inability to have a baby) by blocking the tubes, make you more likely to have an ectopic pregnancy (pregnancy in the tube) or cause you much pain. The symptoms of PID are easy to miss and sometimes there may be no symptoms.

You should see your doctor immediately if you have any of the things on this list:

♦ increased temperature;
♦ tenderness or pain in your pelvis (lower abdomen);
♦ abdominal cramps or lower back pain;
♦ bleeding between periods;
♦ more painful and heavier periods;
♦ pain with deep thrusting during sex;
♦ unpleasant or heavy discharge from the vagina;
♦ feeling unwell, weak or tired.

What about Ectopic Pregnancy?

This is a condition where the fertilised egg grows outside the womb, usually in the tube. If it is not detected early it can cause serious bleeding which can result in death. If you become pregnant whilst using an IUD it is more likely to be ectopic but remember the risk of pregnancy with an IUD is very low. If you miss a period or think you could be pregnant, see your doctor immediately and make sure you are checked for ectopic pregnancy.

Both of these serious conditions can cause infertility.

♦ It is important that if you or your partner ever have casual sex or if you have a new partner that you use a condom every time even though you have an IUD until you have both had a check for sexually transmissable diseases.

> **What are the other side-effects of an IUD?**
> Some women find that whilst using an IUD:
> ♦ periods are heavier and longer;
> ♦ sometimes periods are more painful;
> ♦ Often the amount of vaginal secretions is increased;
> ♦ the IUD is sometimes pushed out of the womb into the vagina. This is more likely to happen in the first few weeks after the IUD is placed in the womb. It is important to check your vagina for the string every month at the end of a period to make sure it is still in place;
> ♦ very rarely—about six out of 1000 insertions—an IUD can pass into the wall of the womb or, even more rarely, into the abdominal cavity during insertion.
>
> If any of these things happen you should have a check by your doctor.
>
> **What happens if a pregnancy occurs with the IUD still in the womb?**
> Occasionally a pregnancy can happen even if the IUD is still in the womb. If you have a positive pregnancy test soon after you miss a period the IUD can easily be removed. You will then have about a 30 per cent chance of having a miscarriage.
>
> If the IUD cannot be removed, because the string has been drawn up into the womb as it enlarges with the pregnancy, the miscarriage risk is higher—about 50 per cent. If carried to term, healthy babies have been born to women where the IUD was left in the womb during the pregnancy. It does not cause abnormalities in the baby.

It is standard procedure of semiotic analysis to explore how it is that readers are constituted by textual moves of one kind or another. It is therefore not breaking new ground to argue that this text is performing its reader in a particular way—and specifically, to argue that it is constituting the potential IUD user as an informed consumer, as a chooser, a centred subject, and then as an agent that will give her informed consent to the insertion of an IUD at a particular moment. As is obvious, the text presents itself as neutral 'information' and a 'you' is made into a centred decision-maker in command of the facts. It is 'to help *you* decide if an IUD is the best method of birth control for you.' (emphasis added)

The 'you' in the leaflet is a woman. Uncoincidentally, it is printed on lavender paper—a colour that stands between—neither the primary colours used to indicate a masculine terrain of decisiveness and action (check any toy store), nor the pink indicative of the feminine but carrying the connotation of a restricted women's role. It constitutes the woman as the decision-making agent in the domain of medicine. This means that medicine is flattened. In particular, the traces of medicine as a professional domain in which the decision-maker is the doctor are lost. And then again, for the choice to be located in the women's head, the leaflet performs itself as both information and everyday knowledge. This is partly achieved through translations: infertility (inability to have a baby), pelvis (lower abdomen), ectopic pregnancy (pregnancy in the tube). And partly by situating the women decider as a reflexive self, a self making a rational decision about costs and benefits, a decision that constitutes her as a subject that weighs up opportunities to advance her interests. Risk data are presented as if they can be plugged into such a calculus: 'The IUD is 95–99 percent effective'; 'If you use an IUD you have a small increase in risk of developing a serious infection . . .'; '[in] about 6 out of 100 insertions [Ö] an IUD can pass into the wall of the womb'.

The leaflet is organized in a question and answer format that sets up the woman's agency as a tree of choices, a series of 'if this then that' decisions. In an earlier section women have decided which category they fall into—'Who could use an IUD?' they are asked (eg, 'Women wanting a reliable . . . method of contraception after having their children'), and 'Who should not use an IUD' (eg, 'Women who have more than one sexual partner'). In the section cited above their decisions are being channelled through a series of choice points. 'What about Pelvic Infection?'; 'What happens if pregnancy occurs with the IUD still in the womb?'; 'Who can use an IUD for birth control?'. 'Choice' is systematic. The leaflet is a machine that produces the reader's decision as a flow to a single temporal point and as an origin that can be referred back to and judged when things go wrong. Did you adequately weigh the risks, 'the possible problems'? With no method of birth control 'absolutely safe' did you make the right choice to fit your lifestyle, your values?

So far so good. The leaflet is a compromise engineered in the committee. And it has made a single and centred subject. But just as the compromises of the committee are better understood as 'oscillations' between singularity and multiplicity—between single and multiple logics, and single and multiple IUDs—so it also turns out that the subject performed in the materiality of the leaflet is oscillatory too (Law, 1998a, 1998b). Centred she is—I have just shown that. But she is also, and at the same time, being inserted into multiple logics. And (I make the argument in the same form as

I did in the previous section) *the centred and the decentred subjects are mutually dependent*. Which means, in a move that is of some importance to all the debates about informed consent, that the success of the leaflet in constituting that informed consent also relies on the production of different subjectivities that disperse the head of the woman and the instant of choice across time and space. (Berg, 1997, 135–136)

For the 'you' of the leaflet is barraged with instructions: 'It is important to check your vagina for the string every month to make sure it (the IUD) is still in place'; 'You should see your doctor if you have any of the things on this list: increased temperature; tenderness or pain in your pelvis . . . [and so through 5 further points to] feeling unwell, weak or tired'; 'If you miss a period or think you could be pregnant, see your doctor immediately and make sure you are checked for an ectopic pregnancy'; 'If you or your partner have casual sex or you have a new sex partner use a condom every time until you both have a check for sexually transmissible diseases.' Here, then the user is being addressed as a subject involved in complex and continuing routines of self-surveillance and self-protection. Which means that the leaflet is performing a future normative body as well as a present disembodied mind.

But in addition to the decentered logics of bodily training, dispersal operates in other ways too. For instance, the leaflet also dissolves the singularity of the chooser by building a future patient-subject. This subject is produced 'in partnership' with medical doctors. The woman and her doctors will together manage her fertility and sexuality. The leaflet is full of exhortations to 'see your doctor immediately' and to 'discuss this with your doctor'. The leaflet puts a doctors-as-carer-and-advisor model of medical practice into play. This disrupts an expert decision-maker model in which the patient is a body to be read and interpreted with interventions being decided by the medical expert. Agency is partially distributed to the patient who must look for signs and symptoms, even if there may be none, and go to the doctor. But th leaflet also builds in a future context of medical care, in which any problems arising from IUD use can be attended to and solved without major medical consequences. It performs a doctor who can bridge an excess, the contingencies that of necessity lie beyond the specifiable (Berg, 1997, 147)

The point location of the consumer-decision-maker also dissolves into the past. The 'information' is framed between the logo of the Commonwealth Department of Human Services and Health on the front, and the logo of the TGA on the back. Under the latter we

Anni Dugdale

learn, in small print, that the leaflet was approved by the Reproductive Devices Panel of TDEC on 27 July 1992, and that it is available from Organon Australia and Medical Industries Australia. These peripheral elements perform a different order and a different logic of decision-making. The decision to use an IUD is dislodged from its instant, and re-located across many sites. We learn, then, that the moment of informed consent implies the existence of a bureaucratic order which approved and registered the IUD. And this is an order in which decisions are distributed elsewhere, and in which the decision of the woman—or even her doctor—is no more than an afterthought.[4]

Again moving backwards from the point location performed in the leaflet, we also find that a commercial ordering is at work. The 'consumer' can only decide to use an IUD because two companies that make such devices went through the TDEC approval process and market them in Australia. The consumer is thus part of a commercial arrangement in which Organon Australia, its multiload IUD, Medical Industries of Australia, its Copper T 380A IUD, the medical profession, and the IUD consumer information leaflet have organized IUD insertion and made it a consumer choice. The leaflet also embeds the changing legal context for manufacturers. Until very recently in Euro-American countries many people relied on their physicians to make choices about which drugs and devices to prescribe, and this is still largely the case. But IUD and other therapeutic device litigation has overturned the 'learned intermediary' defence. This differentiated between medical products and other products precisely by holding the manufacturer responsible only for informing the 'learned intermediary' of any hazards or risks. This person, the doctor, was then considered to have a discretionary responsibility for informing the product user of these, as she judged appropriate (Castleberry, 1990). The overturning of this doctrine is visible in the leaflet which performs the decision-maker as the receiver of information from the manufacturers.

So the decision-making subject is rendered singular—turned into a specific location. But at the same time it is also distributed across time and space into future bodies, future conversations, and into past points of choice or procedure. There is, as it were, continual slippage between presence and absence (Law, 1998a, 1998b). The subject is both centred and decentred. And the possibility of a centred, informed, consenting subject *depends* upon this slippage. It is constituted and made possible by virtue of the fact that decisions have been or will be taken elsewhere, and that these are inserted within, or produce different logics. The consumer information leaflet is not merely a transmitter of information, a reflection of knowledge made elsewhere—in the clinical trials for instance—that will empower the consumer by transforming her into a knower. Rather than simply putting control into the hands of the user, it is a device for distributing control, not once and for all, but as part of many 'modes of ordering' in which it becomes a site for on-going negotiation, a site for articulating the work of manufacturers, regulators, physicians and users (Berg, 1997, 137–8). The strength of the leaflet is that it is a single object but one that intervenes in all of these IUD orders. All of which suggests that *the working of the leaflet and the subject that it produces is no more convergent than the working of the committee, or the object, the IUD*. That the committee's compromises produce, in turn, an oscillatory outcome.[5]

Conclusion

In this paper I have taken a topic that is standard in the literature on policy-making and decision-making: how it is that negotiations, bargains and compromises are hammered out. This is a topic which is also modelled in the literature on science studies as they attend to technical decision-making, scientific closure, and the democratization of technology policy-making. It has not been my object to criticise these literatures: there is much to learn from the ways in which they analyse bargaining and its outcomes. Instead my object has been to explore the *specificities and materialities* of decision-making, and *how* it is that settlements are reached. This focus helps us to rethink both the notions of negotiation and closure. Implicit in most of the ways in which they are modelled is that, at least in successful negotiations and compromises (and indeed the imposition of solutions by force) there is a process of (possibly enforced) convergence. That multiple possibilities are progressively narrowed down until a single outcome is achieved. The model thus implies a progressive shift from instability to stability, or from movement to immobility. Of course it is also understood that decisions that have been made may also be unmade. But for the time being at least, this way of thinking about outcomes implies that stasis or stability has been achieved.

Drawing on a particular case-study, and informed by the semiotics of actor-network theory and related feminist approaches, I have proposed an alternative. This is that *compromise or closure does*

Anni Dugdale

not imply the stability of a single outcome. There are theoretical ways of glossing this that make this suggestion rather straightforward. For instance, it may be seen as an application of the arguments from feminist and other post-structuralist approaches against the possibility—and indeed the desirability—of 'humanist' collapse into self-identity. Nothing reaches stasis. Nothing holds, so to speak, in an internally consistent manner. Which is not, however, to suggest that relatively durable connections are not possible. However, what is unsurprising in the context of non-humanist versions of feminism or such approaches as the actor-network theory, turns out to look a little more surprising when it is applied to bargaining, decision-making, or closure. For the logic tells us that outcomes are not centred either. Which is not to say that they are decentred. Instead the model suggests that we need to avoid polarities such as these, and explore the character of outcomes as oscillatory—or as a simultaneous propensity to centre. To make single and to make multiple. The conclusion is that if decisions, subjects, or indeed objects, cohere, then this is because they are both singular and multiple.

Acknowledgements

This chapter would not exist without the assistance of a University of Melbourne small grant, the hospitality of the National Centre for Epidemiology and Population Health, ANU, and the Centre for Social Theory and Technology, Keele University in 1996, and of course the openness and professionalism of the members of 'the committee' discussed. It owes a great deal to many conversations and intensive collaboration with John Law. I am also much indebted to the Sociology Program, RSSS at ANU, for providing me with the privilege of a full-time research position, and for exemplary collegiality. Judy Wajcman, Lisa Adkins and Dorothy Broom provided useful comments on earlier drafts. Thanks to John Law for his patience and detailed comments on more than one draft.

Notes

1 I would like to thank Suzanne Eastwood for introducing me to the Star Trek series and the salience of Odo to this article. See Paramount Pictures, Star Trek: Deep Space Nine (1996) 'broken link' (story by George A. Brozak) 49962-4.
2 In this paper 'the subcommittee' or 'the committee' is a convenient device that

collapses this change. These terms refer to the operation and work of the two committees on IUDs from 1989 to 1992.
3 For reasons of confidentiality this conversation is fiction. However, in constructing it I have drawn on interviews with two other panel members, my own notes of interventions as a consumer representative, and the minutes of meetings. It is not an accurate record of any part of a particular meeting. Rather, it is a composite sketch that, whilst fictitious, captures the flavour of some of the interactions. All names have been changed. Moreover, the characterizations of any of the persons represented are not based on characteristics and comments of single individuals. As in any work of fiction representations of people are only broadly based on my experience—of diverse members from each committee—and cannot be mapped onto particular individuals. They are also partial and not fully representative of the full character of any person.
4 This is a point explored in some detail by Annemarie Mol in her work on decision-making and normativities in medicine. See her inaugural lecture *Wat is Kiezen? Een Empirisch-Filosophische Verkenning* (Mol, 1997). For related work see the collection edited by Marc Berg and Annemarie Mol (1998).
5 With greater space it would be possible to show that the IUD performed in the leaflet is similarly oscillatory, involving the simultaneous performance of single and multiple objects of the kind discussed in the previous section.

References

ABC TV (1988), 'Tarnished Copper', '4 Corners' programme transmitted by Australian Broadcasting Commission Television, 28th November.
Berg, Marc (1997), *Rationalizing Medical Work: Decision-Support Techniques and Medical Practices*, Cambridge, Mass.: The MIT Press.
Berg, Marc and Annemarie Mol (eds) (1998), *Differences in Medicine: Unravelling Practices, Techniques and Bodies*, Durham, N. Carolina.: Duke University Press.
Bijker, Wiebe E. (1995), *Of Bicycles, Bakelite and Bulbs: Towards a Theory of Sociotechnical Change*, Cambridge, Mass.: The MIT Press.
Bordo, Susan (1993), *Unbearable Weight: Feminism, Western Culture, and The Body*, Berkeley: University of California Press.
Braidotti, Rosi (1994), *Nomadic Subjects: Embodiment and Sexual Difference in Contemporary Feminist Theory*, New York: Columbia University Press.
Butler, Judith P. (1990), *Gender Trouble: Feminism and the Subversion of Identity*, New York: Routledge.
Callon Michel (1986a), 'Some Elements of a Sociology of Translation: Domestication of the Scallops and the Fisherman of St Brieuc Bay', John Law (ed.), *Power, Action and Belief*, London: Routledge Kegan Paul.
Callon, Michel (1986b), 'The Sociology of an Actor-Network: The Case of the Electric Vehicle'. Callon, Law and Rip (eds), *Mapping the Dynamics of Science and Technology*, London: Macmillan.
Castleberry, V. (1990), 'Hill v Searle Laboratories: The Decline of the Learned Intermediary Doctrine in Favour of Direct Patient Warnings of Drug Product Risks', *Arkansas Law Review*, Vol. 43, pp. 821–846.
Commonwealth Department of Human Sciences and Health (1992), 'The IUD Intrauterine Device', Canberra: Therapeutic Goods Administration.

Diprose, Rosalyn (1994), *The Bodies Of Women: Ethics, Embodiment And Sexual Difference*, London and New York: Routledge.

Ellis, James E. (1988), 'Monsanto and the Copper-7: A "Corporate Veil" Begins to Fray', *Business Week*, September 26, p. 50.

Federal Supplement 707 (1989), 'Kociemba v G.D. Searle and Co., Civil No. 3–85–1599, United States District Court for the District of Minnesota, Third Division', 707 *Federal Supplement*, p. 1517.

Foucault, Michel (1979), *The History of Sexuality, Vol. 1, An Introduction*, London: Allen Lane.

Foucault, Michel (1980), *Power/Knowledge* (ed. Colin Gordon), Brighton: Harvester.

Franklin, Sarah (1997), *Embodied Progress: A Cultural Account of Assisted Conception*, London and New York: Routledge.

Gatens, Moira (1996), *Imaginary Bodies: Ethics, Power, and Corporeality*, London: Routledge.

Gillespie, James A. (1991), *The Price of Health: Australian Governments and Medical Politics 1910–1960*, Melbourne: Cambridge University Press.

Grosz, Elizabeth A. (1994), *Volatile Bodies: Toward a Corporeal Feminism*, Sydney: Allen and Unwin.

Haraway, Donna (1991), *Simians, Cyborgs, and Women: The Reinvention of Nature*, London: Free Association Books.

Haraway, Donna (1997), *Modest_Witness@Second_Millennium.FemaleMan©_Meets _OncoMouse^{TM}: Feminism and Technoscience*, New York: Routledge.

Hughes, Thomas P. (1983), *Networks of Power: Electrification in Western Society, 1880–1930*, Baltimore: Johns Hopkins University Press.

Jasanoff, Sheila (1990), *The Fifth Branch: Science Advisers as Policy Makers*, Cambridge, Mass.: Harvard University Press.

Keller, Evelyn Fox (1992), *Secrets of Life, Secrets of Death: Essays on Language, Gender and Science*, New York: Routledge.

Latour, Bruno (1987), *Science in Action: How to Follow Scientists and Engineers Through Society*, Milton Keynes: Open University Press.

Latour, Bruno (1988), *The Pasteurization of France*, Cambridge, Mass.: Harvard University Press.

Latour, Bruno (1996), *Aramis, or the Love of Technology*, Cambridge, Mass.: The MIT Press.

Latour, Bruno (1998), 'On Recalling ANT', this volume.

Law, John (1987), 'Technology and Heterogeneous Engineering: The Case of the Portuguese Expansion', Bijker, Wiebe, Thomas Hughes and Trevor Pinch (eds), *The Social Construction of Technological Systems: New Directions in the Sociology and History of Technology*, Cambridge, Mass.: The MIT Press.

Law, John (1994), *Organising Modernity*, Oxford: Blackwell.

Law, John (1998a), *Aircraft Stories: Decentering the Object in Technoscience*, submitted.

Law, John (1998b), 'On Hidden Heterogeneities', forthcoming in John Law and Annemarie Mol (eds), *Complexities in Science, Technology and Medicine*, Durham, N. Carolina., Duke University Press.

Law, John (1998c), 'After ANT: Complexity, Naming and Topology', this volume.

MacKenzie, Donald (1990), *Inventing Accuracy: A Historical Sociology of Nuclear Missile Guidance*, Cambridge, Mass.: The MIT Press.

Martin, Brian (1991), *Scientific Knowledge in Controversy: The Social Dynamics of the Fluoridation Debate*, Albany NY: SUNY Press.

Mol, Annemarie (1997), *Wat is Kiezen? Een Empirisch-Filosophische Verkenning*, Enschede, the Netherlands: University of Twente.

Mol, Annemarie (1998a), *The Body Multiple: Artherosclerosis in Practice*, submitted.

Mol, Annemarie (1998b), 'Ontological politics: a word and some questions' this volume.

Oudshoorn, Nelly (1994), *Beyond the Natural Body: An Archaeology of Sex Hormones*, London: Routledge.

Richards, Evelleen (1991), *Vitamin C and Cancer: Medicine or Politics*, London: Macmillan.

Shapin, Steven, and Simon Schaffer (1985), *Leviathan and the Air-Pump: Hobbes, Boyle, and the Experimental Life*, Princeton, New Jersey: Princeton University Press.

Staying true to the laughter in Nigerian classrooms

Helen Verran

Abstract

Growing from my years as a lecturer in a Nigerian university in the early 1980s, the stories which begin this paper evoke puzzling, small moments in the life of contemporary Nigerian (Yoruba) classrooms, particularly in the teaching of mathematics and science. Conventional wisdom would pass these by as irrational glitches, yet because they challenged my assumptions about numbers, they shook me, and this effect was magnified because no one else seemed to feel anything amiss. These moments of disconcertment sometimes spontaneously expressed themselves in an up-welling laughter. In responding to the stories I argue that keeping the disconcertment is important, it alerts us that here is an occasion for telling stories which might generate new possibilities for answering moral questions of how to live. I go on to juxtapose three accounts of quantifying: a universalist account; a relativist account; and finally an account of quantifying as realized through embodied routines and repetitions. We can understand the last as a version of an 'actor network' account. I argue that the problem with the universalist and relativist accounts of quantifying is that they explain away the disconcertment in distributing praise and blame and legislating answers to the question 'How should we live?'. An embodied account of quantifying brings with it the possibility of in/foresightful stories and showing how the truths which numbers make, came to be.

Mr Ojo was not the most organized of teachers, but he had good rapport with children. This morning he had excelled himself in his preparations, but my heart sank when I saw how he had set himself up to teach the lesson on measuring length. He had assembled about twenty small cards: thick cardboard 10cm long and about 5cm wide, marked off in 1cm divisions along the length; one card for each group of two or three children. To go with this he had twenty lengths of string about 2m long. It was a lesson we had prepared as a group back in the laboratory in the Institute of Education at University of Ife (now Obafemi Awolowo University). We had begun with one of the 'Measuring Ourselves' pamphlets produced by the African Primary Science Program—a large and prestigious USAID project which sponsored science and maths curriculum development with a focus on practical work in many countries in Africa in the 1960s–70s. Discussing how the lesson might be modified so that it would be suitable for 50 or so Yoruba children, in classrooms quite devoid of resources, helped students to prepare for their practical teaching exercise in the schools around Ile-Ife in Nigeria.

Like the rest of students at the Institute of Education, Mr Ojo was around my own age and a far more experienced teacher than I. After completing primary schooling, these students had attended teacher training colleges, a lesser form of Nigerian secondary school, from which they emerged at aged seventeen or eighteen to take up positions as primary school teachers. They had held those positions for at least ten years before becoming eligible for two years retraining at the University of Ife, after which they often taught in secondary schools. As a lecturer in the Institute I was responsible for at least part of their 'retraining', but given my gross inexperience when it came to Nigerian classrooms, this course in science education was, by necessity, very much a two-way programme of training. As a group, students and lecturer, we worked out a way of negotiating the curriculum we were developing. And the classrooms that these students taught in of necessity entered our negotiations. Given my inability to speak Yoruba, I taught solely in English. The students too were officially obliged to teach in English in the classroom but, for the most part and with my encouragement, they used at least some Yoruba in their lessons, engaging in so called 'code switching' as they felt the need. As part of our group preparation of classroom lessons we spent time discussing how particular notions might be explained to the children in Yoruba.

The lesson Mr Ojo was to teach, 'Length in Our Bodies', involved children using string to record another child's height, leg length, arm length etc, then a metre rule to report the length in metric units. In the lab we had measured each other: string to represent height, lay the string on the floor and use chalk to record the length, then when one of the few metre rulers becomes available, measure the distance between chalk marks and record the measurement in a chart.

Helen Verran

Name	Height
Mrs Taiwo	1m 62cm
Mr Ojerinde	1m 70cm
Dr (Mrs) Watson-Verran	1m 50cm

And we had devised an evaluation exercise. A chart with fictitious children's names and heights. Using the process in reverse, children would show a particular height using a length of string to demonstrate whether or not they had understood. The students were nervous about teaching this way. It meant getting children out of their desks and putting materials other than pencils and exercise books into their hands. It meant children talking to and working with each other instead of working only from the blackboard and speaking only in reply to the teacher. The children were liable to become unruly and noisy at such a departure from the norm, and this could be a serious problem with 45–50 children in a small enclosed space.

I had already watched several other students deliver our jointly devised lesson—and with very mixed results. Mrs Taiwo, for example, had as usual been well prepared. She had twenty 1 metre rulers which she had commissioned a tin smith to produce and paid for with her own money. Using ball point pen she had graduated the tin strips into 10cm and 1cm divisions. And hours had gone into producing charts for the children to record their measurements—hand drawn and carbon copy, no photocopying here. But her lesson had been a disaster. Very few of her carefully drawn charts were filled up with names and numbers representing heights; somewhere between string and chart most children 'lost the plot'. And not one child would volunteer to show, with a piece of string, the height of the fictitious children of our evaluation chart. Mrs Taiwo was most disconcerted at the failure; she blamed the stupid children and the poor teaching of their regular teacher. I was not so sure. I knew these children. I had seen them confidently handling number in Yoruba talk—doing mental calculations in marketing stories. The extraordinary facility that this class of children showed, then, sat ill with the *en masse* incomprehension in Mrs Taiwo's lesson. Was it because her lesson had been delivered mostly in English? When I asked her about this, she insisted that she could not give this lesson in Yoruba. Mrs Taiwo had been well prepared, she was an experi-

Staying true to the laughter in Nigerian classrooms

enced teacher and she had a good grasp of quantification. But she had failed to connect with these second graders.

Mr Ojo, had, it seemed to me, taken a much easier way out in lesson preparation with his 10cm cards, and a chart put up on the blackboard, and I was not impressed with his little cards. Yet I was soon forced to change my opinion. I was not expecting much when the lesson began. Speaking in Yoruba, Mr Ojo demonstrated the procedure. He completely missed out the neat 'lecture' on length that we had collectively prepared back in the Institute laboratory. (Under my instruction, we had come up with a little account of length as a quality that things had, length as infinite etc.) Mr Ojo called a boy to the front: end of string just under the boy's heel, he held his finger at the point on the string which matched the top of the boy's head. Tying a loose knot at this point, he took the other end of the string from under the boy's foot; holding this at one end of a card, he wound the length of string around until he came to the knot. Then he instructed: 'Count the number of full lengths [ie, 10cm lengths] on the card, eg, 9. Write down the number. Multiply by ten. 'How do we multiply by ten? . . . ninety . . . now add the bit of string left over . . . Yes, we have 96cm'. I was scandalised; Mr Ojo was presenting *multiplicity* as constitutive of length. The notion of *extension*, so important for children to grasp as the 'abstract' element of length had been rendered incidental, contingent upon the multiplicity.

The children set to work in pairs or threes. Soon the chart Mr Ojo had drawn on the blackboard was full of names and numbers. Several children very efficiently used card and string to show the height of the fictitious 'Dupe', 'Tunde' and 'Bola' of our evaluation exercise. The lesson could only be judged a complete success; the children had obviously got hold of using the notion of units of extension to express value. The children were pleased with their accomplishment, Mr Ojo was pleased, certain of his success, and so was I. But at the same time I was profoundly confused and puzzled. I had glimpsed the lesson as both the same and different from the one we had prepared, but I was unable to say in exactly what way it was either the same or different. I was disconcerted and felt disempowered by being put out so. But this was no power play against the òyinbó (white) lecturer on Mr Ojo's part. As he saw it, the lesson was a triumph for our group, I was included as one of those who should feel proud at this little success; our lesson had worked well. He was disconcerted by my failure to evince whole hearted and enthusiastic approval for his lesson.

Helen Verran

There were several of my students placed in this school for their practical teaching round. When I went to watch their 'length lessons' the next week, they too produced cards and string, adopting Mr Ojo's technique with minor alterations. Soon all the teachers in my classes were teaching it this way—adopting the technology and using it with or without our little lecture on length. The lessons were routinely successful and, as a group, the students swelled with pleasure at the success of their teaching in this new way by putting materials into children's hands. Generously they ascribed their success to my interventions as they shared with me their new-found pleasure in teaching. As I saw things, the lesson we had devised from the African Primary Science Program cards had been quite transformed, with the demonstration of linear extension compromised in this way of teaching. As the students saw things, it was still the same lesson: children learned to use metric units to measure and were taking pleasure in their learning.

As they found their way into regular practice, the 10cm cards developed into many forms over the next few months of teaching: 10cm strips of tin; regular 30cm rulers cut into three pieces with the numbers erased; bamboo pieces, and plywood strips with or without lugs to prevent the winds of string slipping. And for a short time too the technology even became a craze amongst the children. String and card could be seen in many pockets. In school yards little knots of children could be seen getting the height of children with string, solemnly winding, triumphantly announcing the measurement, and eventually 'the winner'. I even came across children at a roadside stall measuring the yams they were selling; and one enterprising boy had measured something very long, stringing four measuring cards together.

As I write about this episode, remembering my confused feelings of delight and suspicion, failure and success, I am shaking again with a sort of visceral laughter, the same sort of chuckling that often afflicted me as I watched my students teaching this lesson. The sort of laughter that grows from seeing a certainty disrupted to become a different sort of certainty: a certainty that sees itself. I felt as if I 'saw ' length (that serious 'abstract' quality by which we organize so much of our modern lives) and 'saw through' it at the same time whenever I watched my Yoruba students teaching 'length' with this little card with string wound around it. It never failed to 'get' me, to evoke a chuckle of delight.[1]

It is difficult to write this story in a way that accurately captures the subtle and complex power relations that surrounded my participation and the participations of the student teachers and their pupils. And how the power relations are rendered is important. Dealing with them in my narrative comes down to the problem of stopping myself from producing

> 'yet another defensive appropriation of the unfamiliar by means of an "explanation", instead of creating another quite different mode of relation to disconcert[ment] adequate to late twentieth-century patterning of identities and alterities . . . The vertiginous cultural interspace effected by reflection makes many of us desperate to fill it with meaning, thereby defusing disconcert[ment]'.[2]

For me, keeping that disconcertment is important. It is a link to how, working in the complex negotiating arenas of Nigerian classrooms, we can tell in/foresightful stories and understand how truths that these stories evoke, came to be.

An orthodox story of institutional power relations can effectively explain away the disconcertment—as failure and inadequacy. I was a lecturer, accredited with institutional power to teach the canon—in this case the warranted account of length. The teachers I was supervising were students under my jurisdiction. I had the right and the responsibility to tell them they were wrong—award 'pass' and 'fail'. A story which valorizes the institutional power of the lecturer, as the agent of a colonizing modernity, sees only failure in this story. Failure on the part of 'Africans'—children, teachers and whole societies—who adopt 'primitive' ways of quantifying; and failure on the part of the lecturer who did not uphold the standards of modern university teaching and insist on the teaching of length in the 'proper' way. This story legislates a particular answer to the moral question How should we live?[3] We should give up non-modern Yoruba ways, to become full knowing subjects.

Alternatively, an almost equally orthodox story of powerful Yoruba resistance and Western impotence can likewise explain away the disconcertment. In this version Mr Ojo and his fellow students heroically resist Western incursion and teach a Yoruba version of quantification in the school curriculum. Using Yoruba language, they resist and challenge the òyinbó (white) lecturer replacing her prescriptions with indigenous measurement. This story has the school teachers as agents of local resistance 'othering' the impotent university lecturer, the agent of a rejected and resisted Western imposition. It too legislates in a moral arena, only this prescribes the heroism of resistance set against the tragedy of alienation.

These are the 'explanations' tendered by what I call the 'African thought discourse', an academic debate that raged from the mid-1960s to the early 1980s.[4] On one side we had 'realists' and 'rationalists', those committed to a 'physical entities foundationist frame' who, in relentlessly 'othering' explanations elaborated moral legislation over 'Their' primitiveness, and the consequent need for 'Their' up-lifting through 'development' (education). On the other side we had 'relativists', working from the given 'foundations of disparate social practices', who in an equally relentless 'othering', legislated over 'Our' base and spiritually deficient reductionism compared to 'Their' wholeness, emphasising that 'We' (moderns) had lost compared to 'Them' (traditionals).

Of course we recognize the traces of both these alternative causes and effects in the episode I have just related. Explanations adopting either of these possibilities could be convincingly constructed, and such stories as I have just told were grist for both 'realist' and 'relativist' intellectual mills in 'African thought'. And these explanations come along with well-established ways to evaluate and dispute them as knowledge claims, by asking 'Does it give a true picture?' Argument is over the criteria by which this might be judged, as well as the endless argument over the proper nature of the foundation. The foundationist metaphor implicit in these explanations brings with it a particular style of reasoning which establishes its particular propositional notion of truth and falsity,[5] and this is so irrespective of whether the foundation is taken as 'physical entities' or 'social practices'.

But from where I stand, as a participant caught up in the complex power relations and reciprocal indebtedness of being both teacher and learner, at the same time as being a theorist (a story teller) of the episode, to adopt either one of these cause-and-effect stories is to explain away the disconcertment which, as I felt at the time and still feel, is the kernel of whatever truth lurks in the episode and its telling. To tell either of these stories would betray participants in the episode in unacceptable ways. In explaining away the disconcertment, the above explanations foreclose and legislate. They fail to recognize Yoruba classrooms as characterized by a complex and subversive dance of mimesis and alterity in classroom routines, generating new ways to go on, and re-generating old ways of going-on together. In contrast to these two 'foundationist' explanations I want to keep the puzzlement of sameness and difference we can see in Mr Ojo's lesson; to privilege the disconcertment. It seems to me that, this way, we can tell stories which have a chance of articulating how the truths they tell came to be and, also, of understanding how this might be done responsibly.[6]

I want to elaborate on, to translate, to theorize, this story of Mr Ojo, Mrs Taiwo, their classmates, their lessons, their lecturer, and their pupils, using a different, non-foundationist interpretive frame. This utilizes an interpretive frame which, compared to foundationist approaches, amounts to quite a different picture of what the world is. Instead of some sort of foundation (either the 'physical entities of a natural world' or the 'concrete practices of the social world') on which a knowledge-structure of symbols is built, this interpretive frame avoids any separation of the material and the symbolic in proposing worlds as outcomes of mutually resisting/accommodating participants, where participation goes far beyond the human to encompass the non-living as active in routine (and novel) actions which constitute the world. A useful slogan for working this interpretive frame is 'the material is already and always symbolic, as much as the symbolic is already and always material'.[7] Of course this will be recognizable as a description of a cluster of critical approaches including actor network theory.

I am understanding actor network theory as a new interpretive regime invented by Michel Callon, Bruno Latour, and John Law[8]— an approach to studying science and engineering. It is one which 'follows scientists and engineers around' interpreting what they *do* in making scientific facts and artifacts. Latour justifies the interpretive regime as the only one which is supple enough, historical enough and empirical enough to describe the view of generation of technoscientific facts which one gets when one does follow scientists and engineers.[9] But Latour, in particular, and actor network theory in general, has been criticised by those who would work in this new ontological domain, for transferring to it the monologic discursive traditions of foundationism, re-inscribing the separation of knowledge making and ethical-political action.

Coming with feminist sensitivities from the American Sociological tradition of symbolic interactionism, Leigh Star has criticised actor network theory for its obsession and identification with executive action.[10] Showing the natural-social-discursive imbroglios in France becoming Pasteurized, or thyroid stimulating hormone being assembled, become separated from questions of the ethics of the 'doing' and of concerns with distributions effected though the 'doing'.[11] And this significant complicity with distributions of power becomes even more evident when the generation of fighter-bombers[12] is at issue.

Leigh Star and John Law have raised serious issues here, important in going on from actor network theory. In engaging them, I have been inspired by the writing of feminist philosopher Kathryn Pyne Addelson. From symbolic interactionist beginnings, Addelson develops an interpretive frame with similarities to that being worked up by actor network theorists.[13] She begins with the insight that foundationist interpretations have researchers as privileged judging observers offering moral prescription, answering the ethical question 'How should we live?' in a singular authoritative voice. Through consideration of several episodes of social work she evokes an interpretive frame which she calls 'collectivist' to show how outcomes generated in collective action, give an embodied answer to the moral question. This renders researchers/theorists as 'storytelling participants', and Addelson goes on to consider how responsible storytelling might be understood.

In the remainder of this chapter I focus on how, staying true to the generative laughter of Nigerian classrooms, we might construe quantifying in an interpretive frame which has moved on from actor network theory in incorporating a concern with moral issues. Quantifying is a significant issue in this new interpretive frame, for quantifying is an integral part of simultaneously both enabling and hiding the fetishising[14] through which the tropes and metaphors of foundationism work. Or, to use Latour's terms, quantifying simultaneously accomplishes both the mediating and the purifying which is duplicitously achieved in the working of technoscience.[15]

In orthodox foundationist interpretations number use is quintessentially a symbolic practice. There, using numbers is a simple and certain, but also an abstract (symbolic) process. And when we abolish the 'abstract domain' and opt for worlds in which the material is already always symbolic and the symbolic already always material, it becomes difficult to even describe the process of quantifying. In order to appreciate the difficulties here I first consider universalist and relativist accounts of quantifying. This will help us identify the problems involved in giving a detailed account of quantifying in the queered ontological domain I understand as an heir to actor network theory.[16]

Two foundationist accounts of quantifying

Conveniently the logical positivists laid out what might be considered the orthodox universalist account of quantifying. I am thinking here of Carnap[17] and of the more sophisticated version we find in Quine.[18] The underlying assumption here, justified in Quine's version but not in Carnap, is that the world naturally presents already determined as bounded, spatial extensions which endure over time. That is, the world *really* is an array of spatiotemporal entities, which are the given foundation for the symbolic practices of quantification. Quantifying here points first to the universal 'qualities' which are held by these spatiotemporal entities, the first abstract entities of quantifying. Then numbers, a second-order abstract entity, taken to be analogous in form to the extension of qualities held by the concrete spatiotemporal entities, are used to represent a real value of the entity. Spatiotemporal entities are the natural foundation and through quantifying objective value can be derived. Quantifying here is taken as a dual level qualitative abstraction.

On this account of quantifying Mr Ojo is wrong to present an image to the children where length is implicitly portrayed as a multiply divided bundle of string, whose multiplicity can be counted and manipulated to come up with a value for length. Mrs Taiwo who presents an uninterrupted straight line is portraying the proper, and only correct, image for length. Mrs Taiwo's line will be sectioned as a subsequent (an arbitrary) action, but the linear extension is understood to constitute a true image of how (abstract) qualities, and (abstract) numbers really exist in the world. This is the one and only correct way to teach children to understand quantifying with length.

The alternative foundationist tradition, relativism,[19] has social practices as the foundation for the symbolic activity of using numbers in quantification. Possibly the best example of how quantifying is explained here, is some of my own work published in the late 1980s.[20] Although in a confused way I tried to distance myself from Bloor and the Strong Programme in Sociology of Knowledge,[21] the writing does link strongly with that relativist program. The picture of Yoruba and English language quantifying I presented in the past had three sets of social practices as constituting quantifying: practices of referring in ordinary language use, practices of unitizing the material world, and recursive practices of generating numerals. Although I emphasised the physical nature of these practices, in the end I point to them as methods constituting symbols.

The major difference between my account of quantifying as founded on social practices, and the foundationists who take the physical world as a foundation, lies in my disputing the naturalness of spatiotemporal entities as the universal foundation of quantification. Making a comparative analysis of the grammars of English

Helen Verran

and Yoruba languages, and taking language use as a symbolizing practice, I show how Yoruba has its speakers referring to the world as constituted by sortal entities, rather than the spatiotemporal entities that English speakers refer to. These disparate methods of the social practice of referring in language use in English and Yoruba create alternative starting points for quantifying.

In quantification in Yoruba, the abstract referring categories—sortal entities—are used in a further practice of abstracting. Sortal entities are rendered as 'the mode of being collected' which represents the physical practices of unitizing the concrete world in the process of *kà* or *wòn*. And this abstract category of 'the mode of being collected' is then further abstracted by use of a numeral which reports the degree of dividedness of this collected mode, as a mode of a mode. I contrasted these Yoruba practices with quantifying in English which I had beginning with the abstract referring category of spatiotemporal entity, which is abstracted to 'quality of the spatiotemporal entity', which in turn is abstracted to a number which reports the extent of the quality, which can in a way be understood as a quality of that quality. The disparate methods of the social practices constituting English language and Yoruba language quantifying could then be understood as generating numbers which symbolized in different ways.

To make my point I picked up a contrast made by mathematicians working within the alternative 'physical entity foundationist' tradition, I pointed to the contradictions between the work of von Neuman and Zermelo[22] finding that the symbolic codes they used provided an economical way to express the difference between English and Yoruba number. For von Neuman 0 is Ø, the empty set. The set which contains the empty set as its sole member is {Ø}, one; the successor of this number is {Ø{Ø}}, or two; and three is the set of all sets smaller than three {Ø,{Ø},{Ø,{Ø}}}. The successor of any number in von Neuman's version is generated by adding the successor of 0, that is 1. A number in this version is the last number of the series reached through one-by-one progression. I suggested that this was the picture generated in the symbolic process of English language quantification.

In contrast I suggested that a Yoruba speaker would choose Zermelo's account of number as correct. Here the number n is a single membered set, the single member of the set is n–1. Zermelo has 0 as Ø, a set with no members. Then 1 has the empty set as its sole member, {Ø}. The set which contains the unit set, 1, as its sole member is 2, {{Ø}}. Three is the set which has two as its sole member, $\{\{\{\emptyset\}\}\}$. In this version each number is totally subsumed by its successor, and any one number has a unified nature. I contended that for a Yoruba speaker, the model of number which would 'jump out' as the intuitively correct account would be this one, for Yoruba language numbers carry 'the flavour' of a divided whole, there is no sense of a linear stretching towards the infinite here. The two models agree in that each is demonstrably a recursive progression. But for von Neuman and English language number, 14 has 14 members, and for Zermelo and Yoruba language number, 14 has one member only.

On this explanation both Mrs Taiwo and Mr Ojo are correct. We can understand Mrs Taiwo as giving the children an elegant picture of quantifying in English and Mr Ojo as doing a good job in coming up with a neat picture of number in Yoruba quantifying. The explanation presents English and Yoruba quantifying as separate symbolizing domains, and children learn either one or the other: the English one if you take the point of view of conventional schooling, the Yoruba one if you are a traditional Yoruba fundamentalist or a romantic, anthropologically inclined *oyinbo* (white) lecturer in science. We could imagine that learning in the one domain might interfere with learning in the other.

These alternative foundationist descriptions of quantifying both treat quantifying as a set of symbolizing processes generating abstract, symbolic concepts. By extension the set of symbolizing processes is itself taken as an abstract entity: 'quantification'. And this abstract entity 'quantification' turns out to have particular properties, depending on which foundation you 'go for'. By describing these properties knowledge claims over the nature of the foundation can be made. The properties of quantification can be characterized through description, which although necessarily describing particular instances of use, understands itself as making a knowledge claim about quantification in general, not just the particular instance of use presented. These descriptions which claim to be descriptions in general can be evaluated as examples of inductive reasoning: is the evidence sufficient? are the reasoning processes valid? etc.

We can certainly evaluate knowledge claims presented in the foundationist interpretive frame and be content about the certainties we have discursively established but at what cost? Look at the ethical-political prescriptions. We are regenerating the boundary between 'Yoruba' and 'English'; 'traditional' and 'modern'. The individual reasoner must choose to be one or the other, with the 'saved' or the 'fallen'. We are re-making the naturalness of domination; a particular set of colonial institutional power relations. And we are re-inscribing the researcher as a disembodied judging observer[23] who participates in modern spacetime, as an (academic) legislator obliged only to adopt valid reasoning procedures, but who does not participate in the times and places of those who her stories are about. Even if in presenting her work the researcher does include mention of herself and others, this can never be more than a rhetorical flourish.

An account of quantifying as embodied

I want an account of quantifying that will allow me to keep the disconcertment, for it seems to me that this is where truth in this episode lies, a truth which is missed and passed over in the above morally legislative explanations. This is a truth that is an outcome of the collective life of Yoruba schools, and I don't just mean the collective of pupils, teacher, principal, teacher educator etc. I mean also Mr Ojo's cards and string, the scarce metre rulers, the school rooms and playgrounds, and the goats and food-sellers that arrive at recess, the curriculum documents that lie gathering dust on the floor of the principal's office, the pencils and exercise books, parents and report cards. All are participants[24] enacting themselves variously resisting and accommodating; all are already and always both material and symbolic; all outcomes of past collective acting; all participating in generating or regenerating Yoruba (school) life as the same and/or different outcomes in the present; all participating in an answer to the question 'How should we live?'[25]

How can I give an account of quantification that keeps this interpretive frame? How can we understand quantifying fitting into worlds generated in acts? Can we imagine quantifying without the interpretive fame of 'real physical entities' and the 'symbolic representations of numbers', or alternatively without 'concrete social practices' which underlie 'abstract knowledge'? Such an account will necessarily be a story of quantifying as embodied or—to put it more precisely—as routines of collective acting by multiple participants. We will be looking to accommodations and resistances between participants and the ways these have been consolidated as routines, repetitions, and rituals. The outcomes of these routines, repetitions, and rituals are more routines, repetitions, and rituals. The patterned enacting in routines, repetitions, and rituals constitutes a necessary background against which innovation and novelty can occur.

It means keeping in the frame of our interpretation, the original material elements of the patterning out of which the routines of quantifying grew; pointing to the patterning—the sectioning, arraying, and mimicking. Not deleting and hiding the messiness and lack of smooth fit between the 'ideal' and the actual of quantifying. Not retreating with unseemly haste to the easily manipulated words or graphs on paper. It is seeing how when we trace back the patterned actions of quantifying we can recognize them as expressions of embodiment. And embodiment here is not to be understood as the separated individual with an inside (psychology) and outside (physiology) but as a co-constituted embodied participation in collective acting. To the extent that 'quantifying concepts' are generated in these routines, repetitions, and rituals of quantifying, these emerge as orderings or actings-out, as much solidly material as they are symbolic. These 'concepts' of quantification are not entities but routinely (re-)generated tensions between familiar participants.

For example, in this way of rendering things the repetitions of generating number names in English will focus up number making as beginning with one finger and going one-by-one along the fingers. It will keep the fingers there in front of us, not delete and hide this material-symbolic embodiment of number. In contrast, the number making of Yoruba will be identified as beginning with the whole digital complement of a person with fingers and toes, while separating set by set will be understood as mimicked: twenty into tens, tens into fives and fives into ones. It keeps the busy fingers and the (perhaps smelly) toes there, as well as the words and graphs.

Similarly the rituals of imaging what in English we call qualities, and the Yoruba name as modes, will be recognizable as rituals. And accepted in their working, as all rituals do, to hide what is too big to consider routinely (the mystery of originary stories), at the same time rendering it banal in engaging collective memory and constituting ways to go on. We will see that as in all ritual, in the ritual of quantifying there is a set sequence of actions. In Yoruba quantifying, keeping the ritual there before us as ritual, we will see that the routine in Yoruba is to section first into units and then order the units imaging them as nested. In English the ritual actions go in reverse: order first as an image of extension, and then section.

And this retrieving of embodiment in enacting quantifying can go all the way down to our ordinary use of verbs and nouns when we

Helen Verran

talk. Taking words as material and resisting the seduction of assuming them to be only symbols, we can see that they can be joined with each other and set against each other, manipulated as any other material can be manipulated. We can see the using of words as an expression of embodiment, as growing out of the heterogeneous accommodations and resistances out of collective acting. Working at this we will eventually be able to understand 'categories of designating' as bodily expressions.

Massaging quantifying back into the embodied routines, repetitions and rituals through which we learned it, detaching it from its extravagant symbolizing claims, we see quantifying as an impressive accomplishment of ordering. Quantifying makes certain, precise and specific meanings because its meanings are rendered that way in a strenuously regulated and policed array of routine actions. Certainty of numbers is an outcome of the routines by which they are constituted in collective acting, not in their unique capacity to truly represent a foundation in a system of symbols. Quantifying is thoroughly stabilized routines, and for the most part the stabilizing is unseen—except when we work disparate routines together.

When we have quantifying as the 'clotting' of quite heterogeneous routines, repetitions, and rituals of collective acting in this way, we can see that Mrs Taiwo and Mr Ojo are both working particular routines of acting to achieve a particular 'clotting'. The significant difference is not only that Mrs Taiwo works the routines toward the 'clot' of English language quantification and Mr Ojo heads towards the 'clot' of Yoruba quantification, but that Mr Ojo is also mixing and messing with both the routines of English language quantification and Yoruba language quantification. He is combining the constitutent routines of English language and Yoruba language quantifying in novel ways to effect quantification that is, at the same time, both and neither English language quantification and Yoruba language quantification. And this is where the success of his lesson lies. This is also the origin of my disconcertment.

And when we have seen that we can 'muck around' with the routines of quantifying in this way, all sorts of further possibilities open up. Children like those in Yoruba schools can be trained in the routines of both Yoruba and English language quantification, and they can be trained to adopt routines which translate between the domains. When it is a matter of teaching children to use hands, eyes, and words together in routine actions, and no longer a matter of learning 'the concepts' understood as some mysterious function of mind, teaching children to move and switch between logics, multiple ways of making certain, precise and specific meanings, becomes imaginable.

In subverting both English and Yoruba in working them together, blending accepted routines of collective acting in ways that both retain the certainty and reveal the origins of that certainty as located in routines, repetitions, and rituals, Mr Ojo's lesson is a revelation. We experience the certainty at the same time as we experience something else: the amazing hoax of certainty. And at this a great laugh is liable to well up. This laughter, the disconcertment, is vital for it is in that that we can know ourselves as participants who tell stories as part of our participation. Staying true to that laughter will give us better ways of telling true stories in responsible ways.

Notes

1 The gasp or the laughter of such moments is a familiar refrain in postcolonial studies. For example Michael Taussig (*Mimesis and Alterity A Particular History of the Senses*, New York: Routledge, 1993, p. 246) assembles several instances and quotes Benjamin 'The perception of similarity is in every case bound to an instantaneous flash. It slips past, can possibly be regained, but really cannot be held fast' (Walter Benjamin, *New German Critique*, 17 (Spring, 1976), p. 66).
2 Michael Taussig, *Mimesis and Alterity A Particular History of the Senses*, New York: Routledge, 1993, p. 237.
3 That foundationist epistemology brings with it moral prescriptions has been an insight of feminist studies from the beginning of feminist interest in epistemology. I learned to recognize *how* moral prescriptions are generated in 'epistemic' positions from Kathryn Pyne Addelson's work, in particular *Moral Passages*, NY: Routledge, 1994, p. 137.
4 Following the trail of texts we can identify 1967 as a high point in that old debate. In the developing philosophical debate on 'African thoughts' Robin Horton's 1967 'African Traditional Religion and Western Science' was widely recognized as pivotal. Horton took a Popperian line on the analysis of scientific rationality and extended it to 'traditional African religion', purporting to show the 'openness' of science as against the 'closedness' of 'traditional African religion'. 'Open' and 'closed' are terms Popper uses in elaborating his particular brand of positivistic scientific rationality (Karl Popper, *Conjectures and Refutations: The Growth of Scientific Knowledge*, NY: Basic Books, 1962). Rationality had become 'the hot topic' in philosophy of science following the publication of Kuhn's *The Structure of Scientific Revolutions* (Thomas Kuhn, *The Structure of Scientific Revolutions*, Chicago: Chicago University Press, 1962) and perhaps we can credit Winch with the introduction of Africans in to this debate with his 'Understanding a Primitive Society' (Peter Winch, 'Understanding a Primitive Society' *American Philosophical Quarterly*, 1, 1964). In 1970 the edited collection *Rationality* (Bryon Wilson (ed.), *Rationality*, Oxford: Basil Blackwell, 1970) appeared as a contribution to debate in philosophy of science. Horton continued his approach in his

paper in the collection he edited with Ruth Finnegan *Modes of Thought* (Ruth Finnegan and Robin Horton (eds), *Modes of Thought*, Faber: London, 1973). And philosophers at the University of Ife continued to critique Horton's analyses (Barry Hallen 'Robin Horton on Critical Philosophy and Traditional Religion', *Second Order*, 6.1 (1977): 81–92; Barry Hallen and J.O. Sodipo, *Knowledge, Belief and Witchcraft*, London: Ethnographica, 1986). Anthropologists, Geertz and Gellner, had their say (Clifford Geertz, *The Interpretation of Cultures*, NY: Basic Books, 1973; Ernest Gellner, *Legitimation of Belief*, Cambridge: Cambridge University Press, 1974). Kwasi Wiredu was the first African voice to be clearly and widely heard (Kwasi Wiredu, *Philosophy and an African Culture*, Cambridge: Cambridge University Press, 1980). By 1982, when *Rationality and Relativism* (S. Lukes and M. Hollis (eds), Oxford: Basil Blackwell, 1982), which includes a rethink from Robin Horton, was published, the debate had largely puffed itself out.

On the cross-cultural psychology side Gay and Cole published their *New Mathematics and an Old Culture* (John Gay and Michael Cole, *The New Mathematics and an Old Culture*, NY: Holt Rinehart Winston 1967), which reported their work with Kpelle people of Liberia in West Africa, following hot on the heels of the 1966 publication of *Studies in Cognitive Growth*, edited by the well known psychologist Jerome Bruner among others, in which the content was strongly cross-cultural (J.S. Bruner, R.R. Oliver and P.M. Greenfield (eds), *Studies in Cognitive Growth*, NY: Wiley, 1966). We can trace the continuation of this work in Michael Cole and Sylvia Scribner, *Culture and Thought A Psychological Introduction* published in 1974 (Wiley: New York, 1974), and the collection edited by Berry and Dasen, *Culture and Cognition: Readings in Cross-cultural Psychology*, also 1974 (J.W. Berry and P.R. Dasen (eds), *Culture and Cognition: Readings in Cross-Cultural Psychology*, London: Methuen, 1974) and recognize Hallpike's *Foundations of Primitive Thought* (1979) (C.R. Hallpike, *The Foundations of Primitive Thought*, Oxford: Clarendon Press, 1979) as both a definitive work and in some senses a final gasp in this phase of the debate. I have 'lumped' apples and oranges together here. These are rather differently located traditions of psychology. Gay and Cole and Bruner draw inspiration from Dewey and they can be understood as distinct from the strict Piagetians. However they are all alike in juxtaposing 'tradition' and 'the modern' in telling modern stories of modernity.

5 This is Ian Hacking's insight. Ian Hacking, 'Styles of Reasoning', in *Rationality and Relativism*, Martin Hollis and Steven Lukes (eds), Cambridge: MIT Press, 1982.

6 Lorraine Code has considered one aspect of the responsibilities of theorists at length in *Epistemic Responsibility*, Hanover, NH: University Press of New England, 1987 through focussing up the limitedness of the notion of propositional knowledge. She takes up the issue afresh in *Rhetorical Spaces Essays on Gendered Locations*, NY and London: Routledge, 1995, emphasizing that the questions about epistemic responsibility are multiple and 'not uniform in type or in provenance', usefully linking it to the notion of discursive spaces, 'whose climate encourages responsible enquiry', p. 22.

Kathryn Pyne Addelson (*Moral Passages Towards A Collectivist Moral Theory*, NY: Routledge, 1994) understands intellectual responsibility as 'requir[ing] for professionals like myself, devising theories and practices that can make it explicit what the collective activity is and what some important outcomes of the activity might be' (p. 18).

7 I first heard Zoe Sofoulis put the slogan this way at a workshop held in

Department of History and Philosophy of Science at University of Melbourne, in June 1996.

8 I first encountered the term 'actor network' in *Mapping the Dynamics of Science and Technology: sociology of science in the real world*, Michel Callon, John Law and Arie Rip (eds), London, Macmillan, 1986, although the analytic approach was familiar from *Laboratory Life The Social Construction of a Scientific Fact*, Bruno Latour and Steve Woolgar, Sage Publications, London, 1979.

9 'crisscrossing as often as we have to, the divide that separates exact knowledge and the exercise of power—let us say nature and culture . . . choos[ing] to follow the imbroglios wherever they take us. To shuttle back and forth, we rely on the notion of translation or network. More supple than the notion of system, more historical than the notion of structure, more empirical than the notion of complexity, the idea of network is the Ariadne's thread of these interwoven stories.' Page 3, Bruno Latour, *We Have never Been Modern*, (trans. Catherine Porter), Brighton: Harvester Wheatsheaf, 1993.

10 Susan Leigh Star, 'Power, technologies, and the phenomenology of conventions: on being allergic to onions', in John Law (ed.), *A Sociology of Monsters Essays on power, Technology and Domination, Sociological Review*, 38, London: Routledge (1991), pp. 26–56. 'Introduction', in *Ecologies of Knowledge, Work and Politics in Science and Technology*, Susan Leigh Star (ed.), SUNY: NY, 1995.

11 John Law, 'Introduction', in John Law (ed.), *A Sociology of Monsters Essay on Power, Technology and Domination, Sociological Review*, 38, London: Routledge, 1991, pp. 1–23.

12 John Law and Michel Callon, 'Engineering and Sociology in a Military Aircraft Project: A Network Analysis of Technological Change' in *Ecologies of Knowledge Work and Politics in Science and Technology*, Susan Leigh Star (ed.), SUNY: NY, 1995.

13 Kathryn Pyne Addelson, *Moral Passages: Towards a Collectivist Moral Theory*, Routledge: NY, 1994.

14 Here I am using fetishising in the sense Donna Haraway uses it. 'I am arguing . . . about . . . reification that transmutes material, contingent, human and nonhuman liveliness into maps of life itself and then mistakes the map and its reified entities for the bumptious non-literal world. I am interested in the kinds of fetishism proper to worlds without tropes, literal worlds, to genes as autotelic entities.' Donna Haraway, *Modest_Witness@Second_Millenium, FemaleMan© _Meets_OncoMouse*™, Routledge, NY, 1997, p. 135.

15 Latour sees in the workings of technoscience and in modernity generally 'two sets of entirely different practices which must remain distinct if they are to remain effective, but recently have begun to be confused. The first set of practices, by "translation", creates mixtures . . . hybrids of nature and culture. The second by "purification", creates two entirely distinct ontological zones: that of human beings on the one hand; that of non-humans on the other'. Bruno Latour, *We have Never been Modern*, p. 10.

16 I am taking the 'ontic domain' as that infinite domain of things we are committed to there being in the world; the things we go on with. I use the adjective 'ontic' here rather than the more familiar 'ontological', since the latter term, containing an '-ology' within it, implies that we know the sorts of things that are in the world through study. My point is we know them through our doings with them.

17 Rudolf Carnap, *Philosophical Foundations of Physics*, Chicago: University of Chicago Press, 1966.

18 W.V.O. Quine, *Word and Object*, Cambridge: MIT and John Wiley, 1960.
19 Some readers might find it odd for me to construe relativism as foundationist analysis, reserving that adjective for universalist regimes of interpretation, assuming that relativism is distinguished from universalist analysis by not assuming set foundational categories. A full response to the issue would recognize the multiplicity of relativisms which characterize connection between the abstract realm of knowledge and the concrete world of experience in various ways, but as a quick response I suggest that all relativisms are properly identified as foundationist analyses by the very fact of their hypothesizing knowledge as a symbolic realm, inevitably setting up a 'material' realm which either that abstract/symbolic knowledge is in some sense about, or, at the very least, within which it resides.
20 Helen Watson, 'Learning to Apply Numbers to Nature: A Comparison of English Speaking and Yoruba Speaking Children Learning to Quantify', *Educational Studies in Mathematics*, 18 (1987), 339–357; Helen Watson, with the Yolngu Community, Yirrkala and D.W. Chambers, *Singing the Land, Signing the Land*, Geelong: Deakin University Press, 1989. Helen Watson, 'Investigating the Social Foundations of Mathematics: Natural Number in Culturally Diverse Forms of Life', *Social Studies of Science*, 29 (1990), 283–312.
21 David Bloor, *Knowledge and Social Imagery*, Chicago: University of Chicago Press, 1976, 2nd edition, 1991.
22 Von Neuman and Zermelo are attempting to identify the referents of number words. As I see it this is as misguided as an attempt to identify the referent of a section of a ruler would be. What is important about number names is that they form a generative sequence. Within any numbering system it is the place marked and how this is achieved that matters.
23 I am using Kathryn Addelson's phrase here, *Moral Passages, Towards a Collectivist Moral Theory*, p. xi, New York: Routledge, 1994.
24 John Law has been influential in the development of my notion of participants, which I regard as identical to the actants of actor network analyses (see Madeleine Akrich and Bruno Latour, 'A Summary of a Convenient Vocabulary for the Semiotics of Human and Non-Human Assemblies' in *Shaping Technology/Building Society Studies on Sociotechnical Change*, Wiebe Bijker and John Law (eds), Cambridge, Mass.: MIT Press, 1992, p. 259). I adopted the terminology of 'participants' in working with Kathryn Pyne Addelson at the beginning of 1997, as she began work on her forthcoming *Collective Agency*. Addelson's notion of participants comes from a rather different direction than actor network theory. Working in a symbolic interactionist style she explores the ways in which particular ethical positions are the outcome of human and non-human participation in collective everyday action. However, unlike myself and actor-network theorists, I suspect that she does not see herself as completely abandoning epistemology, that is, abandoning the notion of there being a symbolic domain.

In later work Latour, following Michel Serres, calls the thing-symbols I call participants, 'quasiobjects-quasisubjects'. Serres, says Latour wants to describe 'the emergence of the object, [and] not only of tools or beautiful statues' but his problem is that he 'can't find anything in books ... because the noise of discourse drowns out what happened' (Michel Serres, *Statues*, Paris: François Bourin, 1987, p. 216. For Latour 'Quasi-objects, quasi-subjects ... are real, quite real, and we humans have not made them. But they are collective because they attach us to one another, because they circulate in our hands and define our social bond by their very circulation. They are discursive however; they are narrated, historical, passionate, and peopled with actants of autonomous forms. They are unstable and hazardous, existential and never forget Being.' Bruno Latour, *We Have Never Been Modern*, p. 89.

Donna Haraway uses 'cyborg' for what might be understood as a particular subgroup of participants, giving the term a hard political cutting edge 'My cyborg figures inhabit a mutated time-space regime that I call technobiopower . . . the temporal modality pertaining to cyborgs is condensation, fusion and implosion . . . Cyborg figures—such as the end-of-the-millenium-seed, chip, gene, data-base, bob, fetus, race, brain, and ecosystem—are the offspring of implosions of subjects and objects and of the natural and artificial' (p. 12). The cyborg is a cybernetic organism, a fusion of the organic and the technical forged in particular, historical, cultural practices. Cyborgs are not about the Machine and the Human as if such Things and Subjects universally existed. Instead cyborgs are about specific historical machines and people in interaction that often turn out to be painfully counterintuitive for the analyst of technoscience'. (p. 51, Donna Haraway, *Modest_Witness@Second_Millenium. FemaleMan©_Meets_OncoMouse*™, New York: Routledge, 1997.)

25 This is Kathryn Pyne Addelson's insight. Understanding knowledge making and ethical positioning as inseparable outcomes, in her work she shows how collective action, in generating categories to act and know with and through, answers the question 'How should we live?' Kathryn Pyne Addelson, *Moral Passages*, New York: Routledge, 1994, p. 154. Similarly we can understand Bruno Latour's *Aramis. or the Love of Technology*, trans. Catherine Porter, Harvard University Press, 1996, as an extended evocation of a world of actants participating in answering the question 'How should we live?'

What is intellectual property after?

Marilyn Strathern

Abstract

This chapter takes as its starting point ANT's success in overcoming descriptive resistance to dealing even-handedly with persons, things, artefacts and so forth together. It points to a situation which attempts even-handedness, resource transfer in the wake in the Biodiversity Convention, while at the same time re-inventing the very divide between Technology and Society which ANT has sought to demolish. The same may be said of procedures of recompense, and the chapter considers issues in intellectual property rights as they have been extended to the compensation-sensitive milieu of Papua New Guinea: what is intended to balance out interests creates new social divisions. It thus raises questions about processes of social differentiation. It is also intended to show the applicability of ANT models to the practical understanding of what otherwise would just seem too heterogeneous a collection of materials.

In seeking momentary anchorage in actor network theory, I am caught by its formative tussle with the division between technology and society.[1] Surely there is an after-life to its success in overcoming descriptive resistance to dealing with persons, things, artefacts and events all in the same breath? Perhaps we have learnt to treat these heterogeneous phenomena evenhandedly. Fresh divisions, though, seem constantly in the making, and there may be after-life enough in reinventing some of actor network theory (ANT)'s original rationales. It is illuminating to consider a situation where its lessons appear to have been learned, yet where analytical symmetry is challenged by new social differentiations. How evenhanded do we always wish to be? A seminar on intellectual property rights organised in Port Moresby, Papua New Guinea, in the context of policy discussions over biodiversity protection, is my net.

The parliament of brothers

ANT's anchorage in a division between Technology and Society has been its own netting within science/technology studies.[2] Its insistence on treating human and nonhuman entities alike has endorsed the democratic potential of that programme. Humanity should never have been constructed in opposition to extensions of itself, an axiom which Bruno Latour has extended to all kinds of societies and circumstances: a parliament of brothers follows the parliament of things (Latour, 1993:142–3). Yet something akin to a human/nonhuman divide lingers in certain social formulations, evocative of the pains that officers of the British or Australian colonial service once took not to regard peoples under their jurisdiction as different kinds of human beings from themselves. Indeed having to banish any hint of that divide (having to banish because it was still there) was a kind of minimal threshold for entry into the international community after the second world war, endorsed in the United Nations' declaration of rights for the human family.

This gives me half of the present argument. The other half lies in a corollary of sorts: how to apply the insights of ANT to social heterogeneities in the particular absence of a signifying division between persons and things. One would not want the neutralising language and evenhanded analysis of actor network theory to lessen the observer's capacity to perceive loaded rhetoric and persons' far from evenhanded dealings with one another.

From the perspective of peoples of the Papua New Guinea Highlands, continuities of identity between persons and things may be taken for granted. People imagine one another in terms of the food which sustains them or the wealth by which they can be measured. Now to Euro-American ears that may sound a familiar enough situation; however, as we shall see, it is what these imaginings compel people to do with their 'things' which marks them out. In the meanwhile I make particular note of wealth because their former currency (such as the otherwise in animal shell valuable) was held to share many attributes with persons, most notably mobility, reproductive power, attractiveness; it was the machinations which people attributed to other people that rendered these things intractable and obdurate. It is discontinuities between persons that are the persistent objects of local analysis. So while Papua New Guinea Highlanders personify the natural world in the same breath as they reify one another, they do not necessarily presume that these are symmetrical processes. Above all, it is to the actions and intentions of persons that all kinds of effects are assigned. One wonders, for example, which ancestor is blocking a business enterprise or whose persuasion it was that got the election campaign to come to this particular place rather than that. As a result, people are divided not so much by what they possess as by what they do with their possessions and attributes with respect to others.[3] They capitalize on the fact that you cannot tell by looking at a motor vehicle whose it is, or the power it mobilizes. That not being able to tell is a subject on which Papua New Guinea Highlanders elaborate endlessly.

Imagine that radical distinctions hold between persons, then, rather than between persons and things;[4] if one includes the spirit world persons may be both human and nonhuman. So how are distinctions between persons established? Very simply, people achieve division through relations. They are divided by the positions they occupy in relation to one another: male and female, donor and recipient, a clan of this ancestry and a clan of that. Relationships separate out capabilities for action. A speaker holds an audience by virtue of their acquiescence; between them they create moments of (social) asymmetry.

Where interests are the phenomenal form of relations, interests divide people from one another. Different interests are addressed in ANT through Michel Callon's (1986:208)[5] interressements, the devices by which actors detach others from elsewhere in order to attach them to themselves, not to speak of counting allies and the points of passage through which they squeeze debate. Indeed ANT analysis implies that people are always negotiating their relationships with others. If I dwell on persons as actants, it is to plead a special case not for human agency (see Singleton and Michael, 1993:230–1) but for the diversity of social heterogeneities which people create out of extensions of themselves. Consider Callon's (1992:80) definition of an actor as an intermediary regarded as having the capacity to put other intermediaries into circulation. His example of Euro-American ideas on intellectual property—a work being attributed to an author or the right to exploit an invention being attributed to the salary paid to an inventor—has in one sense taken care of anything I might want to say about how Papua New Guineans attribute the appearance of the world to personal intervention. But it is important that Callon's formula allows for controversy and the conflict of interest. The symmetries in which ANT is otherwise interested prompt me to exaggerate the social divisions in this account.[6]

What is intellectual property after?

The situation I have in mind, or rather one half of it, is of people being forced to swallow a set of conceptual divisions long familiar to ANT. Papua New Guineans are being inducted into the mysteries of the divide between Technology and Society. How did this come about? It has come about through a democratizing impulse to render human beings symmetrical to one another. For global interests in sustaining the division are being drawn in with the best of intentions, specifically to ensure an equitable distribution of resources and thus to make sure that people are not (too much) divided by what they possess. Just as national sovereignty is promulgated on an international stage, or appeals to traditional social forms are made in a context of mass education, instruments which actually promote the distinction between technology and society are being introduced into a situation where the distinction did not exist so as to protect the indigenous order from some of its effects (the effects of that distinction). One intermediary here is the very category Callon used for his example, intellectual property rights [IPR]. Already the focus of considerable controversy in the Third World figured through the peasant farmer (eg, Brush, 1993; Greaves, 1994), there are some interesting passages ahead to be shaped by the particular way in which many Papua New Guinean societies deal with persons, their attributes and their effects, and the way as a consequence they also deal with things.

Perhaps part of ANT's after-life will be its effectiveness in having us recognize now familiar confrontations such as these. Being able to see how its very own demon (the separation of technology from society) gathers allies to colonize new terrain may tell us why its analysis remains necessary. And how does this separation combine with the concomitant separations of nonhuman from human or things from persons? John Law (1994) has asked about the difficulty, or ease for that matter, with which phenomena persist and have any durability at all, and that goes for the characteristic distinctiveness of these entities. The seminar on intellectual property rights in Port Moresby promises to mobilize all of these. Along this axis I predict two contrasting passage points for its deliberations. They offer two halves to my commentary on actor network theory. The first, set up by this demon, I have touched upon: the difficulty of aligning different interests in heterogeneous resources and thereby devising the appropriate social procedures for technological development. The second is my other half: in the absence of a hegemonic person/thing divide, the very ease with which all kinds of translations from resources into social claims can be made and the fears of proliferation to which this seems to lead.

First passage point: the Biodiversity convention

Papua New Guinea is a signatory to the 1992 Convention on Biological Diversity [CBD].[7] The convention's objectives include 'developing national strategies or programmes for the conservation and sustainable use of biodiversity ' (article 6), in relation to which the principle of in-situ conservation frames a whole series of recommendations (article 8).[8] Among them is the contracting party's agreement:

> Subject to its national legislation, [to] respect, preserve and maintain knowledge and practices of indigenous and local communities embodying traditional lifestyles relevant for the conservation and sustainable use of biological diversity and [to] promote their wider application with the approval and involvement of the holders of such knowledge, innovations and practices and [to] encourage the equitable sharing of the benefits arising from [their] utilisation [8j]

The category inclusion of indigenous communities is an outcome, among other things, of a decade of NGO campaigning on behalf of indigenous rights. Alongside this has been vigorous debate over indigenous knowledge and its protection[9]—serious attention being given world-wide to this double issue at the very point when Euro-Americans speak of their societies as 'information societies' and of 'knowledge' as industrial capital (see Coombe, 1996a: see Brush n.d.), and when genetic and biological materials come to be treated as informational resources (Parry, 1997).

Intellectual property rights have entered the picture in diverse ways. They comprise an existing instrument for securing the international recognition of copyrights and patents. Papua Guinea (PNG) is also in the process of becoming a signatory to the World Intellectual Property Organization. The international aim is to break down divisions between peoples—to give as much protection to developing nations as to the technologically advanced by extending not just the benefits of technology but the procedural benefits of technology-protection to all. In any case, PNG needs procedures in place to encourage overseas companies who seek protection for product development. There is also the matter of new works of art, music and other exportable 'Papua New Guinean' artefacts.

Then there is the conceptual potential which IPR regimes open up. The notion that creativity could have commercial protection pro-

What is intellectual property after?

vides new scope for indigenous claims to resources. Here Papua New Guinea is being introduced to legislative efforts already attempted on behalf of indigenous peoples elsewhere; representatives from Peru and the Philippines are invited to the Port Moresby seminar [hereafter 'seminar']. After decades of unsatisfactory debate over land claims, come a new set of formulations: the possibility of being able to attribute 'authorship' to products of the intellect, and thus turn debate about property rights from rights of possession to rights of creation. Property in cultural knowledge ('cultural property'[10]) suddenly seems a construct realizable on a new scale. IPR could allow indigenous communities, then, to give voice to new kinds of claims, for example to ethnobotanical knowledge (Greaves, 1994),[11] thereby enabling a beleaguered Third World to assert itself on the international stage. The seminar programme, under the title Intellectual, Biological and Cultural Property Rights, includes 'knowledge, information, inventions and techniques', 'genetic information and products', and 'cultural practices and production'.

On the surface, it would appear that ANT's lessons about symmetry between the human and nonhuman have already been learnt. Intellectual property rights protection promotes human knowledge on a par with other resources. More than that, the Biodiversity Convention explicitly recognizes that knowledge may be embedded in people's practices ('communities embodying traditional lifestyles relevant for . . . conservation'), and seems prepared to deal with a range of entities of both a social and natural kind. There appears a new readiness to accept all manner of phenomena as relevant to agreements. Yet this hybrid embrace entails, as we might expect, new practices of purification (after Latour, 1993). IPR pursues its own differentiations between technology and society.

Differentiation starts with the simple question of profit arising from the utilization of knowledge. Using knowledge to gain knowledge would not qualify for IPR protection; using knowledge to produce a commodity would. For the problem is how to make knowledge socially effective, how to make it transactable—knowledge must be turned into something else with its own independent value. The process of transformation may be attributed to an author of a work ready for consumption (copyright). However, it may instead be embedded in a tool which becomes part of the capital needed to exploit other resources. Any tool thought of as making knowledge useful acquires the attribute of 'technology'; the term points to the human resources contained within it. The more widely available the technology becomes, the more evident the continuing usefulness of knowledge: possessing the machinery to cut down a forest helps to create the interest in doing so. At the point of invention, then, an after-life is given to the application of knowledge (patent). Patents are regarded as crucial to technology development—for technology is both a product and produces products. And it captures people's imagination. One impetus for the proposed seminar is alleged international interest in local resources; outside commercial enterprise is regarded as being able to mobilize the technological base to exploit them. Thus the seminar rubric refers to 'the plans of an Australian biotech company to research and market products derived from snake and spider venom from species unique to PNG'.

So where does Society come in? Copyright and patents are premised on the specific need to give a secondary social effect to 'works' and 'technologies' which are already in themselves social effects. People first author or invent a device and then lay claims to its anticipated utility. They have to mobilize 'society' in order to lay such claims. In Euro-American convention, society here lies not only in commerce but in the procedures, such as legislation and contract, which also govern access.

This is the point at which Society finds more representatives than it thought it had. On its behalf have come trenchant criticisms of IPR as a quasi-legislative device; and criticism has been given impetus by the very challenge of the Convention on Biological Diversity. The movement for Traditional Resource Rights is a case in point (Posey, 1995; 1996; and see n. 8), one of its programmes being dissemination of information between different non-government bodies concerned with these issues. The question they ask is whether IPR could really offer appropriate procedures for aligning social interests with new resources. Far from it liberating the rights of indigenous peoples, many see in IPR only the spread of Euro-American forms of property that will legitimate the extractors of resources and make it more and not less difficult to promote indigenous claims. However useful the notion of intellectual resource remains, the formulation of property right is extremely contentious. The principal criticism which indigenous spokesmen are reported making of IPR is that it confers individual ownership (see the several contributions to Brush and Stabinksky, 1996). International NGOs and others point out that IPR is constructed around the figure of the solitary author or corporate invention, and is likely to work against peoples for whom 'knowledge and the determination of resources are collective and inter-generational' (quoted in Posey,

1996:13). Bringing in the state, from this point of view, does not help. For the Biodiversity Convention only adds to potential injustice in affirming state sovereignty at the expense of local resource holders. Against both market and state, alternative appeals are made to indigenous 'communities' and to the collective basis of knowledge.

Here are old differences rendered anew. This fresh polarization of Society is itself an artefact of international interests: persons are divided by the very debate which provides the key points at issue. For the debate is constituted around apparently axiomatic polarities (frequent candidates are commodity transactions versus sharing, individual interests versus collective ones, companies versus communities, nation states versus first nations). This in turn generates further divisions. If it is agreed that indigenous collective claims are the starting terms of the debate, then the question becomes how to allocate property rights to specific social identities (seniors versus juniors, women versus men, clans versus villages)? Who will be delegated to represent whom? Social difference could proliferate infinitely.

Thus does the hybrid lead to new practices of 'purification'. Entailed in the potential for IPR to extend protection to diverse forms of resources, human and nonhuman, is the way in which knowledge is made effective through technology. Bringing social procedures from technology-rich states and companies to bear on what are perceived to be technology-poor ones perpetuates divisions between world powers/multinationals and indigenous peoples/third world enterprise. Both sides may well attribute to the former an already socialized technological competence (they know how to profit from their knowledge) whereas the latter have to be made to see first that have technology (as in the way they implement knowledge about tree products, for example), and then to realize that they have to develop social institutions to protect it. The chances are that Papua New Guineans will feel that they must temper their internationalism with a specifically indigenous response—a response to endorse a specific sense of national identity. Certainly the language is there in people's talk of 'the PNG way' (see Foster, 1995). Yet the presence of Technology will no doubt remain a point of reference, and Papua New Guineans will in turn no doubt find themselves imaging an 'indigenous' response that summons a 'traditional' (non-Technology driven) Society. For one effect of the international criticisms is to present the Third World as though it were dominated by 'the social' and by community values. Such communities seemingly look towards the past, since it is existing social relations which are being summoned. The social and the ancient are combined in appeals to tradition, and 'indigenous peoples' across the world have responded to IPR for its attack on traditional values.

In short, IPR has become the subject of international debate through enrolling two concepts on which both sides—those who have hopes for it and those who despair of it—agree. One world has knowledge made effective through 'technology'; another world has society made effective through 'community' (see Latour, 1991).[12] The former is driven by the material necessity to produce new generations of products, for the technologically advanced somehow owe it to the intrinsic nature of things to exploit their potential, while latter is, whether as a matter of self-dignity or self-interest, pushing claims of social identity.

And who and what will represent the indigenous order which is the basis of the claims that Papua New Guinea exercise on the world stage? We might look for representatives in their own descriptions of themselves. That brings me to the second half of the argument.

Second passage point: compensation

Papua New Guinea already has a representative of its own indigenous order (so to speak) in the concept of 'customary law', formally part of the underlying law of the country (Law Reform Commission, 1977).[13] It is there (as the seminar intends) to be enrolled in the translation from international agreements to local realization. One particular area generally attributed to 'custom' which has much exercised the implementation of recent claims to resources, is to do with the way claims are negotiated—with procedure. I have been pointing to divisions of interest over the suitability of IPR. There are fundamental problems with how one translates community or collective ownership into internationally valid practice. Indeed, these are imagined exactly as problems of translation. What is to be negotiated? Does intellectual property fit local needs? What appropriate mechanisms can be found? I turn now to the opposite problem and, with it, to the fear that intellectual property could fit all too well into existing practices of negotiation and translation. Mechanisms do not need to be found! However apparently heterogeneous the mix of resources, claims and social groups, the procedure in question will fit almost any contingency. Heterogeneity in matching technological and social means is not an issue; the issue

What is intellectual property after?

is the way procedure itself exaggerates heterogeneity of a social kind.[14]

So what is this universal translator? It is known by the Pidgin/English word *kompensesen*/compensation.[15] Compensation translates persons and things into power-holders with a special competence: they both acquire the capacity to effect further translations.

'Compensation' as it is generally understood in Papua New Guinea does everything which an English-speaker might imagine, and much more. It refers both to the payment owed to persons and to the procedures by which they come to negotiate settlement. It can thus cover recompense due to kin for nurture they have bestowed, as in bridewealth, as well as damages, as in reparations to equalize thefts or injuries. It can substitute for a life, in homicide compensation, or for loss of resources. Car fatalities, war reparations, mining royalties: all potentially fall under its rubric, although since it is generally agreed that people frequently make exorbitant demands, compensation is seen as the enemy as well as the friend of peace-making ceremonies and of commercial exploitation alike. (On might ask, after Latour, how 'exorbitant' is exorbitant). Its outcome is—from a Euro-American viewpoint—hybrid, insofar as it consists in an equally easy translation of persons into things and things into persons. And its procedural capability is of the utmost simplicity. Liabilities and claims are defined by the positions parties take in relation to one another over the issues of compensation itself. I return to this.

The concept of compensation has only recently spread across Papua New Guinea from what is taken as its central Highlands origin (Filer, 1997). Not only was it never ubiquitous, different practices characterized different regional areas; comparative analysis of some of the cultural and social differences in the substitutability of items for one another, for example, may be found in Lemonnier (1991). So wherein lies the ability of Highlands-style 'compensation' to travel? What follows is a synthesis from a Highlands and, in its detail, specifically a Hagen perspective. It suggests two crucial features.

First, compensation enrols a rhetoric of body expenditure,[16] covering both physical and mental exertion, based on an image of body process as the giving out and taking in of resources. What is embedded in artefacts and instruments of all kinds is the energy with which persons have done things. If the fertility of land lies within until it is drawn out in transactions with others, then anything that the land yields—oil, timber, gold—can be taken as evidence of the owner's inner resources. Witnessing foreign ventures in mining and logging, the thought of company profit prompts nationals to construe the counter-idea of recompense. There is thus a logic to current interest in land as an object of investment that commands a price, insofar as wealth (company profits) extracted from it can be taken as evidence of wealth (ancestral fertility) that has gone into it.[17] By this logic, local politicians and businessmen may persuade companies to enter into reciprocal transactions on the grounds that social welfare is at stake. What an economist might call the opportunity cost of lost subsistence production, nationals voice as 'compensation', reimbursements which they can invest for future development. Paying for loss of future benefit can be likened to compensation for bodily injury in warfare or personal payments for nurture. No wonder there is some apprehension among some policy-advisers at what the idea of intellectual property might do in a regime like this: it would add to an already heady mix the concept that knowledge is also an inner resource with a potential price.

Second, and this is the point on which I dwell here, compensation travels by its own means of evaluation. A transaction which transforms human energies into other values, it offers the promise of harnessing any order of material worth to realize them—an insult costs a fortnight's wage, assistance in war is measured by twenty full grown pigs, mother's milk leads to claims over a piece of land. Indeed I would argue that the potential of compensation as a ready mechanism for summoning a modernized indigenous order lies in the very way in which equivalences are set up between persons and things. There are Highlands regimes where one can these days pay for almost anything, because the fact of transaction in and of itself need not drive a wedge between different phenomena.[18] The most intimate acts between persons may materialize in transactions and a wide range of material effects may be laid to people's doors. Moreover the applicability of these procedures is much facilitated by money, which offers infinite scope for drawing new goods into existing facilitations and relationships. This means that there need be no procedural problem about sweeping into the arena of compensation practices all manner of intellectual products—creativity, innovation, work carried out with intention—whatever can be rendered in terms of energy spent. That energy may be stored for the future, and not be immediately disposable (as in many land tenure practices in Papua New Guinea) or it may be detachable from persons through the very process of substitution (that is, compensation) itself. The point is that there is no predetermined discontinuity

What is intellectual property after?

between persons and the products of their efforts (see Gudeman, 1996). One corollary is that almost anything can be attributed to people's work, someone's, somewhere. If not in known human persons, the source may lie in ancestors or spirits or heroes, with a mythology of inventions and interventions to prove the point. In any case, since so many things are the ultimate result of such interventions, there is little that cannot be made to show the imprint of exertion, including the exertion of thought and intent.

Remark again on the simplicity of the procedure. The compensation process itself defines what is transactable (compensatable). This is no tautology. For compensation entails making relations between persons visible through the flow of payments, and making them afresh. The vehicles for compensation (usually conceived as wealth of a kind) are thus pressed into the service of creating, limiting and expanding social relationships. Relations are infinitely open to redefinition and reiteration; their definitive capacity is that of absorbing new transactional moments. IPR would expand by huge volume the number of items that may fall into the category of objects with which Papua New Guineans can transact, insofar as it would be enlisting persons seen in the light of new resources, and thus new categories of social actors and new grounds on which to create relationships.

Unlike claims people make on one another with reference to territorial areas or group membership as some pre-determining set of attributes, compensation itself works as a species of social organization. It can create new social units. For it may be given or received by any order of social entity—an individual or a clan or a district. But that is really the wrong way round. Rather, collectivities differentiate, identify and, in short, *describe themselves by their role in compensation*, a kind of functional heterogeneity. Compensation is part of the wider field of transactions by which social units are defined through exchange.[19] So, for instance, clan or subclan identity may be claimed on the grounds of people's joint action as givers/receivers of bridewealth. If social entities justify themselves through the very act of giving/receiving compensation, collectivities in turn become infinitely divisible, and any order of social grouping can be united or divided through its procedure. Transactions act as a source both of social continuity (actors coming together for one purpose) and of social discontinuity (actors separated either as contributors towards or else as recipients of payments).[20] In short, they bring social units into being and thus offer an indigenous mode of communication through which people describe themselves.

All that remains to be added is that, in its present guise, compensation has become a new passage point, in Papua New Guineans' relations with one another and with outsiders alike. Kirsch (1997:142) has argued that 'economic' explanations of conflict between landowners and resource developers allow 'developers to continue business as usual in the face of landowner complaints about environmental impact, which are redefined as [exorbitant] demands for increased compensation'. They equally allow developers to limit liability to material claims and to avoid other questions about responsibility. Compensation is also new from another point of view. While it works as an intermediary to which actors attribute the value of tradition, its 'traditional' status is questionable. Quite apart from the issue of its ubiquity, Filer (also see A. Strathern, 1993) refuses to agree with people's wholesale equation of compensation and tradition. He argues that despite its reference to old practices of body compensation, the new phenomenon of resource compensation speaks to a very recent history of relations with developers and with the state. In any case, traditional attributes do not bind people to 'traditional' behaviour. Hence Filer (1997:175) observers that expatriate developers may package their relationships with local landowners through 'traditional' compensation agreements intended as signposts to their mutual obligations, while indigenous landowners seek their own private means to remove elements of balance from the relationship—demanding favours on the one hand, resorting to coercion on the other.

Combinations and divisions

The interesting conclusion to derive from this Papua New Guinean sketch is not that people run together technology and society, or things and persons, but that without ideological need for either of these divisions their own prevailing divisions (as ANT makes us see it) are elsewhere. People divide people. What that means is both that old social divisions are used to create new ones, and that the work of division (after Hetherington and Munro, 1997) itself creates social distinctions. Technology is no more nor less at issue here than aesthetics, the spirit world, food, good health and reproductive power. For Papua New Guineans do not have to demonstrate that difference is inherent either in or between any of these kinds of phenomena. Difference is constantly created in the conduct of social life. It has always been a vague puzzle to economists that Papua

What is intellectual property after?

New Guinean Highlanders (among others) should spend so much energy on exchanging like for like, shells for shells or pork for pork—or for that matter money for money. The difference between the items which go back and forth between persons, the significance of their materiality, is precisely a matter of social origin and social destination. They have come from or are intended for specific sets of people. Similarly, the reason why some are lucky and some have power, or have good or bad soil, or advanced technology or not, can be attributed to previous relationships. And, in converse, anything is transactable that can be pressed into the service of the differentiation of persons (after Sahlins, 1976). Perhaps this makes 'persons' different kinds of actants from those persons of Euro-American property thinking who struggle, Thurber-like, with the intractability and peculiarity of things.

Perhaps, too, something like this arises when IPR is criticised for introducing alien forms of possession into indigenous communities. Relations with people become the basis for laying claims; one has a right because one is a cousin or neighbour, and in claiming the right gives substance to being, even sometimes becoming, a cousin or neighbour. Now while we can extend the Papua New Guinean metaphor and speak of Euro-Americans using persons to divide persons, through inheritance for instance, ANT knows that the latter have what is, for them, a far more articulate set of indigenous mediators at their disposal: precisely the properties of 'things'. Kodak cameras, hotel keys: perceived as 'things' with properties of their own these entities require people do something about them.

Take the notorious product derived from the Pacific yew tree, Taxol, as described by Goodman and Walsh (see Walsh and Goodman, n.d.). After years of largely American development with public funds, this emerged as a drug eventually used in human trials for cancer treatment, sometime after which its name became registered as a trademark of the company, Bristol Myers Squibb. Over time, from the first assays of the 1960s to a period between 1982 and 1994 when clinical trials began and nearly 3000 articles on it were published, 'taxol' acquired several identities. These corresponded to the several sets of people who had discrete expert interests in it. To paraphrase the authors, the substance changed from a property of the yew tree that was otherwise unknown and unidentified to a crimson-coloured liquid, thought of as a bark extract to be used in screens to detect potential anti-cancer activity, to a sample of white crystals, which was the 'pure compound' according to chemists, to a chemical formula subsequently revised in a second chemical formula. These diverse attributes are summoned by diverse (expert) interests, although the attributes or properties to which these interests correspond, notably chemical and biological ones, are regarded as inherent or natural to anything which can be classified as an organic substance.

This is a prime Euro-American example of what Law (1994:102) means by relational materiality. If people were not divided into different kinds of experts then we would not have an expert description of the substance divided up like that. Moreover because experts get themselves into permanent positions of competence, as the authority on this or that aspect, they presuppose that there is no substance which could not be divided up thus. Any organic substance can have a biochemical analysis done on it. Whether anyone wishes to will depend on other interests, but properties attributed to the thing will summon forth their own experts, and thus justify the divisions between people. Things come to seem intrinsically heterogeneous this way. So, like the genetic description which bypasses the tedious collecting of medical histories (Wexler, 1992:227), the thing itself will identify what people have to be mobilized. This is what ANT has been telling us all along about (Euro-American) heterogeneity. You do not necessarily want to reopen all the negotiations. You do not reinvent the conventions of commerce with strangers each time you handle money: it is there in the banknote. Of their own accord, things fetishize people's past decisions. It then becomes a matter of surprise or discovery how people rearrange themselves anew around things—the fracas over the private company taking over Taxol is like the difficulty of trying to find the right social constellation, the appropriate protection procedures, for indigenous resources.

In IPR, as it is internationally pursued, a separation between things and persons turns out to be a necessary precondition to implementation—at least to the extent that attributes are taken as independently awaiting discovery or utilization. What is attributed to the thing in question (design, invention, resource) will be used to drive divisions between people (authors or resource holders against the rest of the world). For while an author may claim copyright in a work, the work itself must show, in its makeup, that it has been authored (see Callon, 1986:80). Patent claims rest on showing what bit of nature, or what part of a previous tool or application, has been modified, by technology or by the new invention. Unlike other forms of property, IPR rests crucially in the evidence given by the artefact itself.

This can be imagined in several ways.[21] If IPR rests in the evidence given by the artefact itself, then it disregards other Euro-American possibilities of establishing ownership. People take possession of all manner of things, through purchase, donation, inheritance, and so forth; such property rights (drawing on Macfarlane's formula [1998]) use people to divide things. In other words, each entity is split among the persons who have a claim on it, and has as many parts as there are persons who have rights, like a sum of money divided between several claimants. By contrast, there is a sense in which IPR uses things to divide people, since the claim is specifically to the embedded nature of (intellectual) activity in the product. For IPR can only apply to things (human artefacts) already notionally divided into components, with that part indicating the commercial potential of knowledge or creativity being seen as among several components of the whole. It is as though the money itself indicated which bit was to buy subsistence items and which bit was for luxury expenditure.

It was suggested that if, in the view of the 'international community', IPR were to be extended to indigenous resource claims, it would recreate at one stroke the division between Technology and Society (recognize your technical potential and take social action), and between First and Third Worlds (show new nations the social procedures to cope with commercial potential; biological rights and cultural rights may need different instruments). To this set of views we can now add a division between Things and Persons (the inherent nature of resources as things indicates the appropriateness of the social claim: this is a biological specimen, that a cultural monument). It is likely that the internal relations of indigenous peoples to one another will matter only insofar as they bear on the passage point of their relation to international players; that will no doubt be translated into the 'thing' in which both are held to have an interest.

Sustaining symmetry

Policy makers charged with implementing articles of the Convention on Biological Diversity may search, as do those who resist the extension of the concept of intellectual property, for parallels and comparisons in 'local' and 'traditional' arrangements with which to deal with the new international imperatives. Custom is brought forward as a counterpart to common law. Should not the ANT observer join in? Is there any theoretical interest in that traditional anthropological activity of comparison? How, for example, would one compare networks? Comparison would force the observer to find parallels and equivalences, to treat one's cases symmetrically, within a presumption of difference. Now looking for parallels in the manipulation of Persons and Things will simply reinforce a sense of difference. But that is to start, so to speak, with already purified terms. Suppose we took a cue from a conceptual hybrid, compensation, and looked for other parallels in Euro-American practice. One candidate with an equally limitless capacity for translation suggests itself. It translates knowledge into a powerholder of a now familiar kind, a competence which acquires the capacity to effect further translations. I refer to the Euro-American penchant for self-description.

Self-description is an instrument which, like compensation procedure, encourages social entities to proliferate. And like compensation, which defines the unit that can claim it, such description creates units radically distinct from one another. However similar they all look to an outsider, self-description establishes the uniqueness of each through enrolling the radical divide between self and other. We see this, for instance, in the cascading effect of claims to ethnic identities. Observers who attempt descriptions from the outside are sometimes confused by the hybrid composition of ethnic groups, as though their mixed constitution were a bar to collective identity. But all you need are the instruments for *self*-description.[22]

The Papua New Guinea seminar on intellectual, biological and cultural property rights is a hybrid of a kind, at least as far as its social orientations are concerned (being convened by a new NGo organization in conjunction with a statutory government body). But its own mandate joins these together in its very description of aims and intentions. On the one hand, the Executive Summary states its concern with 'promoting conservation and sustainable management of natural resources at the grassroots level in Papua New Guinea'. It thus targets organizational levels outside state apparatus. On the other hand, it points to its own capacity to articulate that concern, especially in the context of networking with similar organizations in the Pacific, which will make it a voice in the context of any legislative move the government is likely to make. Here it is not 'self and other' which is a motivating factor in the self-description but a definition of competence, the description of the particular power or effectiveness it can deliver, what it can enable others to do. Since the early days of colonization, the Papua New Guinea administration has depended on independent service organizations, most notably

What is intellectual property after?

the various churches, to help implement its policies. This particular alliance of enablement is also part of a late twentieth century global phenomenon. It is a microcosm of the traffic that Willke identifies between interest organizations and the state. In contrast, he writes (1990:235), 'to the liberal format of influence and pressure politics . . . [many] countries are moving towards an officially organized collaboration between the state and large interest organizations in public policy making'. These organizations are resourceful and self-determining, to the extent that the state becomes dependent on them for detailed and specialized information, while having to recognize their decentralizing effect. They act as ('corporated') societal sub systems. Willke argues that the state trades in its competence at policy making for access to the knowledge and skills at these organizations' disposal; they in turn comply with state policies, while gaining the chance to reproduce themselves in numerous fields of expertise.

Their capacity for reproduction is immense. When Posey assembled the documents for his volume on *Traditional Resource Rights*, he drew on a range of organizations, from the U.N., to various bodies in the burgeoning field of 'soft law',[23] to local interest groups. But this is not any random collection of social entities: these groups are mutually recognizable, produce similar documents, speak a common language, and thus communicate with one another.[24] They are all experts. What enables them to multiply is, among other things, *the generative language of self-description* in a field constituted by entities communicating their descriptions to one another. Self-description is a form of self-reference. The self-description which Papua New Guinea produces of itself (the 'PNG way' rendered concrete in customary law) is a description made for a field of similar descriptions circulating in the international community. Each evokes particular competences or sources of enablement. This is the parallel to be drawn with the self-constituting nature of compensation procedures.

Willke argues that modern societies have reached a level of organizational complexity which surpasses the intellectual capacity of individual actors. No one asks, he observes (1990:238), how to link the turmoil of management activity into democratic process— offices of risk assessment, concerted actions, conferences on nuclear plant security, guidelines for experimental work on retroviruses, world trade agreements, and so forth, not to add to his list the CBD. Each writes its own agenda, each develops its own rationales and goals, and the state is at the limits of its powers of guidance. He calls this functional differentiation (after Luhmann).[25] We can also call it social proliferation.

As service bodies informing the state, these quasi-governmental organizations thus contain their own drive to reproduce; they compel social division. What is written, for example, into the UN-led CBD, is endorsed in the interest organizations which spring up to inform states how to take care of social heterogeneity. As Posey says, in his Executive Summary on behalf of the IUCN (the International Union for the Conservation of Nature) (1996:xiii), the intention is to guide the development of *sui generis* systems, that is, locally appropriate mechanisms for protection and conservation, subject only to the requirement that they are seen to be effective. This calls forth, as we have seen in the case of Papua New Guinea, the efforts at self-reference I have been noting: systems have to communicate their uniqueness to others. Customary law is an apt example because 'customs' are axiomatically unique by virtue of the social identities to which they are attached. Arguing that self-referentiality is necessary for a system to deal with its own complexity, Willke observes that systems thereby control their borders, deciding which among myriad contingent operations fit into their own procedure, thus producing some kind of operational closure. That very closure is a condition of heterogeneity.

I have been borrowing from some of the concepts associated with models of complex systems, in order to underline the self-propelling nature of social heterogeneity in international regimes. For while one might say that these proliferating organizations are all the same, they do promote functional differentiation. That is, they have models of themselves as offering distinct and unique, competences, capable of combining with one another, but different from one another by virtue of attributing organizational (operational) closure to themselves. Now Willke seems to take it for granted, that 'systems' are bound to conserve difference. ANT would query that axiom of difference. For it problematizes the attribution of attributes (eg, Law, 1994:23). One response would be to point out that many artefacts, things and events are harnessed to facilitate each organization's self-description, but are not in themselves the source of heterogeneity—each imitates others in their mission statements, databases and executive summaries. But in deploying knowledge about itself, each also makes asymmetrical its claims to expertise *vis-a-vis* these others.[26] In short, the incorporation of self-description into the operational activity of organizations, as at once part of their knowledge about how they work and a currency through which they communicate with others, becomes a precondition for further division. Describing itself is the first move a new organization takes (this is what makes heterogeneity functional). Heterogeneity may thus be communicated though common media and identical looking documents, exactly as Highlands compensation payments mobilize similar items of wealth in an endless round of reciprocities: in both cases the substantive focus of these transactions is the social uniqueness of every participating actant.

The success of ANT is to have overcome descriptive resistance to divisions between technology and society, and everything that follows in relation to things and persons. In actor network theory, anything mobilized in the course of action is an actor/actant: they are all potential agents. One could say that a decade of effort among NGOs and others has overcome descriptive resistance to talking in the same breath about governments, multinationals and indigenous peoples. In this language, these bodies all have rights; indeed potentially they all have expertise, their own competences and above all organizational capacity. Yet people may be as divided by what they share as by what they do not. It may be agreed that everyone has knowledge embodied in their practices: the question becomes how (commercially) useful it is. If claiming access to knowledge leads to functional social differentiation, its utility turns out, like any other resource, to be distributed among people in uneven quantities. The moment one suggests that technology—or procedures for technology-protection—could liberate the usefulness of knowledge for particular social units, one reintroduces the distinction between society and technology which sustains the new international programme. ANT's location within science and technology studies is there as a constant reminder.

Acknowledgements

I owe my introduction to ANT to John Law, whose inspiration is cheerfully recorded. My thanks to Françoise Barbira-Freedman for extensive advice, to Darrell Posey for the stimulus, and for their comments and help, Cyndi Banks, Claudia Gross, James Leach, Pnina Werbner, and Vivien Walsh. Above all I owe the paper to Conservation Melanesia and to the National Research Institute, Papua New Guinea, through their generous sharing of information. A longer version appears in the author's *Property substance and effect: anthropological essays on persons and things* (London: Athlone, 1998).

Marilyn Strathern

Notes

1 Like scallops, one wants to be caught in the right nets. I am not sure that Callon's (1986) Breton scallops would behave like Inuit ones (if there were any). Inuit scallops would yield themselves to fishermen directly (cf Bodenhorn, 1995:187).
2 I am struck by the axiomatic location of Actor Network Theory (ANT) within studies of science and technology. (Callon [1986:197] begins with the hope that the 'sociology of translation' offers an analytical framework for the study of 'the role played by science and technology in structuring power relationships'.) I must thank Vivien Walsh for furnishing me with several relevant papers.
3 Needless to say I have specifics in mind: specifically Highlanders from central Papua New Guinea, and transactions predicated on 'gift exchange'. In my paradigmatic case (from Hagen in the Highlands of PNG), men deliberately put themselves into asymmetrical relationships as donors and recipients within an exchange relationship.
4 On kindedness of human beings see Astuti, 1995.
5 'To interest other actors is to build devices which can be placed between them and all other entities who want to define their identities otherwise' (1986:208). This cutting disassociates actors from their previous associations.
6 ANT's appeal to symmetry requires the enrolment of the social observer him or herself as another neutral party. However here, not neutral at all, I am definitely exaggerating various analytical positions, and especially in relation to the Papua New Guinean material give something of a caricature, in order to press home my own points. Haraway (1997) is the contemporary classic on problems of scholarly neutrality (modest witnesses).
7 The Convention on Biological Diversity was an important component of the UN Conference on Environment and Development (the 'Earth Summit'), Rio, 1992. It also contained other agreements, such as the Rio Declaration and 'Agenda 21', an action plan aimed at the local integration of environmental concerns across a range of activities.
8 The text is printed in Posey 1996.
9 I am grateful to Terence Hay-Edie for several documents here. Instrumental in dissemination has been the Oxford-based Programme for Traditional Resource Rights: see Posey, 1995, 1996; Post and Dutfield, 1996. Posey (1986: chart 1) summarizes UNCED and other UN-based agreements on the rights of indigenous, traditional and local communities. The Appendices of Posey and Dutfield include texts of the following agreements and draft agreements: Declaration of Principles of the World Council of Indigenous Peoples; UN Draft Declaration on the Rights of Indigenous Peoples (1993); Kari-Oca Declaration and the Indigenous Peoples' Earth Charter (1992); Charter of the Indigenous-Tribal peoples of the Tropical Forests (1992); The Mataatua Declaration on Cultural and Intellectual Property Rights of Indigenous Peoples (1993); Recommendations from the Voices of Earth Congress (1993); UNDP Consultation on the Protection and Conservation of Indigenous Knowledge (1995); UNDP Consultation on Indigenous Peoples' Knowledge and Intellectual Property Rights (1995). [1993 was the UN International Year for the World's Indigenous Peoples.]
10 The newly independent state of Papua New Guinea promulgated a Cultural Property Act in 1976. This referred to 'National Cultural Property' and was intended to prevent the export of property of 'particular importance to the

heritage of the country', including objects 'connected with the traditional cultural life' of people (Preliminary). Its target was principally items of art and artefacts which had value in international markets. My thanks to Mark Busse of the National Museum for his help with information here.

11 See Nabhan *et al* (1996: 190–1) who observe that it would be possible for tribal rights to a folk variety of plant to be asserted through the U.S. Plant Variety Protection Act already in place, although no 'tribe' has to date deployed this mechanism. It should be noted that Papua New Guineans are able to equate national with indigenous rights (*vis-a-vis* the international community) in ways unheard of in either North or South America; the concept of tribe is only used in very specific locations, eg, 'tribal warfare'.

12 There are attempts to put these on an equalizing basis. Thus Article 40 of the Charter of the Indigenous-tribal Peoples of the Tropical Forests ('Programmes related to biodiversity must respect the collective rights of our peoples to cultural and intellectual property') is followed by Article 44: 'Since we highly value our traditional technologies and believe that our biotechnologies can make important contributions to humanity, including 'developed' countries, we demand guaranteed right to our intellectual property and control cover the development and manipulation of this knowledge.' However, as Françoise Barbira-Freedman (pers. comm.) adds, one reason why actors cannot be on the same level of agency lies in the history of commoditization which long preceded the IPR debate and has already created a particular kind of 'added value' to products not matched in non-commodity conceptions of products and work.

13 Procedural rather than substantive uniformity has been noted as a feature of Papua New Guinean customary law.

14 For a trenchant critique, which should be compulsory reading for anthropologists interested in these issues, see Coombe, 1996.

15 By 'universal' I mean that under certain circumstances it can translate anything into wealth, not that it is a universal feature of Papua New Guinea societies. I am simplifying a case which be argued in its specifics from the Mt. Hagen area, although it is not unrecognizable elsewhere in the country. However, it is not necessarily accepted everywhere either, and in any case 'traditional' barriers to the substitutability of certain classes of items for one another have long been the subject of anthropological interest (eg Godelier, 1986). I would add that while from the viewpoint of the new generic standing of compensation practices, the synthesis which follows is not out of place, it (the synthesis) does not of course pretend to be a historical accounting of the way in which these ideas have developed (see eg, the contributions to Toft, 1997; Banks and Ballard, 1998).

16 Filer (1997) disputes the connection here [see below]. He is at pains to distinguish the recent politico-economic history of resource compensation from the field of body compensation.

17 By no means the only kind of equation; see for example Leach, 1998, on ideas of place.

18 With the caveat of note 14; different kinds of transactions ('spheres of exchange') may under certain conditions do just this, through setting up restrictions on circulation.

19 The classic statement is Wagner, 1967. Groups come into being through the role they take up in relation to the exchange of wealth or persons, and exist as givers or receivers of specific types of items. There is interplay between what is already

attributed (the outcome of past interactions and performances) and what is created during new interactions or performances.

20 With fluid 'collectivities' goes fluid rhetoric. '[For] when we try to investigate or conceptualise the substance of their mutual conduct, we may find that we are no longer dealing with any actual pattern of relationships between real individuals in concrete social settings, but only with snatches of rhetoric which, like the abstract opposition of "landowners" to "developers", are applied to "development discourse" in a certain type of public forum.' (Filer, 1997:174).

21 I borrow from an analytical conundrum observed elsewhere (eg, M. Strathern, 1991a). A reminder of Macfarlane's formula: Roman law emphasized the divisibility of material things among persons [people divide things (into different shares)], while feudal and English common law emphasized the divisibility of persons in the multiple 'bundled of rights' held in entities themselves indivisible [things divide people (into different right-holders)]. We might say that scientific classification (as a project that divides by inspection, that is, by virtual or intellectual partition as in componential analysis, without having to divide the entity) transposes 'bundles of attributes' onto the things.

22 The reproductive power of combination and recombination which produces 'cultural hybridity' (Werbner, 1997) does not go away with fundamentalisms in identity when identity summons a division between self and other (c.f. Yuval-Davis, 1997).

23 Posey and Dutfield (1996:120) draw attention to the development of soft law: 'strictly speaking it is not law at all. In practice, soft law refers to a great variety of instruments: declarations of principles, codes of practice, recommendations, guidelines, standards, charters, resolutions, etc. Although all these kind of documents lack legal status (are not legally binding), there is a strong expectation that their provisions will be respected and followed by the international community.' They add that the evolution of 'customary international law' can be accelerated by the inclusion of customary principles in soft law agreements and nongovernmental declarations. These become hardened through use and world wide acceptance.

24 Both in terms of their participation in the culturally recognizable activity of document production, and (as Riles (in press a) describes in detail) in terms of relations between specific sets of organizations among whom the documents products by one may be crafted so as to encompass the documents of others (Riles in press b). Françoise Barbira-Freedman (pers. comm.) notes the virtual nature of claims and counter-claims (as between landowners and developers) which may be inherently incapable of locking into the social constellations called for by IPR practice.

25 Luhmann (e.g. 1990:100) describes the systemics of society as a 'network of communication'; within that system Euro-American societies have a huge investment in communicative sub systems whose function is to describe (communicate information abut) society.

26 Willke's point is that there is no common (or transcendental) basis for the exchange of systems: any exchange involves intervention into the otherwise autonomous organisations of other bodies. This is most acute for the state: 'the traditionally basic guidance function of the state is severely limited because any type of societal guidance predominantly means self-guidance of resourceful organized actors' (1990:248, italics omitted).

References

Astuti, Rita (1995), *People of the Sea: Identity and Descent among the Vezo of Madagascar*, Cambridge: Cambridge University Press.
Bodenhorn, Barbara (1995), Gendered spaces, public places: public and private revisited on the North Slope of Alaska. In B. Bender (ed.), *Landscape: Politics and Perspectives*, Oxford: Berg, 169–204.
Brush, Stephen (1993), Indigenous knowledge of biological resources and intellectual property rights: the role of anthropology, *American Anthropologist*, 95: 653–86.
Brush, Stephen and Doreen Stabinsky (1996), *Valuing Local Knowledge: Indigenous Peoples and Intellectual Property Rights*, Washington DC: Island Press.
Callon, Michel (1986), Some elements of a sociology of translation: domestication of the scallops and the fishermen of St Brieuc Bay. In J. Law (ed.), *Power, Action and Belief: a New Sociology of Knowledge*, 196–233.
Callon, Michel (1992), The dynamics of techno-economic networks. In R. Coombs, P. Savitotti and V. Walsh (eds), *Technological Change and Company Strategies: Economic and Sociological Perspectives*, London: Academic Press, 72–102.
Coombe, R.J., (1996b), 'Left out on the information highway', Oregon Law Review, 75: 237–47.
Filer, Colin (n.d.), Compensation, rent and power in Papua New Guinea. In S. Toft (ed.), *Compensation and Resource Development*, Canberra: ANU Press.
Foster, Robert (ed.) (1995), *Nation-Making: Emergent Identities in Postcolonial Melanesia*, Ann Arbor: Michigan University Press.
Gibbons, Michael *et al* (1994), *The New Production of Knowledge: the Dynamics of Science and Research in Contemporary Society*, London: Sage.
Greaves, Thomas (ed.) (1994), *Intellectual Property Rights for Indigenous Peoples: a Sourcebook*, Oklahoma City: Society for Applied Anthropology.
Gudeman, Stephen (1996), In S. Brush and D. Stabinsky (eds), *Valuing Local Knowledge: Indigenous Peoples and Intellectual Property Rights*, Washington DC: Island Press.
Haraway, Donna (1997), *Modest_Witness@Second_Millennium. FemaleMan©_Meets_OncoMouse^{TM}, Feminism and Technoscience*, New York: Routledge.
Hetherington, Kevin and Rolland Munro (eds) (1997), *Ideas of Difference: Social Spaces and the Labour of Division*, Oxford: Basil Blackwell.
IAITTF (International Alliance of Indigenous-Tribal Peoples of the Tropical Forests) 1995, The Biodiversity Convention—the Concerns of Indigenous Peoples, London, Draft.
Latour, Bruno (1991), Society is technology made durable. In J. Law (ed.), *A Sociology of Monsters: Essays on Power. Technology and Domination*, London: Routledge, 103–131.
Latour, Bruno (1993), *We Have Never Been Modern* (trans.) C. Porter. London: Harvester Wheatsheaf.
Law Reform Commission (Papua New Guinea) (1977), *The Role of Customary Law in the Legal System*. Port Moresby. LRC, Report 7.
Law, John (1994), *Organizing Modernity*. Oxford: Blackwell.
Luhmann, Niklas (1990), *Essays on Self-Reference*, New York: Columbia University Press.
Macfarlane, Alan (1997), The mystery of property. In C. Hann (ed.), *Property relations: Sharing, Exclusion, Legitimacy*, Cambridge: Cambridge University Press.

Posey, Darrell (1995), Indigenous Peoples and Traditional Resource Rights, Conference Proceedings, Oxford: Green College Centre for Environmental Policy and Understanding.

Posey, Darrell (1996), *Traditional Resource rights: International Instruments for Protection and Compensation for Indigenous Peoples and Local Communities*, Gland, Switzerland, and Cambridge: IUCN [International Union for the Conservation of Nature].

Posey, Darrell and Graham Dutfield (1996), *Beyond Intellectual Property: Toward Traditional Resource Rights for Indigenous Peoples and Local Communities*, Ottawa: International Development Research Centre.

Riles, Annelise (in press), *The Actions of Fact: The Aesthetics of Global Institutional Knowledge*. Ann Arbour, MI: Michigan University Press.

Sahlins, Marshall (1976), *Culture and Practical Reason*. Chicago: Chicago University Press.

Singleton, Vicky and Mike Michael (1993), Actor-networks and ambivalence: general practitioners in the UK cervical screening programme, *Social Studies of Science* 23: 227–64.

Strathern, Marilyn (n.d.), Environments within: an ethnographic commentary on scale. Linacre Lecture (Oxford, 1996).

Wagner, Roy (1967), *The Curse of Souw*, Chicago: Chicago University Press.

Walsh, Vivien and Jordan Goodman (n.d.), Cancer chemotherapy confronts biodiversity and public property: the case of the anti-cancer drug taxol. Manchester, 1997.

Werbner, Pnina (1997), introduction to P. Werbner and T. Modood (eds), *Debating Cultural Hybridity: Multi-Cultural Identities and the Politics of Anti-Racism*, London: Zed Books, 1–26.

Wexler, Nancy (1992), Clairvoyance and caution: repercussions from the human genome project. In D.J. Kevles and L. Hood (eds), *The Code of Codes: Scientific and Social issues in the Human Genome Project*, Cambridge, MA: Harvard University Press.

Willke, Helmut (1990), Political intervention: operational preconditions for generalised political exchange. In B. Marin (ed.), *Governance and Generalized Exchange*, Frankfurt: Boulder Co, 235–254.

Yuval-Davis, Nira (1977), Ethnicity, gender relations and multi-culturalism. In P. Werbner and T. Modood (eds), *Debating Cultural Hybridity: Multi-Cultural Identities and the Politics of Anti-Racism*. London: Zed Books, 193–208.

Actor-network theory—the market test

Michel Callon

Abstract

It is often argued that ANT fails to offer a satisfactory theory of the actor which is allegedly endowed either with limitless power, or deprived of any room for manoeuvre at all. The aim of this paper is to show that the absence of a theory of the actor, when combined with the role attributed to non-humans in the description of action, is precisely one of the strengths of ANT that it is most important to preserve. This is because this combination makes it possible to explain the existence and the working of economic markets. Any particular market is the consequence of operations of disentanglement, framing, internalization and externalization. ANT makes it possible to explain these operations and the emergence of calculating agents. *Homo economicus* is neither a pure invention, nor an impoverished vision of a real person. It indeed exists, but is the consequence of a process in which economic science places an active role. The conclusion is that ANT has passed one of the most demanding tests: that of the market.

Before embarking on an active and positive critique of the Actor-Network Theory (ANT), I will start by highlighting some of the results obtained by the approach, results which I do not believe we should lose sight of in any debate about what might follow ANT.

One of the shortcomings about ANT which is most often mentioned is the inadequacy of the analysis which it offers in respect of the actor. I shall consider this point at greater length in what follows. However, before proposing ways of enhancing this analysis, I wish briefly to recall a number of positive points which, in my view, should be retained. The most important is that ANT is based on no stable theory of the actor; rather it assumes the *radical indeterminacy* of the actor. For example, the actor's size, its psychological make-up, and the motivations behind its actions—none of these are predetermined. In this respect ANT is a break from the more orthodox currents of social science. This hypothesis (which Brown and Lee equate to political ultra-liberalism[1]) has, as is well known, opened the social sciences to non-humans. It has also freed them from the sterile individualism/holism dichotomy and, by using the notion of a spokesperson, has made language an *effect* of distribution and not an inherent property. My friend John Law has had the opportunity of developing this notion of distribution and of revealing its richness (Law, 1994; 1998 a and b).

The indeterminacy of the actor naturally entails a number of difficulties. ANT is so tolerant that it ends up presenting an actor which is an anonymous, ill-defined and indiscernible entity. Since everything is action, the ANT actor may, alternately and indiscriminately, be a power which enrolls and dominates or, by contrast, an agent with no initiative which allows itself to be enrolled. It is certainly this aspect which has produced the most negative effects and led to the frequently repeated accusation of relativism. Another way of formulating the critique is to say that ANT's main shortcoming is that it is everything but a theory—which explains why it cannot explain anything!

What I would like to do in this paper is to show how ANT can explain actors' competencies, without however denying its basic hypotheses and, in particular, without calling into question the refusal to give an a priori definition of the actor or the role of non-humans in action.

In order to do this—and in order to put ANT to a test—I will offer an analysis of the economic market. The market is an institution which mixes humans and non-humans and controls their relations. What economic theory describes is, among other things, the circulation of goods and the allocation of resources between human agents. It would be worrying if ANT had nothing to say about the market when it was all along designed specifically to describe and analyse those imbroglios in which humans and non-humans alike are involved. Yet the market is a considerable challenge for ANT because it introduces a strict separation between what circulates (goods which are inert, passive and classified as non-human) and human agents who are active and capable of making complicated decisions (producers, distributors and consumers). Moreover, on the market, whether we are referring to real markets or those of economic theory, the agents involved are characterized by very specific and highly demanding competencies: they are calculating, know and pursue their own interests, and take informed decisions. In short, the market seems to undermine ANT's hypotheses. ANT was developed to analyse situations in which it is difficult to separate humans and non-humans, and in which the actors have variable forms and competencies. Whereas the market is diametrically opposed to this situation; everything is delimited and roles are perfectly defined.

The question is then: is ANT of any use to us for understanding markets? And if so, in what ways will it have to be modified?

1. The market as a network

What is a market? There are numerous answers to this question but Guesnerie's definition seems well-suited to our argument (Guesnerie, 1996). According to him, a market is a co-ordination device in which: a) the agents pursue their own interests and to this end perform economic calculations which can be seen as an operation of optimization and/or maximization; b) the agents generally have divergent interests, which leads them to engage in c) transactions which resolve the conflict by defining a price. Consequently, to use his words:

> 'a market opposes buyers and sellers, and the prices which resolve this conflict are the input but also, in a sense, the outcome of the agents' economic calculation'

This definition has the merit of emphasizing the essential. That is:

— the decentralization of decision-making;
— the definition of actors as calculating agents;
— conflicts of interest which are resolved in transactions that establish an equivalence measured by prices.

The point that needs to be borne in mind is that the agents enter and leave the exchange like strangers. Once the transaction has been concluded the agents are quits; they extract themselves from anonymity for a moment only, slipping back into it immediately afterwards.

As this definition shows, the market as a method of co-ordination implies the existence of agents capable of calculation. This is confirmed by Williamson in his discussion of the notion of trust (Williamson, 1993).

> 'Calculativeness is the general condition that I associate with the economic approach and with the progressive extension into the related social sciences'.

Michel Callon

Let us accept this hypothesis and ask ourselves the following question: Under what conditions is calculativeness possible? Under which conditions do calculative agents emerge?

In order to write and conclude calculated contracts—that is to say, to go into the content of goods and their prices—the agents need to have information on the possible states of the world. More specifically, for calculative agents to be able to take decisions they need at least to be able to:

i) establish a list of the possible states of the world;
ii) rank these states of the world (which gives content and an object to the agent's preferences);
iii) identify and describe the actions which allow for the production of each of the possible states of the world.

Thus, if market co-ordination is to succeed, there have to be not only calculative agents but also agents with information on all the possible states of the world, on the nature of the actions which can be undertaken and on the consequences of these different actions, once they have been undertaken.

Market co-ordination encounters problems when uncertainties about the states of the world, on the nature of the actions which can be undertaken, and on the expected consequences of these actions, increase. Problems are at their worst when the uncertainties turn into ignorance, pure and simple. Now, such situations are the rule and not the exception. This is even more obvious with the uncertainties generated by technoscience. The general question is thus the following: how are agents able to calculate when no stable information on the future exists? (Eymard-Duvernay, 1996)

In order to maintain the possibility of co-ordination, economists have proposed several solutions which—they assure us—are, or ought to be, applied in concrete market situations. The most 'orthodox' solution is that of *contingent contracts*. Contingent contracts are revisable contracts; their renegotiation is planned, thus taking into account the occurrence of events specified beforehand. The greater the uncertainties, the more difficult it is to use this approach. It implies that agents spend a considerable amount of their time renegotiating their contracts, that is to say, interacting and exchanging information as it is produced. In this case market co-ordination as such disappears, leaving room for uninterrupted social interaction involving many different agents. These agents, no matter how much they wish to do so, are no longer able to become strangers; they are entangled. I shall return to this notion in a minute.

Another solution is that of a *focal point*. Here it is assumed that agents share common knowledge which guarantees their co-ordination. The nature of this knowledge is highly variable. It may pertain to a shared culture, rules, procedures, routines or conventions which guarantee the adjustments and predictability of behaviour. Socio-economics has studied these intermediate realities in detail in order to explain the co-ordination of market action. But it is easy to show that these different solutions suffer from the same limits. Whether we talk about a common culture or of shared rules or conventions, we encounter the same stumbling block: rules, conventions or cultural devices do not govern behaviour completely since they imply irreducible margins of interpretation. Here again, these margins of interpretation can be removed only during interaction, negotiation or discussion.

A third, and opposite, solution to the question of co-ordination is to assume that beneath the contracts and the rules, there is a 'primitive' reality without which co-ordination would not be possible. An understanding of this ultimate basis is the purpose of the notion of a social network (Swedberg, 1994) or, more broadly, the notion of embeddedness as initially formulated by Polanyi (1957) and later refined by Granovetter in two brief but seminal articles (Granovetter, 1973; 1985). If agents can calculate their decisions, it is because they are entangled in a web of relations and connections; they do not have to open up to the world because they *contain* their world. Agents are actor-worlds (Callon, 1986).

It is useful to recall these two articles for they have been the source of many misinterpretations which prevent us from seeing both the originality and the true limits, of Granovetter's solution. His solution lies in his definition of the notion of a network. Granovetter first does away with the classic opposition between *homo sociologicus* and *homo economicus*. He shows, convincingly, that beyond their often-asserted differences, they have in common the characteristic of both being individual agents with perfectly stabilized competencies. The thesis of over-socialization and that of under-socialization, share a common hypothesis: that of the existence of a person closed in on himself—*homo clausus*, to use Elias' expression. This hypothesis precludes any solution to the problem of co-ordination in a situation of radical uncertainty.[2] For Granovetter the only possible solution is that provided by the network; not a network connecting entities which are already there, but a network which configures ontologies. The agents, their dimensions, and what they are and do, all depend on the morphology of the relations in which they are involved. For example, a very simple variable such as the length of the network, or the number of connections that an actor has with different networks, determines what the actor is, wants and can do. There is thus in Granovetter's work an emerging theory of the actor-network. We find in it the reversibility of perspectives between actor and network, as well as the variable geometry of identities (for example interests, projects, expectations and preferences).[3]

The consequence of this approach is radical. What needs to be explained is precisely that which we consider as obvious in the usual description of the market: the existence of calculative agents who sign contracts.

The break introduced by Granovetter—albeit one that he does not follow through to the end—lies in this reversal. What needs to be explained is not the fact that, despite the market and against it, person-to-person interaction has to be developed in order to produce shared information. On the contrary, we need rather to explain the possibility of this rare, artificial latecomer composed of agents which are generally individual, calculating humans, foreign to one another and engaged in the negotiation of contracts. The evidence is the flow, the circulation, the connections; the rareness is the framing. Instead of adding connections (contingent contracts, trust, rules, culture) to explain the possibility of the co-ordination and the realism of the calculation, as in the various solutions proposed by economists, we need to start out from the proliferation of relations and ask how far the bracketing of these connections—which below I call 'framing'—must go to allow calculation and co-ordination through calculation.

As we shall see, to explain the emergence of calculating agents and of a great divide between agents and goods, we have to fit out and to enrich the over-social networks of Granovetter. This leads me back to some of the achievements of ANT.

2. Framing and disentanglement

In this section I will show that if calculations are to be performed and completed, the agents and goods involved in these calculations must be *disentangled* and *framed*. In short, a clear and precise boundary must be drawn between the relations which the agents will take into account and which will serve in their calculations, on the one hand, and the multitude of relations which will be ignored by the calculation as such, on the other.

Economic theory has already addressed this question very specifically through the notion of externality which allows the introduction of the more general question of disentanglement.

Economists invented the notion of externality to denote all the connections, relations and effects which agents do not take into account in their calculations when entering into a market transaction. If, for example, a chemical plant pollutes the river into which it pumps its toxic products, it produces a *negative externality*. The interests of fishermen, bathers and other users are harmed and in order to continue their activities they will have to make investments for which they will receive no compensation. The factor calculates its decisions without taking into account the effects on the fishermen's activities. The externalities are not necessarily negative, they may also be positive. Take the case of a pharmaceutical company which wants to develop a new molecule. To protect itself it files a patent. However, in so doing it divulges information which becomes freely available to competitors and can be used by them to shape their own R&D.

These examples help to explain the following definition of externalities: A, B and C are agents involved in a market transaction or, more generally, in the negotiation of a contract. During the transaction or negotiation of the contract these agents express their preferences or interests and proceed to evaluate the different possible decisions. The decision taken has positive or negative effects, called externalities, on a series of agents X, Y and Z (distinct from A, B and C) who are not involved in this transaction to promote their interests.

The notion of externalities is essential in economic theory because it enables us to underline one of the possible shortcomings of the market, one of the limits of its effectiveness. But it is also very useful for understanding the meaning of the expression 'constructing a market'. This is where the joint notions of framing and overflowing fit in.

Granovetter—and on this point he is at one with ANT—reminds us that any entity is caught up in a network of relations, in a flow of intermediaries which circulate, connect, link and reconstitute identities (Callon, 1991). What the notion of externality shows, in the negative, is all the work that has to be done, all the investments that have to be made in order to make relations calculable in the network. This consists of framing the actors and their relations.

Michel Callon

Framing is an operation used to define individual agents which are clearly distinct and dissociated from one another. It also allows for the definition of objects, goods and merchandise which are perfectly identifiable and can be separated not only from other goods, but also from the actors involved, for example in their conception, production, circulation or use. It is owing to this framing that the market can exist, that is to say, that distinct agents and distinct goods can be brought into play since all these entities are independent, unrelated and unattached to one another.

What economists say when they study externalities is precisely that this work of cleansing, of disconnection, in short, of framing, is never over and that in reality it is impossible to take it to a conclusion. There are always relations which defy framing. It is for these relations which remain outside the frame that economists reserve the term externalities. The latter denotes everything which the agents do not take into account and which enables them to conclude their calculations. But one needs to go further than that. When, after having identified them, the agents, in keeping with the predictions of Coase's famous theorem, decide to reframe them—in other words to internalize the externalities—other externalities appear. I would suggest the term 'overflowing' to denote this impossibility of total framing. Any frame is necessarily subject to overflowing. It is by framing its property rights by means of a public patent that a pharmaceutical firm produces externalities and creates overflowing. It is by purifying the products that it markets that a chemical firm creates the by-products which escape its control.

The impossibility of eliminating all overflowing has, in reality, a profound cause which I shall merely point to in this piece (Callon, 1998). To ensure that a contract is not broken, to delimit the actions that can be undertaken within the framework of this contract, the agents concerned have to mobilize a whole set of elements; these are, to use Leigh Star's expression, boundary-objects (Star & Griesemer, 1989). These objects make possible the framing and stabilization of actions, while simultaneously providing an opening onto other worlds, thus constituting leakage points where overflowing can occur.

Let us take the simplest example, that of a market transaction concerning a motor car. The transaction is possible because a rigorous framing has been performed. This framing has reduced the market transaction to three distinct components: the buyer, the producer-seller, and the car. The buyer and the seller are identified without any ambiguity, so that property rights can be exchanged. As for the car, it is because it is free from any ties with other objects or human agents, that it can change ownership. Yet even in this extreme and simple case not all ties can be cut. Something passes from the seller to the buyer: the car, which conveys with it the know-how and technology of the producer. All the property rights in the world cannot prevent this overflowing, except by eliminating the transaction itself. If the buyer is a firm, reverse engineering becomes possible. This is a general point which can be expressed as follows: the simple fact of framing the transaction leads to overflowing because it mobilizes or concerns objects or beings endowed with irreducible autonomy. Complete framing is a contradiction in terms.

The framing/overflowing duo suggests a move towards economic anthropology and more specifically towards the entangled objects of Thomas and the careers of objects of Appadurai (1986).

I shall settle for recalling Thomas's thesis, noting that it expands on and enhances Appadurai's: one is not born a commodity, one becomes it. It is also Thomas who gives the best explanation for this reconfiguration in his discussion of the distinction between market transaction and gift. His argument is fairly complex and sometimes even obscure. I think, however, that it is summed up in the following citation (Thomas, 1991):

> 'Commodities are here understood as objects, persons, or elements of persons which are placed in a context in which they have exchange value and can be alienated. The alienation of a thing is its dissociation from producers, former users, or prior context' (p.39).

The last sentence of this citation is obviously the important one. To construct a market transaction, that is to say to transform something into a commodity, it is necessary to cut the ties between this thing and other objects or human beings one by one. It must be decontextualized, dissociated and detached. For the car to go from the producer-seller to the customer-buyer, it has to be disentangled. It is only if this can be achieved that the calculation can be looped; that the buyer and the seller, once the transaction has been concluded, can be quits. If the thing remains entangled, the one who receives it is never quits and cannot escape from the web of relations. The framing is never over. The debt cannot be settled.

This notion of entanglement is very useful, for it is both theoretical and practical. It enables us to think and to describe the process of commoditisation which, like the process of framing or of disentanglement, implies investments and specific actions to cut certain ties and internalize others. The advantage is that this analysis applies generally, and enables one to escape from the risk of essentialism. Anthropological studies of money are most informative from this point of view. Money seems to be the epitome of the commodity; it is pure equivalence, pure disentanglement, pure circulation. Yet as Viviana Zelizer showed so convincingly, agents are capable of constantly creating private money which embodies and conveys ties (Zelizer, 1994). This is the case of the grand-mothers who gives her grand-daughter silver coins, or supermarkets which give fidelity vouchers to their customers. To entangle or disentangle are two opposite movements which explain how we move away from or closer to the market regime. Both movements can apply to any entity. No calculation is possible without this framing, a framing which makes it possible to provide a clear list of the entities, states of the world, possible actions and expected outcome of these actions.

3. Framing and the construction of calculative agents

Very few studies exist in which analyse the work of framing which allows calculation. To my knowledge the best study is that of Marie-France Garcia on the transformation of the table strawberry market in the Sologne region of France (Garcia, 1986). This transformation occurred in the early 1980s and resulted in the constitution of a market with characteristics corresponding to those described in political economy manuals:

— the existence of a perfectly qualified product;
— the existence of a clearly constituted supply and demand;
— the organization of transactions allowing for the establishment of an equilibrium price.

Garcia analysed all the investments required to produce the frames allowing for the construction of this market. First material investments were needed. Un-coordinated transactions between producers and intermediaries engaged in interpersonal relationships were replaced by interactions held in a warehouse built for this purpose. The producers took their product there daily packed in baskets, and exhibited it in batches in the warehouse. Each batch had a corresponding data sheet which was immediately given to the auctioneer.

The latter entered the data into his computer and compiled a catalogue which was handed out to the buyers. Producers and shippers then went into the auction room which was designed in such a way that buyers and sellers could not see one another but nevertheless had a clear view of the auctioneer and the electronic board on which prices were displayed. The display of the strawberries in the hall and the catalogue enabled all parties concerned to have precise knowledge of the supply in terms of both quality and quantity. Moreover, the fact that the different batches were displayed side by side highlighted differences in quality and quantity between producers. The latter could compare their own production with that of their competitors, something which had not been possible formerly when collections were made locally. As Garcia notes: 'those growers who had been caught up in personal relationships with intermediaries and shippers entered into impersonal relationships' (Garcia-Parpet, 1996).

All of these different elements and devices contributed to the framing of transactions by allowing for the rejection of networks of relations, and thus by constructing an arena in which each entity was disconnected from the others. This arena created a space of calculability: the technique of degressive bidding, the display of transactions on the electronic board, the relative qualification of batches of strawberries on their data slips, and knowledge of the national market all made the transactions calculable. As this example clearly shows, the crucial point is not that of the intrinsic competencies of the agent but that of the equipment and devices which give his/her actions a shape.

The importance of the introduction of such tools is starting to be well documented. It is unquestionably one of the essential contributions of science studies. The work of Peter Miller has, for example, highlighted the role of accounting tools in the construction of agents capable of calculating (Miller, 1998). What Garcia clearly shows is all the devices—material (the warehouse, the batches displayed side by side), metrological (the metre) and procedural (degressive bidding)—which give these instruments their power and effect.

Garcia's study serves moreover, to specify the respective roles of the instruments of calculation, of material investments and of economic theory in this process of framing and of constructing spaces of calculability. In the construction of the strawberry market, a young counsellor of the Regional Chamber of Agriculture played a central part. The remarkable thing is that his action was largely inspired by his training in economics received at university and his knowledge of neoclassical theory. The project, which he managed to launch through his alliances and skills, can be summed up in a single sentence: the construction of a real market on the pure model of perfect competition proposed in economics handbooks. As Garcia says, it is no coincidence that the economic practices of the strawberry producers of Sologne correspond to those in economic theory. This economic theory served as a frame of reference to create each element of the market (presentation on the market of batches which account for only a small portion of the supply; classification of strawberries in terms of criteria which are independent of the identity of their producers; unity of time and place making the market perfectly transparent; and, finally, the freedom of wholesalers and producers alike who are not obliged to buy or sell).

This case provides an outstanding example in that it enables us to follow the birth of an organized market. Above all, it is the purest and most perfect example of market organization. The conclusion that can be drawn from it is extremely simple yet fundamental: yes, *homo economicus* does exist, but is not an ahistorical reality. It does not describe the hidden nature of the human being. It is the result of a process of configuration, and the history of the strawberry market shows what this framing consists of. Of course it mobilizes material and metrological investments, but we should not forget the essential contribution of economics in *performing* the economy (Callon, 1998). The study of this contribution constitutes a vast project for the future. ANT and, more generally, science studies, provide an invaluable resource for studying this contribution.

4. Conclusion

So what does ANT contribute to the understanding of economic markets?

On the whole I find the assessment positive and encouraging. ANT enables one to go further than do traditional socio-economics or analyses in terms of networks proposed by people like Granovetter. Markets are not embedded in networks. In other words, it is not a question of *adding* social, interpersonal, or informal relations in order to understand their functioning. A concrete market is the result of operations of disentanglement, framing, internalization and externalization. To understand a market it is necessary first to agree to take what it does seriously; that is to say, the construction of calculative actors who consider themselves to be quits once the transaction has been concluded. This does not mean that everything has been framed and internalized and that no relations other than market relations exist. I have suggested that complete disentanglement is impossible; framing can function and survive only if there is overflowing, and connections have not been internalized. But it is one thing to see these links and relations as having been voluntary and actively rejected from the framework of market relations, with the precise aim of locally and temporarily purifying market relations; it is quite another to say that the market is possible and functions only because these relations are present and form, in a sense, the substratum of market exchange.

The metaphor of framing and externalization (taking into account only those relations which make it possible to conclude the calculation) is not the same as that of embeddedness and of social construction (taking into account informal relations in order to account for the possibility of a calculation). In one case the configuration of market relations and of the market is taken seriously, while in the other case all the overflowing that the market cannot prevent is highlighted. In one case we believe in *homo economicus*—although a *homo economicus* that is variable, configured, framed, etc.—and in the other case we denounce him as an abstract invention. ANT, which allows entities to define and construct one another, is well suited to observing the construction of *homo economicus*. With its focus on the role of technical devices and scientific skills in the performing of the collective, ANT highlights the importance of the material devices and of natural science but also of the social sciences in general and economics in particular, in performing the economy.

A final remark regarding the actor. As I mentioned earlier, ANT has often been criticised for presenting actors guided by the quest for power and solely interested in spreading networks and their influence. We have probably sinned, although it was a venial sin. What is shown by the study of the market—and hence of the gift—but also by the exploration of other regimes such as that of political representation, is the variety of possible configurations of action and actors (Hennion, 1993). In a network of pure scientific mobilization, the actor resembles that dreadful white male enamoured of power and aligning the world around himself. In a market network he is calculating, selfish and impersonal. The good news is that in a network of gifts, s/he gets tangled in links and relations that s/he does not want and from which he cannot disentangle him or herself.

Michel Callon

Suddenly he is generous and altruistic. In political representation s/he makes words proliferate and renders the world talkative, which is not necessarily unpleasant. This amounts to saying that there are no model actors. The identity of the actor and the action depends precisely on these configurations, and each of them can be understood only if we agree to give humans all the non-humans which extend their action. It is precisely because human action is not only human but also unfolds, is delegated and is formatted in networks with multiple configurations, that the diversity of the action and of the actors is possible.

At the start of this paper I was ready not only to recall Actor-Network Theory, but possibly to change the model and to launch a new range. In concluding it I am more optimistic. In short, it has passed one of the most demanding tests: that of the market. And if it has passed it is because ANT is not a theory. It is this that gives it both its strength and its adaptability. Moreover, we never claimed to create a theory. In ANT the T is too much (*'de trop'*). It is a gift from our colleagues. We have to be wary of this type of consecration especially when it is the work of our best friends. *Timeo danaos et dona ferentes*: I fear our colleagues and their fascination for theory.

Notes

1 See Lee and Brown (1994).
2 Elias (1978).
3 This point is addressed by Burt in a formal manner (Burt, 1993).

References

Appadurai, A. (1986), *The Social Life of Things: Commodities in Cultural Perspective*, Cambridge: Cambridge University Press.
Burt, R.S. (1993), 'The Social Structure of Competition', in R. Swedberg, *Exploration in Economic Sociology*, New York: Russell Sage Foundation, 65–103.
Callon, M. (ed.) (1998), *The Laws of the Markets*, Oxford: Blackwell.
Callon, M. (1986), 'The Sociology of an Actor-Network', in M. Callon, J. Law and A. Rip, *Mapping the Dynamics of Science and Technology*, London: Macmillan.
Callon, M. (1992), 'Techno-economic Networks and Irreversibility', in J. Law, *A Sociology of Monsters*, London: Routledge, 132–164.
Elias, N. (1978), *A History of Manners*, Oxford: Blackwell.
Eymard-Duvernay, F. (1996), 'Les supports de l'action dans l'entreprise: règles, contrats, engagements', in *L'état des relations professionnelles. Traditions et perspectives de recherche*, Presse de l'Université de Montréal et Octarès.

Garcia, M.-F. (1986), 'La construction sociale d'un marché parfait: Le marché au cadran de Fontaines-en-Sologne', *Actes de la Recherche en Science Sociales*, no. 65, 2–13.
Garcia-Parpet, M.-F. (1996), 'Représentations savantes et pratiques marchandes', *Genèses*, 25, Décembre 1996, 50–71.
Granovetter, M.S. (1973), 'The Strength of Weak Ties', *American Journal of Sociology*, 78, 1360–1380.
Granovetter, M.S. (1985), 'Economic Action and Social Structure: The Problem of Embeddedness', *A.J.S.*, 91, 3, 481–510.
Guesnerie, R. (1996), *L'économie de marché*, Paris: Flammarion.
Hennion, A. (1993), *La passion musicale*, Paris: Métailié.
Latour, B. (1987), *Science In Action. How to Follow Scientists and Engineers through Society*, Cambridge, Mass.: Harvard University.
Law, J. (1994), *Organizing Modernity*, Oxford: Blackwell.
Law, J. (1998a), *Aircraft Stories: Decentring the Object in Technoscience*, submitted.
Law, J. (1998b), 'Political Philosophy and Disabled Specificities', *mimeo*.
Lee, N. and Brown, S. (1994), 'Otherness and the Actor Network: the Undiscovered Continent', *American Behavioral Scientist*, 36, 772–790.
Polanyi, K., Arensberg, C.M. et Pearson, H.W. (ed.) (1957), *The Economy as Instituted Process*, New York: Free Press.
Miller, P. (1998), 'The Margins of Accounting', in Michel Callon, (ed.), *The Laws of the Markets*, Oxford: Blackwell Publishers Ltd, 174–193.
Star, S.L. et Griesemer, J. (1989), 'Institutional Ecology, "Translations" and Boundary Objects: Amateurs and Professionals in Berkeley's Museum of Vertebrate Zoology, 1907–1939', *Social Studies of Science*, 19, 387–420.
Swedberg, R. (1994), 'Markets as Social Structures', in N.J. Smelser and R. Swedberg, *The Handbook of Economic Sociology*, Princeton: Princeton University Press, 255–282.
Thomas, N. (1991), *Entangled Objects, Exchange, Material Culture and Colonialism in the Pacific*, Cambridge, Mass.: Harvard University Press.
Williamson, O. (1993), 'Calculativeness, Trust and Economic Organization', *Journal of Law and Economics*, XXXVI, April, 453–486.
Zelizer, V. (1992), *The Social Meaning of Money*, New York: Basic Books.

Good passages, bad passages

Ingunn Moser and John Law

Abstract

This chapter explores the relation between subjectivities, materialities (including technological arrangements) and bodily competencies. Starting from the assumption that all material and bodily arrangements are specific, it considers some of those specificities, and the 'passages' through which these specific arrangements are fitted together for a particular person, Liv, who is physically disabled. It explores the character of some of Liv's 'passages'—some are 'good', some 'bad', some public, and some discrediting—and the ways in which they are shaped to produce personal and biographical continuity and relative autonomy for her—an autonomy and capacity discretionary decision making which she highly values. The paper thus uses some of the tools developed in the actor-network approach, but also in feminism, to interpret the material and corporeal relations involved in the formation of contemporary subjectivities.

First story

Ingunn is ringing the front door bell of Liv's flat, and there's nobody at home. Indeed she has been ringing for some time. It's getting monotonous. Then she hears the sound. It's the sound of an electric wheelchair. She turns round. There's a woman coming towards her. The woman is driving the wheelchair. And she's looking at Ingunn. She's wondering who Ingunn is and what she's doing there. The wheelchair rolls to a halt. Later it will become clear how it works, the wheelchair. And how this woman—it turns out that she is Liv—lives, spends much of her day, in the wheelchair.

Apart from the fact that she is confined to a wheelchair, Ingunn knows almost nothing about Liv. She knows that she can't answer the phone but that's about all. For instance, she doesn't even know how Liv controls the wheelchair. Liv is going to explain that she steers her wheelchair with a switch. She doesn't work the switch with her fingers: she does not have the use of her arms and her hands. Instead she works it with her chin. It takes the form of a long stick—perhaps we should say a joystick—which is attached to the back of her chair. It goes from the back, over her right hand shoulder and arm, and ends just beneath her chin. If she leans her head forward a little then she can move it, move it forwards and backwards, to the left and the right If she holds it to the left, then the chair turns left. And if she holds it to the right, then, well, it turns to the right. To start it she uses a key, which takes the form of another switch, attached to the same stick that goes over her shoulder to the back of the chair. The key has a green button on top. Having unlocked the chair, she can start it by moving the first—black—switch in the direction she wishes to go. To stop, she simply releases the switch. To make it go faster, she knocks the switch to the right. This moves the three-level speed regulator one step upwards. But she says that she doesn't do this very often.

Extension

The story is prosaic—though vital, of course, for Liv. The joystick and her wheelchair give her mobility. But, at the same time, it's prosaic because Liv has been living with it since 1983. But at the time, well, it was an extraordinary event, the arrival of this wheelchair and its joystick. It was, she remembers it well, 'the greatest day of her life'. Until that moment she'd only had a manual wheelchair. Well, actually, for much of her life she'd not had a wheelchair at all. At first there was nothing, then her parents laid her out, flat, in a home-made carriage. Later there was an equally home-made wheelchair, a series of such wheelchairs, homemade wheelchairs, followed finally by one that was manufactured.

The 1983 wheelchair spelled a revolution for Liv. At an age of 44 she could move by herself for the first time in her life. She could control where she went. She could stop and start at will, turn left or right, move faster or slower, into the sun or into the shade, indoors and out of doors. She could, as we say, go for a walk.

So by now it is part of the mundane, the everyday, for Liv. And, to be sure, it's a prosaic story in technoscience studies too with its stories about extensions, prostheses and heterogeneous actor-networks.

We know about the ways in which different materials interact to produce cyborgs, and the way in which we are more than bodies, bodies alone.[1] But we are, perhaps, less clear in other ways. In this paper we want to focus on the material specificities—corporeal and otherwise—which lead to or affect the character of dis/ability. It is our argument that dis/ability is a matter that is highly specific: that people are dis/abled in endless different and quite specific ways. But we are also interested in the ways in which dis/ability is linked up with identity or subjectivity. Indeed, we take it that the links between dis/ability and subjectivity are close—which means that any study of the materialities of dis/ability is incomplete unless it also attends to the continuities and discontinuities of subjectivity—a topic that has attracted rather little attention both in actor-network theory and, more generally, within the field of science and technology studies.

Second story

So Liv is looking at Ingunn. There's a question written on her face. Ingunn explains who she is and asks her: 'are you Liv?' Yes, she's Liv, though it turns out she's not expecting Ingunn today. But it's okay to visit anyway. 'No, it won't be inconvenient. Yes, you can come in. Yes, we can talk'. So now she's opening the door.

Opening the door? Again it isn't clear how she's doing this but Liv is going to explain. She's going to explain about a third joystick, this time with a red button. She can move it, again by shifting her head, her chin. But this time it's different. Because this joystick is working something called an 'environmental control'. So what happens?

The answer is that once she sets the environmental control running it moves through a series of functions, click, click, click, a different function each time. Liv knows the order in which they come. It turns out that it is the first sub-option within the fourth main function, after the fourth click, that is going to open her front door. She moves her chin at the right moments, moves the joystick. And finally the door opens. And then Liv is rolling forward. Her wheelchair is taking her through the door. Ingunn is following her, and once they are both through, a few seconds later, the door closes. It closes automatically. They're in the flat and they're ready to talk.

Specificities

Altogether there are five joysticks. That is, five long switches which branch out of a single support. One of these works the environmental control. Click, click, click, this shifts itself through its functions. So what *are* its functions? Well, that depends on the set-up, on how it's been arranged. Liv's environmental control works a series of functions: it answers the telephone; it makes telephone calls; it switches the lights in her flat on and off; it turns the television on and off; and it operates a series of what they call 'apparatuses'. That's the first level. But there's more than one level. Go down one step and you can control the specificities. For instance, the specificities of the television. What channel does she want to watch? How loud should the sound be? Or, on this level, again under apparatuses, you can turn the radio on and off, you can open or shut the front door and the patio doors, lock or unlock the front door, and call for help if an emergency should occur. The environmental control is a little—or not so little—hierarchy of controls, commands that work this and that in her flat.

Specificities. A command to do this. The capacity to do that. Liv is able, she is *able* to control the television, to open her front door, and all the rest. And, we've seen this, she can move, move around in her wheelchair. Mobility, specificity. She can work parts of her flat. The door, that's a specificity. The television, that's another. But she can't work the blinds, not for the moment. They're not hooked up the environmental control, not yet. They're not hooked up to it because she hasn't got round to it yet. So the blinds don't have the electric motor they'll need if they are to be worked from the wheelchair. She's planning to get this. Does she want anything else? Well, possibly, though she's not bothered about having an alarm. No, she says, she doesn't need that, there's always someone around. 'There'd be someone around if something went wrong. And I could ring them anyway.' Liv's flat is one of eighteen in a new and relatively unstitutionalized local authority home for people with disabilities. This means that her flat is her private home—her personal territory. Care workers come in—but as visitors—though Liv can get help around the clock.

The environmental control is a set of specificities. It is like the wheelchair, which is another set of specificities. Forwards, backwards, left or right, movement is possible on a surface that is reasonably solid and reasonably smooth. These are specificities about mobility. Dis/ability is a set of specificities—which means, to be sure, that we might imagine ourselves as abled, but abled in a million ways. Just as Liv is dis/abled in million ways.

Opening doors. Going up and down stairs. Brushing our teeth. Reading the newspaper. Using the telephone. Writing a letter. Cleaning the kitchen. Making a meal. Eating in a restaurant. Going to the cinema. Doing up our shoelaces. Sitting a granddaughter on our knee. And so on. And so on.

Specificities.

Third story

So Liv has got it worked out—but then again, Liv is a pretty determined person. She's 56 and she's been dis/abled since birth. She was born at a time when there was no formal education for severely dis/abled people in many parts of Norway. It was her mother who taught her to read and to count—her mother and friends of the family. She has battled her way towards relative ability for decades.

Here's another story. Liv is from Trøndelag which is hundreds of kilometres from where she lives now. But she's still got family there, family and friends, and she likes to visit them. Though visiting isn't so easy she's determined about it. She was determined, for instance, to go back and visit the institution she'd lived in for years which was having a celebration. So she and her carers made the arrangements. She bought the train ticket. She told the railway she was dis/abled, confined to a wheelchair. No problem, they said. The trains are built for people in wheelchairs too. There's a lift, a hoist, at every station. You roll the wheelchair onto the hoist. It lifts the wheelchair up. And then you roll into the train.

The day arrived. Liv was there at the station. She was waiting for her train. The train arrived. But where was the hoist? Answer: it was missing. They tried hard and found a kind of a ramp with rails. Then they tried to haul the wheelchair up the ramp but it didn't work because the wheelchair was too heavy, and the ramp was too steep. The train left without Liv.

Passages

Movement between specificities. Between, for example, the platform of the station and the train itself. Or her home town and her destination. We need to say that the movement between specificities is also a specificity in its own right. Here it takes the form of a hoist and a taxi—for though the railway had got it wrong and failed to make the specificity needed to bridge the gap between the platform and the train, they did do the next best thing. They ordered a taxi and paid for it too, though the story doesn't have an entirely happy ending, because, on the way back, there *was* a hoist. So they lifted Liv and her wheelchair into the train, but then they parked her in the only place where there was room for a wheelchair: in the goods compartment. Liv found herself travelling with the baggage.

So the argument has to do with specificities and the relations between specificities. Once we start to attend carefully to specificities, the passages between those specificities also come into focus. We find that we need to pay attention to them too. We need to look into how they are done, done, or not done, these passages which are also specificities in their own right. And talking with, talking of, Liv, already tells us quite a bit about the character of some of those passages. It tells us, for instance, that some are easy and some are difficult. It tells us, for instance, that for Liv the passage between opening her front door and switching on the lights is pretty straightforward, as is the passage between controlling the front door and moving her wheelchair. Whereas, on that day in that railway station, it turned out that the passage between platform and train was insurmountable.

Note that: on *that* day, and in *that* railway station. Because we're dealing with specificities here, specificities, and the equally specific passages between specificities. Specificities—let's remind ourselves— that are specific because they come in the form of networks of heterogeneous materials. To repeat the standard lesson from STS: if the networks are in place, if the prostheses are working, then there is ability. If they are not, well then, as is obvious, there is dis/ability. So here's the proposition. Dis/ability is about specific passages between equally specific arrays of heterogeneous materials. It is about the character of the materials which en/able those passages. And it is about the arrays which secure or don't secure them—like absent lifts.

Fourth story

We said it earlier: Ingunn knew almost nothing about Liv before she visited her for the first time, except that Liv couldn't answer the telephone. So she knew that Liv couldn't talk so well, and the question was: how would they communicate?

It turned out Liv could talk. Ingunn discovered this in the first five seconds, at the moment when they met outside her front door. But could they have a proper conversation? Could they talk for two or three hours? Would Liv be able to respond to her questions? And in turn, how well would Ingunn understand her answers? None of this was clear as they entered Liv's flat. Ingunn looked around for the aids which she had become familiar with in the course of other interviews. For instance, the portable computer with its little screen or the little box with its menu of chosen sentences—devices which speak the words when words made by voices break down. But she couldn't see any such devices. It seemed that they were going to talk to one another face to face. Voice to voice.

And so it turned out. Liv asked Ingunn to take a seat—and she sat on her sofa. Liv moved her wheelchair to the right of the sofa. Liv started to speak and Ingunn concentrated—and though it wasn't easy Ingunn understood what Liv was saying. She was asking about the study, about the reason for Ingunn's interest in her disability. And so the conversation started. Indeed it started well, though, to be sure, sometimes it came unstuck.

Came unstuck? Well yes. For every so often even with concentration it wasn't possible to make sense of Liv's words. Ingunn was looking at her face, her expression, her mouth, her lips, attending to her voice, to her words, but also to her intonation, to the emotions carried in her voice, the intonations of pleasures and sadnesses. She was listening, for instance, to the moments when her voice trembled or became thick. For Liv had much to tell, and she conveyed it well, yet sometimes, even so, it wasn't possible to make sense of what she was saying.

How much did it matter? Answer: it didn't matter much—but it also mattered a lot. It didn't matter much because Liv was watching Ingunn and could see if she wasn't following. Or Ingunn would repeat what she thought Liv had said, and ask her: 'is this what you mean?' And she'd agree, or not. And then, at least sometimes, it would be turned into a joke and there would be laughter to relieve the tension of failing communication.

Which meant that communication also mattered very much to Liv. Here is a excerpt from the interview notes:

'I feel myself so handicapped', she says, with a voice that is moved to tears . . . She says this to me, and asks me whether I understand her, do I understand her when she speaks?

Good passages, bad passages

'Yes', I say, 'if we sit opposite one another.'

'For not everything understands me when I speak', says Liv, with sorrow and pain in her voice, a lump in her throat. 'That is so . . . Yes.' She speaks, and then there is a long pause. It is not easy for her to say this.

Bad passages

So talk is another set of specificities. Each moment in a conversation is a moment that joins together the moment before and the moment after. Artful work, well, yes, there is artful work in holding on to incomplete meanings, in joining them together, in making the necessary passages. Harold Garfinkel showed this thirty years ago,[2] all the business of repairing indexicality by means of reflexivity. But then there is breakdown. If you go beyond a particular point and the words no longer make sense. The words that you didn't make out can no longer be retrieved, rebuilt and inserted back into a context, and then sense is lost.

Which is all very well, and no doubt right, but perhaps it also pays insufficient regard to the materialities of words.[3] So what of the materiality of words? If they are spoken then these have to do with air and acoustics. But also with ears and with tongues. With throats and voiceboxes. With stomachs and breaths. With heads and cheeks and tongues and lips. With the way in which the mouth is held. With many muscular abilities. With the co-ordination and ordering of no less than fifty eight muscles in the tongue alone. There are so many muscular abilities, abilities that are so important, that there is a whole profession called speech therapy which reorders the disciplines of the voice when these are disrupted. But the materialities of words also have to do with the way in which speakers face each other, or don't, with what they are able to see of one another. And with ears and the sense of hearing. So once again we are dealing with specificities, specific material heterogeneities and the passages between those specificities. Which brings us to Liv's urgency, her desire to be understood. And to her self-evident pain when she is not understood.

The reasoning is so: pleasures and pains, or so we are suggesting, have in part, perhaps in large part, to do with passages. They have to do with difficult passages that are then made easy, or easy passages that are then made difficult. Or they have to do with what we might think of as 'necessary passages'—by which we mean passages that are, as it were, set for subjects in the material and discursive conditions which order relations. Which help to constitute normative subjectivity. Which order what will come to count as the passages that are important. Or simply taken-for-granted, at any rate by those who are normatively competent. Or, to put it differently, by those who happen to take the form of relatively standardised technico-bodily packages. Such as, for instance, the business of opening and closing a front door for someone who has voluntary control of their hands. Or not. Going for a walk for someone who can indeed, use their legs. Or not.[4] Or speaking to someone else, having a conversation by using the voice. Or otherwise.

There are passages that are presupposed, normatively prescribed: if these turn out to be bad passages for the subject, then they make lacks. And if such passages are made better then this, perhaps, makes for pleasure.[5]

Fifth story

This is Ingunn's second visit to Liv. By now things are different. Liv has acquired a computer which she uses to write. Of course she cannot use a keyboard. So Ingunn is asking how she works the computer. The answer is that it has a special control, a further joystick. This controls a special program called Wivik that replaces the keyboard. The program has its own window on the screen—the bottom half—while the text she's writing is in a second window in the top half of the screen. Liv can't control the cursor in the text window directly—only the way it moves in the special program in the lower window. But how does it work? Here is an excerpt from Ingunn's fieldnotes:

> 'How do you start, for instance?' I ask. And she says 'I push the blue joystick till I hear a click, which means that I am connected to the computer.' By pushing the joystick in four directions Liv can move the cursor within the Wivik program. This has four big boxes with four arrows. And each of the big boxes is subdivided. So the whole thing is like a Chinese box. And then Liv is demonstrating to me how she uses this system. She says 'I'll write my name'. She pushes the joystick to the left to get into the upper left square of the Wivik window where there are four smaller squares. She pushes the joystick away from her chin to move the cursor into the square for 'l'.

So that's the 'l'. Turning this into a capital involves further moves. She has to move the cursor down into the big box at the bottom on the right of the screen. This is subdivided into something like sixteen boxes. One of these is a function called 'sp'. 'sp' means 'special functions'. Once she is inside this she can open up another menu, or another display in the form of four further boxes where she chooses between special functions such as 'capital letters', 'save', and 'print'. Now she chooses 'capital letter' and the 'l' turns into an 'L'. This done, she has to get back up again to the boxes with the letters of the alphabet. So she continues to write, first an 'i', and then a 'v'. She's written 'Liv'. All of which means that there are a lot of operations involved in writing a single symbol or word, not to mention a sentence. And if she wants to correct things it is similarly complicated. She has to find a special sign to get into the equivalent of the backspace function on the keyboard.

However Liv works it all okay. It's almost in her body by now, an embodied skill. It's almost in her chin, the ability to work the system without thinking explicitly about every move. But it takes time. Even writing her name is a very long operation. 'It is very slow,' she says. 'But I can write more now, and I can write alone.'

Better passages

So good passages have to do with moving smoothly between different specificities and their materialities. Bad passages are about awkward displacements, movements that are difficult or impossible. So what, then, of this Wivik program? First let's note that it isn't really very easy to use—or, more precisely, it is pretty laborious. It is much easier for someone who has the use of their hands to sit and type at a keyboard. Liv takes several minutes to write the three letters that make up her name. And it takes her two days to write a two-page letter to her friend. So we wouldn't want to say that Wivik is actually a way of making good passages.

But. But we can approach the argument the other way round, and then it looks rather different. Before Liv was given the computer and the Wivik program—indeed at the time of Ingunn's first visit—she couldn't write on her own at all. She could dictate what she wanted to write to her teacher or perhaps to her carers. But her writing time was limited. There were two hours with the teacher a week—and however much time she could beg or borrow from her carers. Most of the time, then, she simply couldn't write at all. Which was, so to speak, the literary equivalent of her inability to get onto the train. A passage so bad that it wasn't really a passage at all.

Now hoists and Wivik programs are not that wonderful. In the case of Wivik she has to chase up and down the hierarchy of commands dictated by the structure of the program. On the other hand, she *can* chase up and down that hierarchy. She *can* write letters and sentences when no-one else is around. The *can* spend a weekend writing a letter to one of her friends. The passages it affords, then are not that wonderful. But they are a great deal better than what there was before. They are a great deal better than nothing.

Sixth story

At that first interview Ingunn is with Liv for three hours. They talk, and near the end Liv sends Ingunn to the canteen where she is given something to eat and drink. She returns to Liv's flat to eat it and drink it. That's it: Ingunn eats and drinks, with her hands and her mouth, but Liv does not join in. Instead, she sits there, and she watches.

And what is the significance of this? Of course, there is a severely practical matter. Liv cannot feed herself. But there is something else going on too. The Norwegian custom runs so: if you visit someone's house then you are offered something to eat and drink. It is a part of the custom, the ritual, a part of playing the role of a good host, a gesture of friendship. Liv cannot play every aspect of that role. She cannot get up and go to the kitchen to make a cup of coffee. But she can send—she does send—Ingunn to the cafeteria to get a sandwich and a cup of coffee. And, note this, it is understood that Ingunn will not pay. She is a guest, Liv's guest.

Orderings

Does Liv want to eat with her guest, or does she prefer to wait, wait until she has gone? Empirically, the question is one that is open. And, no doubt, it is in part a matter of discretion: Liv's discretion. For it she chose to eat with Ingunn then she would need her help, and perhaps she would prefer to avoid that. Perhaps for her this is a personal matter—something that she does not want Ingunn to see. Though what counts as personal is, of course, a tricky matter, one of negotiation and discretion as the story about the role of the host suggests.

Here perhaps, we are all students of Erving Goffman, or Norbert Elias, or Judith Butler, or Leigh Star,[6] with their lessons about the division between private and public, visible and invisible, back stage and front. This is an oblique way of saying that not everything is as it seems, that the public smoothnesses always conceal work, and indeed may also conceal private disruptions. So the good passages which we see are concealing other passages—the hard work, for instance, and all the time that goes into a two page letter. Of course, some of these secret passages are good, but some of them may also be bad. To say it again, the apparently effortless movement from one specificity to the next conceals work. It conceals pain, the effort, of arraying the materials of successive specificities, of ordering them[7] or, perhaps, the shame involved in the materialities of their arrangement.[8] So there are front-stage slickness and back-stage complexities, difficulties, or bad passages.

So Liv? Well, isn't it like this? She is like any person. For any person is, after all, a set of more or less complex and difficult passages. And an economy that distributes those passages between visibility and invisibility. Not all of those distributions have to do with difficulty or ease—or (which is not necessarily the same thing) to do with pain or pleasure.[9] Not all. But some of them do. For instance, what we think of and perform as the 'intimate' bodily functions. These passages, passages which are taken to be difficult, are certainly not visible for most of us, most of the time. And if Liv's dis/ability requires that here she needs the help of carers, then they are certainly invisible to Ingunn, a visiting sociologist. They are back stage.

If our lives are the performance of specific passages between specific material arrays, then no doubt we might tell stories about the ways in which they are ordered, about the various ways in which they follow one another, and the degree to which they do so smoothly. There are, to be sure, whole literatures on this. For instance, thanks to Leigh Star, in STS we know something of the difficulties of being allergic to onions: yes, it is usually better to be a standardized bodily package,[10] one that is normatively approved, where the norms are embedded in the ramifications of the networks of specificities, and the passages between them. Of course, what it is that counts as 'standardized', what it is that is *made* to be standardized, are also matters that deserve inquiry. And then, again as we know well, packages that are standardized also prefer to imagine themselves, perform themselves, as unmarked categories. Or are imagined and performed in this way as the invisible body, the corporeal-technical body that is 'naturally able', that has been normalized to the centre. The unmarked normativity that is standard, that is standard and invisible—and is therefore invisible.[11] Is made invisible by being made smooth, made standard, or not. For passages are smoother for some than others. Stairs don't mix with wheelchairs. They mix better with legs—but legs, for instance, without the pain that comes with lower limb atherosclerosis. And non-standardized bodies, some of them, don't mix so well with onions. So there is the question of the materialities of passages—those materialities that are assumed, normative materialities, those which are provided like stairs, and those that are not like ramps or hoists.

Seventh story

Here is another excerpt from the interview notes. Ingunn is asking what Liv is able to do now, that she couldn't do before, without technology?

> 'Decide for myself', Liv says with emphasis 'I can decide when I want to get up, and when I want to go to bed. What and when I want to eat. I can prepare and cook my own food—with help. I can decide how to decorate and arrange my flat. I couldn't do that before, not where I lived earlier. There I only had a single room. Here I have decided about everything in my flat. Every flat here is different', she adds. And she repeats; 'I can eat at home myself here, I can have visitors, prepare the food myself—with help. Those who want to can go to the canteen and buy their food there instead. And I can go out for a walk whenever I would like.'

'Where I lived earlier'. Liv is making a contrast between her current living conditions and the home where she used to live, which was much more institutionalized. Elsewhere she tells stories about this, about the grey and white, the walls that were painted in interminable tones with different greys and whites. And of the single light in every room, hanging from the centre of the ceiling, that cast a harsh glare over everything. Every room was the same. There was no individuality. It was a world of institutional regimes, going to bed and getting up at fixed times, the meals at the same times each day, the menus on a weekly schedule, rigidly fixed—the same, week in and week out.

Good passages, bad passages

So life is different now. Liv can decide about time, about when to do things. Though, of course, since she often needs someone to help her, she may have to wait if the carers are already busy. Which, she also adds, is usually no great problem.

Discretion

So there are smooth passages, and then there are passages that are more awkward. And then there are public passages and those that are private. All of this has to do with ordering. But then there is also the matter of order. Literally, we mean that. The questions of what comes before what, and crucially, how it is determined, what comes before what. Which brings us to the vexed question of discretion, of choice, of centred decision-making, questions that have to do with the final triumph of the modern subject in all his glory.

But before we get completely carried away into irony, let us note that this is what Liv, who is scarcely an unmarked category, is seeking and is talking about. It is what she has been struggling for. Indeed, it is what she has been struggling for, for most of her life which has, as a consequence, dramatically improved in quality with its computers and its intelligent flats and the creation of new forms of care for people like Liv, forms of care that are no longer scheduled like life in a barracks. With huge institutions. With everyone the same, stripped of individuality, stripped of discretion, without the slightest ability to choose, to make decisions.[12]

Eighth story

A further excerpt from the field notes.

'Is there something you miss or wish you could do?'
Liv instantly replies: 'To write'. She says this with some force. She goes on, 'because it has always been so cumbersome. I learned to use a word processor, and got help with it, in the place I lived before. At that time I had a PC with a special mouse. I still have it in the school in the old building here'. . . . Then Liv confides to me: 'I am writing my memoirs, my autobiography'. She says this in a low voice and with a big smile on her face. I have the sense that if she had been able to lean forward as she said this, then she would have done so. This is obviously very important for her. It turns out that Liv has written over 25

chapters!—'I have so much in my head', she says with another smile. 'Recently I have been writing about my time here, what happened after I moved here. I have two school hours each week and then I write. That means that what I do is to dictate, since it is so cumbersome to use the writing system that I have got. And the teacher writes down what I say. . . . I really think it is important for young people to know how it is to be handicapped, and how it was to be handicapped in the old days.'

Indeed, Liv has written twenty five chapters of her memoirs. She's been working on it hard—ever since she moved to her new home. It isn't her only priority, but it is near the top of her list, perhaps even at the top.

Ingunn has looked at the autobiography and discussed it with her. Many Norwegians are interested in their family origins, and Liv is no exception. So the memoirs start with a family tree, and then describe what it was like to live on a farm in Trøndelag in the 1940s: bringing in the harvest; slaughtering the animals; curing the meat and making sausages; Christmas celebrations. The round of the year. And then woven into this, Liv is telling the story of her own life: her premature birth; the fact that against all the odds she survived; the fact that in celebration of this, she was christened Liv (in Norwegian this means 'life'); the virtual impossibility of getting an education for someone as disabled as her; the first primitive technical aids; the purchase of her first manufactured wheelchair. An important moment, of this Liv remembers: 'it was shiny, green and beautiful'. Then the move from home to an institution at the moment when her father fell ill and her mother could no longer cope, which was a moment of great anxiety, the night she first slept alone—but also, or so it was to turn out, a moment of release and liberation. The moment when it became possible to make new social contacts, to build a new social life. And then the trials and tribulations—we have already touched on these—of living in a large institution with all its interminable routines. But also a whole chapter devoted to her new electric wheelchair, to the freedom and mobility that it brought, and the pleasures that followed.

And the story continues to grow.

Continuities

We want to talk about the *importance* of the act of writing for Liv.
What is happening as she writes is that Liv is building a life. Let

us emphasise that: she is *building a life*. She is *building* it. And it is also the narrative of a *single* life, of a life that holds together, a life that has grown, grown through a series of narrated passages. There are good passages. Her life has grown out of a family context that can be traced back—she has done this—to the sixteenth century. It has grown out of the context of a rural family history and has unfolded, to be sure, through endless struggle and adversity. This means that there are bad passages, her birth in the winter and her survival against all the odds. But then there are better passages, the things that she did, Liv did, on the farm, in her home, in her commune. For there is a strong sense in her autobiography of *agency*. Of Liv as a positive agent. Of someone who is able to act in a way that is independent of others. Move from place to place, metaphorically. Of someone who is able to ignore her physical dependence on her carers and enablers. Who knows perfectly well—to put it in actor-network language—that she is inserted in a series of heterogeneous networks, human and non-human. But for whom—how should we say this?—this is not morally important.

'Morally important?' We have some anxieties about the term. We don't want to build a dualism between the moral on the one hand and the pragmatic on the other. Though it is perhaps difficult to avoid some kind of divide: we have seen this already in the difference between back-stage and front, between the somewhat disembodied agent and the difficult passages that she conceals. But in talking this way, we want to follow Goffman and catch something about the interdependent importance of both independence and unity for Liv as a moral agent. For what we might think of as Liv's 'moral economy'? Her sense of self. Her sense of herself, to repeat, as an active and autonomous agent. Her sense of herself as a unitary agent. A unitary agent? This takes us into deep waters. But we are tempted to tell a story about activities or narratives of continuity, of good passages, of stories that are 'rational'. Which means that they are planful and coherently ordered—and no doubt, in fair measure, centrally controlled. Which is the point about discretion, the normatively desirable state of discretion in the modern discourses of Western subjectivity.

Rationalization: of course the term has a double sense. The act of making rational, of ordering. And the act of pasting coherence on after the event. No doubt storytelling, autobiography and memoirs lie somewhere between the two: retrospective and prospective. What will happen, what the agent will do, these are made in large measure by the narratives of the past; the genres of telling and sensemaking, of which, to be sure, autobiography is only one, all be it one that is important for many—and not least Liv.

So Liv is performing herself as a rational agent. This means that she is also performing herself as a continuity. Liv in 1939 leads to Liv in 1997. The one grows out of the other. It is in some sense a continuous passage, or a continuous set of passages. The earlier and the later Livs are both part of a single chronological narrative, a narrative in which Liv as agent makes herself, struggling against all the difficulties of a dis/abled body. Against or with all the everyday contingencies, there is nevertheless a real coherence in which she has some degree of control.

Autobiography, then is a prosthesis. It is an extension to the person. Or the person is an extension to the autobiography. Cyborg-like, they are partially connected, internally related, and irreducible to one another.

Ninth story

Towards the end of our first interview, there was a knock on the door, and a care worker came into the flat. She'd expected Liv to be alone, and was a little surprised to see a visitor. However, she wanted to talk with Liv about two or three things, and went ahead and talked about them anyway. There was the matter of Liv's laundry, but also a question to do with her personal finances. In an earlier correspondence, Liv had said that she wanted to take full responsibility for running her personal finances. Now a letter responding to this had arrived from the administration of the home. The carer read it out to Liv. It turned out to be a question about Liv's earlier letter. How important was it for her to control her own finances? Did Liv really mean what she had said? Did she really understand what was involved?

As the carer did this Liv got very upset. Ingunn's fieldnotes say:

Afterwards I ask her if she is angry. And what kinds if things maker her angry anyway.

'Yes,' says Liv, 'when people want to make decisions for me. When they overstep the boundaries. For instance, when they involve themselves in my financial affairs. I want to manage my money for myself. I have always done so. I will not have them interfering in my private life or in my finances.'

Discontinuities

Here Liv is making herself separate. She is insisting on the performance of a discontinuity. Of course we have come across discontinuities already. Liv separates herself from her environment in physical ways. She has her own flat with its environmental controls. As we have seen, she can close the door on the flat. It is her private space.

But separation is not simply a physical matter. Indeed, the physical separations are significant because they point to what we have referred to as 'moral' divisions and distinctions: Liv as an autonomous and discretionary agent. Which is of course the point of the last story. Here another agent is invading Liv's space both physically and morally. Physically she has come into the room and started a conversation despite the fact that someone else was already there, and despite the fact that another conversation was already going on. And if this is also a moral intrusion, then it is perhaps doubly so because the intruder wants to talk about Liv's personal finances.

Note that: we write 'personal' finances. We scarcely need to create a full-blown narrative of the development of normative rationality and that of the modern Western subject to appreciate that something rather sensitive is going on here. The competent subject is indeed one that can count, can calculate, can plan, can exercise discretion and so take responsibility for the decisions it has taken. And if decisions about matters of finance are particularly important within this paradigm of subjectivity, this is perhaps not so very surprising given the links between the formation of normative subjectivity and the development of market relations.

All of which is a way of saying that this intrusion performs Liv as an incompetent subject. Which means, in turn, that here the performance of *discontinuity* is the essence of competence.

Tenth story

Well perhaps we don't need to make another story, because what we want to do is to point to some of the complexities of Liv's situation. She is totally dependent on care for many of her daily activities. She is totally dependent on the environmental control in order to work her flat. She is totally dependent on her wheelchair in order to achieve mobility. The list of continuities that are also dependencies is endless, as it is for all of us—though, so be sure, it is the fact of Liv's dis/ability that witnesses this, that makes her passages, good, bad and indifferent, so much more visible than would be the case for a person with a normatively standardised bodily package.

All this means that at the same time (again like all of us) Liv is indeed independent. She can write. She can go out for a walk when she wants. She can watch the television like anyone else. And, we haven't mentioned this, she can knit—she knits caps and legwarmers. She can paint—her flat is full of her own paintings. She can bake cakes. She makes Christmas decorations with the help of an assistant. Her life is full, she is a busy person. And she is indeed in a real sense, a person who is independent.

Dis/continuities

Here it seems we are faced with a puzzle, or a paradox. Somehow or other, if we are to understand what is going on for Liv, then we have to hold together both continuity and discontinuity. Or, to put it a little differently, it seems that continuity and discontinuity are being performed together.

Paradox? No doubt, the paradox is more apparent than real. Empirically it is obvious enough what is happening. Indeed, perhaps it is obvious at more than one level. For instance, first, it seems that moral continuity also depends on—indeed performs—moral discontinuity. To be a competent agent, is in some sense to be separated from other agents at times. We have just seen that. But, at the same time, it is also to extend the moral continuities of planful action and sustained identity into both the past and the future. Hence the importance of Liv's autobiography, not to mention her artistic and craft activities mentioned above.

Moral continuity/moral discontinuity, an oscillation or alternation. But then, second, there is a link of a similar kind between the discontinuities of moral agency, and the continuities of material support. We've made the point above, so it scarcely needs labouring. Liv is able to move, able to write, able to act as an autonomous agent, only because she is embodied in and performed by an endless network of heterogeneous materials, human and non human.

Perhaps, then it is something like this. Liv is a *cyborg*. She's not simply a cyborg in the easy sense that she is part machine, part human. That this is the case is self-evident—though it is self-evident for all of us, inserted into and produced by the specificities of heterogeneous networks. No. She is also a cyborg in another and yet more important sense. She is a cyborg in the sense that she is irreducible, she is irreducible to a unity—*even though 'she' is also a unity*.

Perhaps there are various ways of saying this—though no doubt our languages with their preferences for singularities or binarisms strain away from the possibility, make it/them difficult to say.[13] We need to exercise the imagination in order to elbow away at the conditions of im/possibility. And this, or so it seems to us, is what Donna Haraway is trying to do with this metaphor, the cyborg. For a cyborg is a unity but also a composite of parts that cannot be reduced to one another, which are different in kind, and which are not homogeneous. *But which are also internally related to one another*. Which would not be the way that they are, individually, if it were not for that link, that internal relation.

How to press the point? Perhaps this will help. Marilyn Strathern recounts that there are two Stratherns: Strathern the feminist and Strathern the anthropologist. And notes that there are *partial connections* between the two. The anthropologist is not the same as the feminist—but it would not be the way it is if it were not connected to the feminist. And vice versa. Note that: Strathern's argument, which tells of her as a cyborg, does not depend on the material heterogeneity of a woman/machine assemblage. Heterogeneity, partial separation, may come in quite other forms. Prosthesis does not necessarily have to do with artificial limbs.

Except we should end, where we began, with Liv, who more visibly than most of us lives in a place and performs herself through physical prosthesis. She is indeed a cyborg, yes, in an obviously material sense, but is a person, yes, a modern western subject, whose struggles to achieve that normative form of subjectivity make it easier to see what is at stake for all of us. For all of us as we make, are made by, good passages and bad passages. As we make and are made by the desires for continuities and discontinuities. As we weave, are woven, in the partial connections, in the particular oscillations and dis/continuities of normative subjectivities.

In which case Liv is made, created, within an economy of non-coherence, a heterogeneous economy, an economy that cannot be told and performed in one place at one time. Which cannot be drawn together. Absence and presence, yes, these go together. That is the character of subjectivity.[14]

Ingunn Moser and John Law

Acknowledgements

This chapter draws on interviews with Liv conducted by Ingunn Moser as part of a larger study of dis/ability funded by the Norwegian Ministry of Health and Social Affairs and the University of Oslo. We are grateful to the Ministry, the University of Oslo, the Research Council of Norway, and the British Council for the financial support which has made this work possible. We are grateful to Brita Brenna, Mark Elam and Annemarie Mol for sustained intellectual support and discussion. But most of all we are grateful to Liv for her interest, support and encouragement, and her willingness to describe and explore important aspects of her life.

Notes

1 The relevant STS literatures include publications by Madeleine Akrich, Michel Callon, Charis Cussins, Donna Haraway, Karin Knorr-Cetina, Bruno Latour, John Law, Annemarie Mol, Vicky Singleton, Sandy Stone, Leigh Star, Sharon Traweek and Sherry Turkle. See Akrich and Pasveer, 1996; Callon and Latour, 1981; Cussins, 1998; Haraway, 1989; Haraway, 1991a; Latour, 1988; Latour, 1990; Latour, 1993; Law and Mol, 1995; Mol, 1998; Mol, 1999; Singleton, 1993; Singleton, 1996; Star, 1991; Stone, 1995; Turkle, 1996.
2 See Garfinkel (1967).
3 'Perhaps': for Garfinkel was also deeply interested in the materialities of ordering, at least in many cases. For instance, in the records kept by jurors, or the materialities of Agnes' performance of female gendering.
4 Going for a walk. Here we think also of the people who turn up at hospitals suffering from pain when they go walking, pain which in the textbook stories, is caused by artherosclerosis in the blood vessels of the legs, which means that the blood supply is impaired. How do doctors decide whether to not to operate? There are a thousand and one indicators and contingencies. But one has to do with the style of life of the patient. If she always walked everywhere then this is a specificity to do with an important passage. Or to put it a little differently, she is dis/abled in a way which is not the case if she is happy to sit in a chair in a home all day. For details of this case see (Mol, 1999a). A similar logic applies to the passage towards pregnancy: as is obvious, not every women wishes to have a baby. But those who really wish to get pregnant and are unable to do so unaided, are under certain circumstances, now able to secure technological intervention to achieve this passage. See (Cussins, 1998).
5 For further discussion of forms of pleasure and pain, see (Moser and Law, 1998).
6 See: (Butler, 1990; Elias, 1978; Goffman, 1968; Goffman, 1971; Star, 1991; Star, 1992).
7 Perhaps the point is made in a similar manner within the work of the actor-network theorists when they talk about 'black boxing'. In which case an agent is one who comes to stand for, to speak for, a lashup of heterogeneous bits and

pieces, awkward and disruptive passages which are, for the moment, pushed into the background. See (Callon, 1986; Callon, 1997; Callon and Law, 1995; Latour, 1988; Law, 1994).

8 Which is, to be sure, a somewhat different point: the making of back-stage front-stage distinctions is also a 'moral' matter in which certain aspects of corporeality and embodiment are taken to be discrediting. There is a large feminist literature on this, and it is also developed in an historical context in the writing of Norbert Elias. We will return to the question of the 'moral' below.
9 After all, sexualities, often backstage, are equally often sources of pleasure.
10 The reference is to (Star, 1991).
11 As has been extensively considered in some of the literatures of feminism. See, for instance, Donna Haraway's writing: (Haraway, 1991b; Haraway, 1996), and also in the writing of Annemarie Mol, which explores the normativities that are implicitly performed in devices and organisational arrangements.
12 Ordering. Deciding what comes first. Deciding what comes first? Well, that is the way we have set it up. As a matter of choice. But if we put it this way, then it also implies that matters are drawn together, arrayed and displayed at a single place and a single time. As, for instance, on the screen of a computer, whose material arrays and specificities perform the possibility of centring. But this is only one possibility, and there are others. Perhaps, then, we might imagine subjectivities built in other ways: subjectivities made in alternatives to centred discretion: subjectivities performed in indeterminacy, undecidability. See, for instance, Émilie Gomart and Antoine Hennion, this volume.
13 A binarism is *also* a simplicity or a homogeneity. That is, the parts of the binarism perform themselves as parts of a whole. The same argument applies to pluralities. Pluralities are made up, in the standard stories of political economy, by primitive and homogenised simplicities. Donna Haraway wrestles with these linguistic difficulties, as do Marilyn Strathern, Annemarie Mol and John Law.
14 The heterogeneities of absence/presence are discussed at some length in: (Law, 1998; Law, 1999). But the metaphor of partial connection draws on (Haraway, 1991a) and (Strathern, 1991).

References

Akrich, Madeleine, and Bernike Pasveer (1996), *Comment la Naissance Vient aux Femmes: le Technique de l'accouchement en France et aux Pays Bas*, Collection les Empêcheurs de Penser en Rond, Le Plessis-Robinson: Synthélabo.
Butler, Judith (1990), *Gender Trouble: Feminism and the Subverison of Identity*, New York and London: Routledge.
Callon, Michel (1986), 'Some Elements of a Sociology of Translation: Domestication of the Scallops and the Fishermen of Saint Brieuc Bay', pp. 196–233 in John Law (ed.), *Power, Action and Belief: a new Sociology of Knowledge? Sociological Review Monograph*, 32, London: Routledge and Kegan Paul.
Callon, Michel (1997), *Representing Nature. Representing Culture*, Paris: CSI, Ecole Nationale Superieures des Mines.
Callon, Michel, and Bruno Latour (1981), 'Unscrewing the Big Leviathan: how actors macrostructure reality and how sociologists help them to do so', pp. 277–303 in Karin D. Knorr-Cetina and Aaron V. Cicourel (eds), *Advances in*

Social Theory and Methodology: Toward an Integration of Micro- and Macro-Sociologies, Boston, Mass.: Routledge and Kegan Paul.

Callon, Michel, and John Law (1995), 'Agency and the Hybrid Collectif', *South Atlantic Quarterly*, 94: 481–507.

Cussins, Charis (1998), 'Ontological Choreography Agency for Women Patients in an Infertility Clinic', pages 166–201, in Marc Berg and Annemarie Mol (eds), *Differences in Medicine: Unravelling Practices, Techniques and Bodies*, Durham, N. Carolina.: Duke University Press.

Elias, Norbert (1978), *The History of Manners*, Oxford: Blackwell.

Garfinkel, Harold (1967), *Studies in Ethnomethology*, Englewood Cliffs, New Jersey: Prentice Hall.

Goffman, Erving (1968), *Asylums: Essays on the Social Situation of Mental Patients and Other Inmates*, Harmondsworth: Penguin.

Goffman, Erving (1971), *The Presentation of Self in Everyday Life*, Harmondsworth: Penguin.

Haraway, Donna (1989), *Primate Visions: Gender, Race and Nature in the World of Modern Science*, London: Routledge and Chapman Hall.

Haraway, Donna (1991a), 'A Cyborg Manifesto: Science, Technology and Socialist Feminism in the Late Twentieth Century', pp. 149–181 in Donna Haraway (ed.), *Simians, Cyborgs and Women: the Reinvention of Nature*, London: Free Association Books.

Haraway, Donna (1991b), 'Situated Knowledges: the Science Question in Feminism and the Privilege of Partial Perspective', pp. 183–201 in Donna Haraway (ed.), *Simians, Cyborgs and Women: the Reinvention of Nature*, London: Free Association Books.

Haraway, Donna (1996), 'Modest Witness: Feminist Diffractions in Science Studies', pp. 428–441 in Peter Galison and David J. Stamp (eds), *The Disunity of the Sciences: Boundaries, Contexts, and Power*, Stanford, California: Stanford University Press.

Latour, Bruno (1988), *The Pasteurization of France*, Cambridge, Mass.: Harvard.

Latour: Bruno (1990), 'Drawing Things Together', pp. 19–68 in Michael Lynch and Steve Woolgar (eds), *Representation in Scientific Practice*, Cambridge, Mass.: MIT Press.

Latour, Bruno (1993), 'La Clef de Berlin', pp. 33–46 in *La Clef de Berlin, et autres Leçons d'un Amateur de Sciences*, Paris: Law Découverte.

Law, John (1994), *Organizing Modernity*, Oxford: Blackwell.

Law, John (1998), *Aircraft Stories: Decentering the Object in Technoscience*: submitted.

Law, John, and Annemarie Mol (1995), 'Notes on Materiality and Sociality', *The Sociological Review*, 43: 274–294.

Law, John (1999), 'On Hidden Heterogeneities: the Design of an Aircraft', in John Law and Annemarie Mol (eds), *Complexities in Science, Technology and Medicine*, Durham, North Carolina: Duke University Press.

Mol, Annemarie (1998), 'Missing Links, Making Links: the Performance of Some artheroscleroses', pp. 141–163 in Marc Berg and Annemarie Mol (eds), *Differences in Medicine: Unravelling Practices, Techniques and Bodies*, Durham, N. Carolina: Duke University Press.

Mol, Annemarie (1999), *The Body Multiple: Artherosclerosis in Practice*: Durham, N. Carolina: Duke University Press, forthcoming.

Moser, Ingunn, and John Law (1998), 'Notes on Desire, Complexity, Inclusion", page in the press in Brita Brenna, John Law, and Ingunn Moser (eds), pp. 181–197 *Machines, Agency and Desire*, Oslo: TMV, Universitetet i Oslo.

Singleton, Vicky (1993), 'Science, Women and Ambivalence: an Actor-Network Analysis of the Cervical Screening Campaign', PhD, University of Lancaster.

Singleton, Vicky (1996), 'Feminism, Sociology of Scientific Knowledge and Postmodernism: Politics, Theory and Me', *Social Studies of Science*, 26: 445–468.

Star, Susan Leigh (1991), 'Power, Technologies and the Phenomenology of Conventions: on being Allergic to Onions', pp. 26–56 in John Law (ed.), *A Sociology of Monsters? Essays on Power, Technology and Domination, Sociological Review Monograph*, 38, London: Routledge.

Star, Susan Leigh (1992), 'The Sociology of the Invisible: the Primacy of Work in the Writings of Anselm Strauss', pp. 265–284 in David Maines (ed.), *Social Organization and Social Processes: Essays in Honor of Anselm Strauss*, New York: Aldine de Gruyter.

Stone, Allucquère Rosanne (1995), *The War of Desire and Technology at the Close of the Mechanical Age*, Cambridge, Mass.: MIT Press.

Strathern, Marilyn (1991), *Partial Connections*, Savage Maryland: Rowman and Littlefield.

Turkle, Sherry (1996), *Life on the Screen: Identity in the Age of the Internet*, London: Weidenfeld and Nicolson.

A sociology of attachment: music amateurs, drug users

Emilie Gomart and Antoine Hennion

Abstract

After describing objects as networks, we attempt to describe 'subject-networks'. Instead of focusing on capacities inherent in a subject, we attend instead to the tactics and techniques which make possible the emergence of a subject as it enters a 'dispositif'. Opting for an optimistic analysis of Foucault, we consider 'dispositifs' and their constraints to be generative: they do not simply reduce but also reveal and multiply. The generative power of 'dispositifs' depends upon their capacity to create and make use of new capacities in the persons who pass through them. Drawing upon a diverse body of literature and upon fieldwork among drug addicts and music amateurs, we show how this point of entry into the question of the subject immediately and irredeemably undoes traditional dichotomies of sociology. It becomes impossible to continue to set up oppositions like those of agent/structure, subject/object, active/passive, free/determined. We also have to look beyond studies of 'action' and describe 'events'. Through the words and trials of the music and drug lovers, it becomes clear that the subject can emerge as she actively submits herself to a collection of constraints. These actors describe necessary yet tentative techniques of preparation to produce this 'active passion', this form of 'attachment' which we attempt to describe as that which allows the subject to emerge—never alone, never a pristine individual, but rather always entangled with and generously gifted by a collective, by objects, techniques, constraints.

Introduction: from action to passion?

In twenty years of ANT practice, objects have been turned into networks and thereby radically re-defined. An analogous project is now starting to take shape: the study of 'subject-networks'. This is not a critique of the 'construction' of the subject. Rather, it is an attempt to offer an alternative account of the ways in which subjects may be seized, impassioned and swept away. How to describe the devices by which amateurs (in the widest sense) are able to put their passion into practice? This version of actor-network theory switches focus from the (albeit decentred) subject to what one might think of as the socio-technical 'dispositifs'[1] of passion. Unlike the pessimistic interpretations of 'discipline' and bodily techniques of power, we opt for a version of Foucault in which techniques of discipline are not just to do with prohibition, regulation and reduction. Discipline may also be productive: it may reveal and multiply. And the power of the 'dispositif' rests on the proliferation of new competencies that it lets emerge.

> 'We must cease to always describe effects of power in negative terms: it 'excludes', it 'represses', it 'buries', it 'censors', it 'abstracts', it 'masks', it 'hides'. In fact power produces; it produces the real; it produces domains of objects and rituals of truth. The individual and our knowledge of this individual come from this production.' [our translation, Foucault 1975, p. 196]

'Constraints' become the generous aspects of things which, if prepared for, create existence and initiate transformation. In this chapter we extend this analysis of the collective production of agencies by describing the invention of 'dispositifs' of passion. This process does not fit the limited sociological dichotomies. Passive/active, free/determined, or subjugated/dominant, such dualisms do not work.

In what follows we consider two forms of passion, the love of music and of drugs. The first is positively valued while the second is not. But both reveal similar conditions for the emergence of 'addiction'. The attachment each involves takes the form of a surprising consensual self-abandonment. Both have to do with entering into a world of strong sensations; of accepting that 'external' forces take possession of the self; of being 'under the influence' of something else; of bracketing away one's own control and will in order to be expelled or rendered 'beside oneself'. To talk in this way implies that there are techniques, settings, devices and collective carriers which make this active dis-possession possible. But to talk about these we need stop asking, temporarily at least, about the sources of action. Questions such as 'who acts?' no longer work. Instead of focusing on the subject, we consider the mechanisms through which this kind of 'active passion' is performed. This shift leads both to theoretical questions about the person and emotions, and to tricky methodological problems to do with observation and the status of people's narratives about sensations and self-dispossession. In this chapter we first link the two addictions and show that the drug user, like the music lover, is a competent amateur who puts his equilibrium at risk in the name of an non-communicable experience. He or she takes risks, exercises judgement (including moral judgements) and makes choices. This means that the addict no longer appears to be a more or less tolerated or frustrated binger in need of treatment. In the first section, then, we discuss the methodological advantages and limits of this comparison.

Second, we describe the common modalities of passion (or attachment). Our argument is that each is a mode of realization of the mix between active and passive. This mix calls into question a theory of action which can only hold one term of the dichotomy at a time. We suggest that there are events or occasions in which activity and passivity enable each other.

Third, we characterize each composition of activity and passivity more precisely. Our object is to go beyond the idea that events are conditioned or prepared by skilled users by describing some actions as being *left to and made to arrive* (*'faire faire'*), an expression we use to draw attention away from the source of action, and to suggest instead that action is an unanticipated gift from the 'dispositif'.

Does 'ANT' need its 'a'? ANT and theories of action

We are not interested in Maoist self-criticism of ANT but neither do we simply want to 'apply' ANT to music and drug addiction. Our interest is in continuing to use and develop ANT by using it to study a new area. By taking it beyond its original domain of action of science and technology studies our hope is that we can challenge the reformed yet resolutely traditional (distributed, situated) theory of action which has been, we claim, too hastily associated with ANT. No doubt, this association was useful at first, but it also obscured key aspects of ANT. The shift to different objects of study—outside science and technology—makes it possible to highlight discrepancies between ANT and interesting trends in 'action theory', from ethnomethodologists and interactionists to people like L. Suchman, D. Norman and E. Hutchins. For action theory and ANT share similar goals:

1) Both seek to go beyond an oscillation in social analysis between action as determining and action as determined. This debate is possibly as old as sociology itself, for this is a discipline that has largely constituted itself by criticising the free subject postulated by philosophers. Both the European critical tradition and Anglo-American positivist empiricism took sociology to be a way of removing action from the person and returning it to the determinations of a structure or the invisible hand of a system. Action is either the unproblematic basic unity of a complex game of construction, with all its perverse effects and paradoxical systems results,[2] or the enemy, the illusion of power which the human actor entertains when in fact (or so it is suggested) he or she is the plaything of forces that s/he cannot see.[3]

Here, then, action is not treated as a problem in its own right. It is a by-product of theoretical orientations, often associated with political engagements. As a result, sociological debates have long been informed by dualist oppositions: holism *vs.* methodological individualism, agency *vs.* structure, critical *vs.* liberal orientations . . . However, it is striking that the different positions in the debate do not offer different conceptions of action. All concur that the action of a free subject needs to be replaced, only differing about what form this replacement might be (social class, blind functionalism, an invisible hand, an effect of structure). And all assume that the action of the subject needs to be covered into something *else*.

One significant benefit of the 'networkization' of the 'actor' was that philosophers, psychologists and cognitive scientists interested in action were now joined by a number of sociologists. For instance, Callon and Law [1997] suggest that each element of the network 'relays' and 'prolongs' the action of the collective without ever being a (or the) source of action in itself. They conclude that (for instance) the capacity to be strategic cannot be assigned to a human actor within a network but should be described as the effect of the association of a heterogeneous network (corporate manager+fax+secretary+. . .). In this way, sociologists started to be able to speak again about the action of the collective without reducing it to the effect of a system or structure.[4]

2) Both action theory and ANT also seek to describe the actions of humans and non-humans symmetrically. Lucy Suchman's early work serves to make this point. In her seminal book on plans and situated action, Suchman explores instances of breakdown in communication between humans and machines. Her analysis makes it possible to think of non-humans as partners in interaction. However, objects are *inferior* partners: the poverty of the resources

available to objects in communication 'substantially limits the scope of interaction between people and machines' [Suchman, 1987, p. 181]. Though her analysis of non-humans is highly original, it assumes that there is radical asymmetry between objects' and humans' communication resources. An impermeable barrier between human and non-human is maintained and action is not shared or co-produced.

3) Action theory and ANT also strip the subject of its cognitive, cultural, common sense capacities and return these to its surroundings. However, our attempt to explore how an effect may be achieved does not completely mirror that of the action theory. For instance, interactionists describe 'passages' in which what occurs at a local level explains and reifies the global.[5] ANT tells a different story in which local and global, agent and 'dispositif', mutually incite each other into existence. This is closer to work—especially in cognitive psychology—which argues that action is the performance of a specific collective, rather than of an individual agent or member of the collective [Norman, 1988; Hirschauer, 1991; Hutchins, 1995]. Hutchins for example undoes the myth of the captain who 'masterminds' the trajectory of his ship. The properties of the collective (humans and ship) are unlike those of any single individual member or of the sum of the individuals. Competencies are shaped by the social and material organization of work, the lay-out of the instruments, the means of communication . . . Such accounts of situated action shift analysis from the individual to the collective actor. ANT similarly describes actors as *associations* of a myriad of little elements, human and non-human.

However, it also seems to us that ANT seeks to do something different. Exactly what this is has been blurred and overlooked as a result of ANT's proximity to theories of action. One key idea of ANT—its analyses of networks, mediations and translations—has nothing to do with criticising the subject of action or demonstrating its distribution. It is not a gory explosion of the subject nor an attempt to spread it ever wider and thinner across the landscape into more and more heterogeneous networks. ANT cuts a thread that is crucial to the theory of action: the link between action and an (albeit distributed) actor. For ANT this means that the 'radicalization' of situated action is not radical enough. This is because it continues to ask—in an appropriately deferential voice to be sure— 'who acts?'. But this assumes that 'action' is there to be distributed, while the definition and limits of action itself are not questioned.

A sociology of attachment

Thus in even the most original theory of action assumes that the events that take place are indeed 'actions'—distributed, involving more and more non-humans, yet just actions with actors as their source. To put it bluntly, the approach does not undo the model of human action, but allows the cognitive capacities of humans to migrate to objects. These in turn become efficient, intelligent, coordinated, or 'purposive'. Qualities which had been the privilege of humans and guaranteed their distinctiveness from non-humans are simply recycled to characterize the heterogeneous 'hybrid' collective which become the new source of action.

By contrast, ANT seeks to describe the composition of heterogeneous elements in networks which produce emerging action from an indeterminate source. This means that 'action' is no longer the primitive unit of analysis, nor the only kind of event which might be described. 'What happens' only sometimes takes the form of an action that may be distributed to circumscribed sources. The usual fieldwork topics, science and engineering, show this very well. This is because scientists, like engineers, insist on 'doing something'. In such cases 'action' theory works because what is at issue for the actors is the fabrication and validation of objects and theories 'that work'. Science and technology studies describe modes of action, tentatively stabilized through specific networks, which came to replace the unique 'action' of action theory. However, they do not allow access to events that are not actions. We wish to shift the field of study in order to focus on events that 'just occur'. And these are effects which occur at moments when amateurs enter a certain dispositif and are transformed by their attachment to that collective.

From 'who acts?' to 'what occurs?': an 'event-network theory'

We are not seeking, then, another theoretical oscillation between agent and structure as source of action. Instead we want to give up 'action' and turn towards 'events'. The goal is to study other configurations of 'what occurs' and to highlight an idea already suggested by work on 'mediation' [Hennion, 1993]: first, delegations and inscriptions into objects render these as prolongations of actions already initiated elsewhere; and second, these object-mediators do not just repeat and relay actions but also transform these in surprising ways. To say that objects are 'mediators' is a way of noting that something 'happens' without falling back to action and actors. The world is not exactly as it was before. An 'event' occurred and it has a positivity of its own which is limited neither to its origins and determinants, nor to its effects.

Art provides the model: mediations (like frames, museums, mediums) are neither mere instruments of a work of art, nor substitutes which dissolve its reality. To talk of mediation is to step away from the European critical tradition mentioned earlier: it is not an act of unveiling which reveals the illusion of the object.[6] Mediation is a turn towards what emerges, what is shaped and composed, what cannot be reduced to an interaction of causal objects and intentional persons. The network is not a black pool in which to drop, dilute, criticise and lose the subject. It is on the contrary an opening—pried lose with a partly rhetorical liberation of things and an attentiveness to spaces, dispositions, and events—which releases us from the insoluble opposition between natural determination and human will. 'Mediation' allows the course of the world to return to the centre of analysis.

In order to do this we have chosen objects of study which cannot easily be treated as actions. Objects which insist on that which 'arrives', not on that which is 'performed'. This distinction between 'performance' and 'emergence' is found in semiotics and in authors who draw on it. Thus, Callon [*et al.* 1982] talked of this distinction when they described the different elements involved in a scientific text as *'actants'*.[7] The notion of 'actant' allows us to explore the heterogeneity of elements which inflect the course of things. It allows the types of relations between elements of a network to proliferate far beyond the usual sociological terms such as influence, power, exchange, domination, conflict, or strategy. This semiotic approach has made it possible to circumvent sociological explanations in which action refers either to structures (cognitive, psychological) within the agent or to structures (social class, social worlds, cultural paradigms) which surround and determine it. Actants do not have to chose between obliging and being obliged, domination and submission, individual action and causation. Semiotics makes it possible to describe the emergence of an effect by referring not to agents but to 'that which lets/makes happen' (*'ce qui* fait faire', Greimas and Courtès, 1986k). For semioticians, this *'that which'* is the predicate of the sentence; for us, it is the mediating object, the dispositif.

Abandoning oneself?

Passion, emotion, being dazzled, elation, possession, trance, all of these are instances of events in which there is no action—in either a traditional or a radical sense of the term. They describe movement in which loss of control is accepted and prepared for. One's hand is given over to an other, and one abandons one's being to what seizes it. As we have noted, we do not take 'passion' to describe the subject's instrumental mastery of things, nor her mechanical determination by things. Rather, *passion is the abandonment of forces to objects and the suspension of the self.*

In our examples we do not reintroduce subjects that are (in the example of art) pure subjectivity, or objects which are (in the example of drugs) pure chemical determination. The subject is neither glorified, nor nullified in its abandonment. 'Action' is not reintroduced because there are no pure causes, no pure intentions. Instead human activity is 'made possible', 'potentialized', 'conditioned' by the activity of drugs or the pull of music. The *conditioning* of the amateur by cocaine or Bach's partitas requires that she meticulously *establish conditions*: active work must be done in order to be moved. 'Conditioning' is a paradoxical expression, referring both to original determinations and to the creation of these determinations. It is very close to what we are looking for if we want to speak of passion. Likewise, to 'abandon yourself to a tune' is a phrase in which 'yourself' denies the possibility of 'pure' abandonment. It is not exclusively passive; it involves the participation of both the person and the object. Ignoring the mutual exclusion of 'passion' and 'passivity' imposed by the theory of action, the human 'actor' might pass through a series of peculiar states (being open, patient, receptive, sensitive). These models of being/acting weave together what had seemed to be polar opposites—passivity and activity, determining and determined, collective and individual, and intention as against causality.

This understanding of passion has emerged from our reading of existing literature on art and drugs as well as from analyses of debates among amateurs themselves. Thus passion is not a concept that is limited to these two cases, but nevertheless seems to fit them well:

- *Music*: Obeying the dualism described above, social critiques of art and taste have aimed to identify the aspects of a phenomenon ('beauty', 'pleasure') attributable to properties of the object itself or to cognitive structures within the individual, and those that should be traced back to natural, social or cultural constraints.[8] Thus, on the one hand, certain analyses lead to an internal aesthetics, and on the other, sociological analyses consider works and tastes to be socially constructed and determined. The latter describe relations to patrons and sponsors, organizations and markets, professions and academies, codes and rites of social consumption. These descriptions, a form of critical sociology, are important because they focus on objects and devices, and pay specific attention to the materiality of intermediaries. In a sense, sociology of art has always been a sociology of mediation [Hennion, 1996]. Nevertheless, they are somewhat limited. We want to question the way in which they avoid both the work of art itself and aesthetic experience. These are simply dismissed as stakes in a game about identity and distinction. As a result of their opposition to aesthetics—a mirror of the polar opposition between agency and structure described above—in critical sociological analysis any account of artistic experience in terms of beauty, sensation, or aesthetic feeling is considered misleading, because it presumably reflects actors' illusions about their own beliefs. Moreover, like Durkheim's totems [1912], art works have no effectivity of their own; they 'do' nothing since they are 'nothing but' the material production of 'ourselves' as a collective entity.

In contrast to this, amateurs ignore this polar opposition when they describe how they prepare for an event. In showing this we need to come closer to art lovers' own tastes and practices, to their descriptions of art as an experience of pleasure, as an expression and emotion collectively lived by subjects and bodies through specific objects and procedures. Their descriptions suggest that we cannot be satisfied with explanations of 'beauty' as the conventional products of collective activity [Becker, 1974, 1982] or of art as belief, an *il-lusio* [Bourdieu, 1980, 204]. Amateurs' own descriptions thus contribute to a growing literature which documents the different ways humans and dispositifs might participate in inducing what occurs (for instance in the literature on embodiment[9]). Taste is neither the affirmation of a free subject nor the action of a determinism. Instead, it is a concrete activity whose modes, dispositifs and practices can be described. A rock concert, or a sculpture exhibit, does not bring together already existing objects, subjects and social groupings—rather, this is a conjunctural event in which the relevant objects, subjects, and social groupings are co-produced [Hennion and Grenier, 1998]. This turns classical stratification analysis of determined tastes for determined categories into a new ethnography of amateur practices.

- *Drugs*: Recent developments in the treatment of addition have led to new discourses and practices. Drugs at the beginning of the

A sociology of attachment

debate in the mid-80s were principally defined by repressive legislators and psychologically-oriented treatment specialists. Legislators, backed by advisory pharmacologists, were engaged in 'the War on drugs', describing drugs themselves as the source of harm. By limiting their circulation, they sought to limit a drug 'epidemic'. By contrast, for treatment specialists addiction both generates and reveals 'physical, psychological and social' difficulties. They identify three agents of change: the therapist, the addict and society. The patient is defined as a 'man of the Enlightenment' with rights and freedoms but also duties and the need to submit to 'the laws'. Harm-reduction promoters emerged in the 1990s, as important critiques of the nature of these laws: are these (as the 1970 French law penalizing drug use) social laws, revocable and perhaps 'harmful' to the individual? Are they psychological norms? Do they include biological predispositions, or the pharmacological transformations occasioned by chronic drug use? Harm-promoters have argued that addiction specialists ignore the 'concrete' action of drugs on the bodies of users; specialists ignore the 'concrete' action of drugs on the bodies of users; specialists have countered that they have deliberately focussed on the 'free' aspect of the individual, that is, on the psychological plasticity of individuals and not on biological and social determinisms. Thus the harm-reduction promoters introduced the substitute drug as a crucial element in change. Drugs were re-defined not as simple chemical determinisms but as objects which could not be assigned properties until the dispositif and apprenticeships for their use had been identified. The description of drug 'effects' preserved their contingent character: the definitions of heroin, for example, had to be moderated by recognition that effects varied depending on where it was used. What was compared were 'injectability', legality of circulation, desirability for users, and rigidity of modes of prescription (in cases when a drug was medically available). So in the specific situation of France at the beginning of the 1990s drugs were defined not in a list of 'properties' but rather as affording different concrete relations between drug and user, user and doctor, and user and law-officials.[10]

A final remark about the status of laws and constraints. These were depicted as unethical by psychologically oriented specialists.[11] By contrast, the harm-reduction promoters explicitly offered a different interpretation of Foucault and 'social control'. Constraints might lead to change and not simply to the destruction of the individual. Methadone, in the words of one, was 'an experiment on constraint'. Fears of 'medicalization' were not entirely forgotten, but the *productive* effect of drugs had to be explored. Drugs could then be described and techniques be tried out where these did not just impact *upon* users, but were elements of a dispositif *through* which the user passed and which tentatively modified his modes of existence. Substitution drugs were that element which permitted a dispositif to become '*ce qui* fait faire'.

Music and dope: comparing instances of attachments

Our attention to the actors' own debates might suggest that we want to treat the sociologist, the music amateur and the drug user as 'colleagues'. Promoting actors to the status of sociologists or philosophers is, to be sure, a politically sympathetic goal. However, to proclaim *equality* (that is, identity) between sociologists on the one hand, and drug and music amateurs on the other, is to ignore the techniques the sociologist needs to use if the interviewee is to become a communicative and competent witness. For the competent amateur is not a neutral guide. Neither is s/he a filter. Instead s/he is a relevant co-experimenter, concerned with a livable and constructive attachment. She/he must not only be seen as involved in the same kind of experiment, but as *participating* in a sociological experiments. Both we and they follow real-time experimental trials in which different hypothetical answers to this question are tested. Whether, to what proportion, and in which combinations the passions or the pleasure finds its source in chemistry, in the composer, in the situation, in the shared rituals, in the techniques of self-preparation, is precisely what amateurs' knowledge and experiments are all about. But also what our theoretical debates between sociologists or therapists are concerned with. Even if this means that we go about finding answers in very different ways.

Another clarification. We have linked drugs and music in a deliberate attempt to maintain comparability between two kinds of 'attachments', 'addictions', or 'obligations' which are morally quite distinct. This stops us from slipping into discourses of praise or blame. The danger is that the music amateur's meticulous composition of pleasure, his abandonment, would quickly become a point of entry into the sublime, a realm of superior sensibility; while the drug user's equally meticulous composition of pleasure and abandonment would look like the decline of the subject into slavery or an inferior level of intentionality. Attending to and comparing the similarities in the practices, the gestures, the tricks, the words and the skill of drug and music amateurs, is an effective antidote to this moral dualism. For the same qualifications which might serve to condemn the drug user who is risking health, autonomy, and his bank account, apply just as much to the musical amateur who also invests his resources and allows his relations to be organized by a passion—this time for music.

Even so, we are not suggesting that the two forms of addiction are identical. Chemical flashes and drumming sounds are not the same. Neither are social reprobation and highly valued artistic connoisseurship. To risk jail, or to break relationships of trust with those to whom one is close, is not the same thing as to acceding to the many secondary benefits of belonging to a select club. Being initiated into a world to which not everybody has access does not lead to the same consequences, even if initiation passes through similar steps. Yet for reasons that we hope are by now apparent, here we will insist on the common features of the two 'addictions'.

'Passings'

The amateur experiments with the efficiency of diverse 'technosociologies'. With a peculiar form of reflexivity, *she* writes her sociology for *us*. She circulates in different registers and in both directions: from collective to individual; physical to ritual or symbolic efficiency; discretionary freedom to determinism by external causes and higher collectives. These registers are not infinite, and they can easily be related both to theoretical debates in the sociology of culture or on drug addiction. Here are the more recognizable 'passings' that we can find in interviews:

- from the body to the 'head' (mechanical, physical, corporeal effects and feelings/personal psychology of the user)
- from the lonely user to the social and technical setting (what's on my own/what comes from the whole thing)
- from the expertise of 'making' to the abandonment of 'feeling' (what I do/what happens to me)
- from the material efficiency of objects 'themselves' to objects as mediations (what comes from the properties of things/what happens through things)
- from the technical mastery of time and organization to loss of control (what procedures must be obeyed/what requires its own overwhelming) . . .

These suggestions are intended to lead (in later elaborations) to an exploration of:

- the specialized vocabulary used to describe and perform sensations;
- the necessity for all the rich procedures and dispositifs (settings, devices) created to make things happen;
- the (difficult) ways of characterizing the amateur's modes of presence to what happens, just before being 'seized' by his/her passion.

We will now analyse these 'passings' in our material. This section offers excerpts from interviews with music amateurs (M) and drug addicts (D) and, informed by their juxtaposition, attempts to show how these different 'passings' involve practices, uses of time and objects, relations to the group, indigenous theories of what happens, what works, and what is at stake.

1. *Passing from the body to the 'head'*:

> M12 [m, 45, classical record collector]: I always say that music is carnal. People will always say that the criteria is the shudder, the hair that stands up on the back of the neck. But it also means that we listen with our bodies, that it is not good to be knotted. But you know, we could also deduce the inverse from this. That if one is not ready in one's head, the ear will want to hear nothing ... It is a play between both, in fact. You dispose yourself, and then it is just something physical. I feel that people always start out with the sublime—this is the work of a genius, the interpretation was fantastic, etc. For me, music is almost a form of gymnastics. But I exaggerate, it is not just physical of course. Still the armchair, the hi-fi installation, the records or a good seat at the concert ...

The very uncertainty of this reflection which seems to correct itself as it goes on points to the refusal to choose, to the feeling that available discourses miss the peculiar articulation which musical pleasure finds in the play between body and spirit rather than in the cancelling out or the overcoming of one in the other. This passage from physical forces to intentional or higher order forces is also described by drug users. It can of course take diverse forms. Here, the patient at a substitution clinic describes the efficacy of methadone, where the drug's causal power to fix the body depends on the person's readiness. He holds both on to the chemical pertinence of the drug and to his intentional activity as a subject.

D [A male patient on methadone, U, and a counsellor, B, himself as ex-user]:
B: How long have you been on methadone?
U: 6 months. But I was two years on another substitution, ®Temgésic. I tried everything: abstinence, ®Tranxène 50, the psychiatric hospital, ®Moscontin . . . in the past 15 years. And nothing worked.
B: Methadone is the most comfortable drug.
U: Yes. Before, I tried to leave the country, and to burn bridges with (drug using and dealing) people. I tried everything to get out. But now I also realize that if I don't want to get out of it, no one will get me out . . . At first, no one put a gun to my head to force me to take drugs. It's you and you . . . When I arrived here (at the methadone programme) I was finally mature enough. I was 30 years old . . . If I don't do it now, I'll never do it. I've had enough . . . And to top it off, I found a wonderful woman. She's even more understanding than people who use. Now methadone that's the product that stabilizes me. I had three or four days where I goofed up a little (with drugs) three months ago. But now I'm OK . . . I get up in the morning happy and my wife is too. I'm feeling happy to be alive again.

The patient makes a case against a radical social construction of efficiency: leaving the context of use is not sufficient to stop using and make the treatment work. He also argues against a purely pharmacological solution: substitution with just any opiate-like substance (Temgésic) had not worked for the first two years of treatment. Neither is his addiction problem purely pharmacological: 'No one held a gun to my head'. For him, the effect of methadone, 'stabilization', his new capacity to 'take on anything', articulates the activity of both a physical mechanism and an intentional person.

2. *Passing from the lone actor to the socio-technical dispositif*

The second passage is between a lone actor and the set-up in which he uses. For there is no choice to be made between agent and structure. The actors offer their own hypotheses about the relation between the two, sometimes defining structure as social group and at other items as technical context, sometimes defining the agent as a psychological structure and at other times as a legally responsible person. As we shall see, musicians and drug users deploy and articulate different versions of this divide. Thus, the origin of pleasure is located between the two, in their interplay. It is in their encounter and the trial which co-ordinates them that the appeal of taste and pleasure emerges. This is a composition which the amateurs test and try out in diverse variations, not an interpretation given by sociologists from outside.

One instance of this sort of passage is provided when expert users locate the source of their pleasure between personal choice and the mimicry of other experts. Thus, the musicians try out diverse sociologies of taste based on rational choice, on cultural determinism, and on personal influence:

M2 [m, 37, jazz]: With Paulo and Michel, we really got to working well musically. I think it is the best ensemble in which I ever played. Jean-Luc is good but he does not make me do things that I would not have thought I was able to do. That's the problem with groups. The equilibrium is quite unstable, to get the perfect thing, it's difficult, you look around, you don't find it right away. Me, it's especially the relation with Michel that matters, as a friendship. I mention this, though among guys we don't talk about it much in general. At the same time, that does not mean at all that music is in the background, or just a way to get together, a pretext to do things together. They are two important things, but distinct. There must be something happening on the level of the music, if we played badly, we'd continue to see each other as friends but we'd no longer play together. In the other direction too, could we play together if there were no friendship or relation? . . .

M4 [m, 29, baroque choir]: It was exclusively the leader of the choir who chose (what we sang), but for me that was perfect. It was the first time that I like what I did, as a taste, that I learned to like, even if at the same time I say to myself perhaps it was the other way around, perhaps I liked it especially because I was doing it. My boyfriend too was in the ensemble. I suppose that played a role . . . Maybe finally it is sufficient that I sing something to like it! . . .

The music amateurs attempt to co-ordinate with other people in a setting in which tastes, preferences and appreciations as effects of the individual within the group are tried and constituted. Drug users too admit the importance of social setting and do not try to distinguish it from their own activity in the construction of pleasure. The source of action is not narrowed down to either of the sociological alternatives. Further, it appears that the individual's participation in the phenomenon's emergence is articulated to and conditional upon the effects of the setting. Like the amateurs above, users sometimes associate (but do not reduce) their preference for a drug to the social group with which they use. This user describes the effect of methadone and heroin as being linked to personal experience and socio-technical activity.

> D [m, 36, militant in self-support group]: Before (being accepted to a methadone program) I took heroin every day. I always used to be in a state of emergency. The dealers, the cops, everyone was after me. And I was like the addict who didn't see further than two hours ahead . . . Methadone, now, it's to make me learn how to manage drug use . . . But methadone is really a drag. It is so boring. Because with heroin, it's not just the shoot, it's also the excitement of the ripping and running. It's always being vigilant, cunning, smart. That excitement, that's the vice. Trying to get the dough for the next dose and succeeding. It's also the atmosphere of the street. The adrenaline. It's dirty, gory. It's the anguish of getting caught and of trying to dig up the bet dope . . .

In his attempts to describe the source of his pleasure or displeasure, this user passes between the effect of the drug, the revelations of a trial in which he stopped taking methadone, the activity and rhythm of life under each product, etc. Personal experience is not detached from the setting in which it emerged. Like the object, the person is not distinct a priori from the set-up which fabricates it. It is not the analysts—the sociologists—who need to decide which actor (human/collective/technical?) to which to attribute the source of pleasure. The amateurs and addicts do this very well themselves—and are more innovative about it.

3. *Passing from striving to 'make' an effect to laying back and 'feeling' the effect*

It is common sense to say that expert appreciation or taste is a mix between: a developed activity intended to achieve one's 'blue note', the achievement of the sublime moment of the *aficionado*; and a subjugated and unreflexive state of 'primary' passivity, of the moment of pleasure which this patient work has prepared:

To listen to three notes, sometimes that's all that is good, I'd travel kilometres . . . [M5, m, 54, fan of lyric].

The passage ranges from full agency to passivity, to being determined by. The point is not intended as a eulogy to passivity, but rather to highlight a different register in which action and passivity are not the only alternatives. The actors act upon a mediator, and then await the effect which it might return to them: the 'rendition' of the setting.

This musical fan suggests a passage between a critically sophisticated search for the setting for a musical event (in the full sense of the term) and the 'three notes' that take him over with pleasure:

> M1 [m, 42, jazz group]: What attracted me really what that it was hard, serious, that we did things we never thought we could do. We played Tenor Madness, for example, I was so happy, it was copied almost note for note, no, not 'almost', exactly note for note; I would not do that anymore—to play it exactly as is—but at that time, it really helped me pass to another level, and I still remember that I was beaming with pleasure . . .

This 'mix' is sometimes found among drug users though in a different form. Users talk a great deal about how to get 'high'. They discuss among themselves techniques of administration and deals for quality substances, and they devise 'potentializing' cocktails of drugs (methadone is mixed with alcohol or benzodiazepines to enhance its usually dull 'opiate' effect). Users also discuss and set up locations (geared towards the activity they intend to accomplish, ie. theft or hard work), times (night/day), human company (friends, few cops, etc.). Might we say then that in those moments the user is only *making* the drug arrive? The descriptions of the 'high' show that skilful preparation is a condition for the drug's taking over.

> [My] initiator feverishly prepares his pipe, a chipped Pastis doser. On the mouth which serves as an oven he places filter, pressed electric wire, heats it and then puts on it a piece of the precious rock [crack] which melts immediately on the incandescent wire [. . .] and impregnates the filter. All there is to do now is to heat the whole thing and to breath in the vapour. I take in the smoke all at once, hold it a few seconds in my lungs. Then all of a sudden it's the hit in the face [*la baffe*]. My mouth is anaesthetized, my brain is enveloped in an electric fog. Everything is flashing on and off in my head. From a tap, music flows, 'superbe', I'm strong, the

world belongs to me. But no so long. The state of grace lasts two
minutes. What is left is an excitement close to that of a simple
sniff [cited in J.-R. Dard, 1998].

Here the crack high is described in a switch from active to passive
tense, from description of what he does to what happens to his
body. In other instances, the user describes the high as a moment
when he himself is surprisingly different. There, is seems, the mix
between active and passive is not just sequenced and mutually
enabling; the distinction between what is caused by the drug, what
is the person under influence, and what the person 'naturally' is are
blurred. The 'naturalness' of the transported and transformed user
who suddenly does things he would never have otherwise done,
suggests that the source of action is neither entirely the drug nor
the person (as he was before he took the drug). This user of
Rohypnol (or 'Roche', a barbiturate taken at high doses and often
mixed with alcohol) describes how she becomes a 'natural' thief
with the drug.

D [f, 25, cited in Jamoulle 12, 61–24]: Roche, it changes my
personality completely. I catch a big mouth, I am afraid of
nothing, I'd do anything. I don't stop thieving. Everything that I
feel like, I take. I am not discreet but people don't pay attention
because I pretend like nothing is going on . . . I steal so naturally
when I take Roche.

4. *Passing from the objectivity of objects to objects as mediators*

Leigh Star's and James Griesemer's concept of 'boundary object'
will serve as a contrast to another definition of the role of objects.
According to them, the boundary object 'means' different things in
different 'worlds of practice'. Star and Griesemer's description of
these objects is based on a desire to account for both heterogeneity
of 'viewpoints' and co-operation in the scientific world. They suggest
that objects must be both 'local' and 'general' [1989, 388]. The
management of diversity proceeds with the use of objects which
'originate in and continue to inhabit different worlds' and which
'incorporate radically different meanings' to make them coherent.
Boundary objects must be 'plastic' enough to adapt both to 'local
needs' and to the constraints of the different groups employing
them; yet they must also be 'robust' enough to maintain a common
identity across sites. Examples of the boundary object are diagrams
or atlases. Star and Griesemer's boundary object is vague and the

actors are near-sighted. This myopia explains the smooth circulation of the object in different worlds.

In this analysis methadone would change 'meaning' as it circulates among users and staff, while during their interaction the two groups' 'interpretation' would (superficially) resemble each other. Methadone would 'pass' because during the interaction no difference appears. However in practice the opposite occurs: when different users, care givers, etc. encounter each other they discuss with great sensitivity and at considerable length the different ways of using methadone; detailed and divergent meanings proliferate. The detail of the object is not blurred but rather deployed. Its geometry is exactly the inverse of the boundary object: methadone is precise, unanticipated and its careful inspection reveals properties contingent upon the user's discovering movements. Unless these are carried into the situation with clear markers, what is blurred are precisely the different 'worlds' to which methadone might belong.

Amateurs of both drugs and music claim that their objects are grasped only through a 'hyperaesthesia' or 'hyper-aesthetics', a particularly developed competence to perceive, combine and elaborate them. There is no distinction between or sequencing of natural and social effects. No idea that there is first the moment of the pure action of the object, and then the moment of its socialization. The musical masterpiece or the user's favourite cocktail 'itself' is not slowly diluted with technical methods, rituals, and discourses 'on' the object. Thus, it seems to us, when symbolic interactionists distinguish between the 'content' and the 'performance' effects of drugs, when Becker for example writes that vague impulses and desires are transformed into definite patterns of action through social interpretation of action [1963, 30], they miss a crucial characteristic of drugs. Indeed, there is slow interpenetration and reciprocal enabling between procedures, skills, and properties of the object on the one hand, and the ever finer capacity of the amateur to perceive them on the other. The verbal and technical virtuosity of the user are co-produced in the same experience as the pleasure and the 'purity' of the drug. Only to an expert user is there 'pure' heroin, or 'pure' Bach. In competent use, the propensity of drugs and music unfolds. Expertise is not achieved, then, in spite of, or alongside, the materiality of the object. A music amateur says:

> M6 [m, 44, classical]: I listen to Bach cantatas especially while working. Why the cantatas? Because they form an open ensemble,

impossible to grasp in a single breath of memory, there are about 200. I've got the Harnoncourt-Leonhardt complete collection, and I don't choose this or that cantata, I listen to the CDs at my own little rhythm, box after box, in order, one time going up then going down, vol. VIII record 5, then 4, etc. Of course it's alternated with other records. I do not choose for example to listen to this or that excerpt, famous, or particularly good, on the contrary, those are the ones I risk getting tired of: I let them arrive with joy at their own time and in their own place; I rarely need to re-focus on listening, the moments of attention are more or less 'already in there'.

Just like Gibson's 'affordance' [1977], the propensity of music refers to and unfolds with the habits and embodiment of the creature listening. Beautiful music is heard only by the amateur. The specific form of the object commands a response—but only from an expert user. The object 'itself' is made powerful through the apprenticeship of the amateur. Drug users too note that the efficacy of methadone is shot through with social strategies, intentions, etc.:

> [Two ex-users, now counsellors, discuss with a generalist in a substitution clinic]
> Counsellor: The [methadone] treatment is working. It's been holding (*ça tient*) for the past two weeks!
> Generalist: Yes, but he's taking lots of pills.[13]
> Counsellor: *Ça tient!*
> Other Counsellor: Yeah well you've also got to see that he's soon going to the judge for trial for custody of his kid (so he's strategically reducing in view of this event). The judge told him that he had to be clean [not on illegal drugs]
> Counsellor: Whatever! For an old user who's been taking pills and heroin for 10 years, to quit for two weeks is great!

For the first counsellor, the strategic character of the patient's abstinence cannot detract from the fact that 'methadone is working' when and because it is shot through with social motives, intentions. Like drugs, music acts neither 'socially' (ie, in spite of its materiality), nor 'physically' (ie, 'after' a social apprenticeship). Thus the amateurs suggest a sociology which is neither radically social contructivist, nor materialist—but which allows that potential sensorial effects of music and drugs are conceivable only in relation to a skilled consumer and that this skilled consumer is only conceivable in relation to these 'potentialized' effects.

5. Passing from the technical mastery of time and organization to a loss of control

Expert drug and music users trace a continuum between the physical and mechanical aspects of the drug or piece of music, and the surprising, uncontrolled emergence of certain states.

> M1 [m, 42, jazz group]: I do not have an easy rapport with music. I always have the impression that I am not talented, that it is easier for other people. I don't just get things (without effort), I've got to work on them, it's very mechanical, I've got the impression that I can only play when I've assimilated everything, by repeating it dumbly until it comes, it disgusts me sometimes, but anyway I like it, to work I mean, fortunately I like it, and then when it comes, it becomes fluid, I don't fight with it anymore, I play . . .

The musical effect is not simply standard or correct playing. It 'arrives' with repetition. For addicts too the question arises. The drug is used because it offers surprising and open-ended effects: 'to goof off' (*'pour faire des conneries'*), 'to be more (frank/serious/active/violent . . .)'. Like music for amateurs, attachment is sought because you are suddenly able to do more and differently than you had thought you were able to do. An ex-user, now turned substitution centre co-ordinator, describes different drugs (or cocktails of drugs) as ways of achieving different degrees or distributions of 'control' or 'management':

> D [40, ex-user, clinic staff member]: I take his search for pleasure into account and I see it as a period which will pass. Then I search for ways for him to keep his head in the sand, but ways that are the least dangerous possible, the most sanitary possible (by devising with him a different cocktail of substitution plus drugs, or by prescribing substitution products which do provide some pleasure, like morphine sulphates). Someone under morphine, you can talk to him, you still know what you are doing. With alcohol and benzos, you don't. With morphine, you don't remember everything but . . . The most terrifying is coke. It's a breathless pursuit. The only thing you can manage is (pharmacological) dependence . . .

Thus, according to this ex-user, the cocaine user freely puts himself in a situation where he will no longer control, where he will be unfree. The impossibility of controlling is paradoxically exactly that

A sociology of attachment

which was intentionally sought, without 'any gun pointed to [the] head'. Thus if the drug is 'functional', it is so in a strikingly original way: not because control and manipulation of the drug's properties increases the quality or desirability of an effect, but because—when used by an expert—it fabricates a person who will no longer have the intentionality necessary to functionalist theories. The 'management' of drug use is but the act of 'passing users from the category of people sticking their heads into the sand [. . .] or of pleasure-seekers to the category of people who are dependent.' The user does not go from addicted to free but shifts from one form of attachment to another.

Musicians and users both describe a kind of 'availability', the prepared openness to an event. For musicians it might be that moment when exhaustion overcomes you and you are no longer expecting anything.

> M2 [m, 37, jazz]: We rehearse twice a week at Michel's, Friday night, usually very late and also Tuesdays, it's harder, they are teachers but I work the next day, so usually we do it less late, until midnight on Tuesdays. We learn new chord grids (accords), we do solos, or we work together on parts we know well to find new things for improvement, it's calm, I like the atmosphere of Tuesday nights, then the success is really to those that work (on their music), I am not handicapped, and it is very friendly. Fridays it's more the day before the week-end, either we play the next day and then it's like a general rehearsal, or a last moment adjustment, stressed out, no, that's not the word, tense, we are thinking more about the result; or else we do not play and then we compensate a little, it's more an atmosphere like in a jazz-club, we smoke (well, I don't) and we drink more, we say we're not going on too late, but then at two in the morning we do another one we really like, etc. It's important, that, too. It bonds us together. It's also the moment when you see what you're worth, as guys, simply, the notes are not the only important thing, it's the correct attitude (*tenue*), the fact that you can hold up, I don't know, any musician will tell you that, it's that you hold up, to make something come out good just when you are exhausted . . . Why do you think they all shot up (drugs), hey?, there's no miracle!

In this beautiful excerpt there is no break between the methodical work and long collective organization of the amateurs' practice, and their tentative expectation of a possible event. (In addition, there is the explicit parallel with drugs at the end, a classical topic, both as a metaphor and as a common practice of musicians). For drug users, there are also several ways to prepare for and let ecstasy arrive. They devise cocktails, as mentioned above, that multiply pleasure in accordance with the skill of the user. Users also remain prepared for surprise by managing their dependence on certain drugs. One very experienced patient on methadone describes this management during his using years:

> D [50, charismatic ex-gangster and favourite substitution patient at the clinic]: In the summer I'd go away with my family. We'd go South to the sea. There was no dope there. I barely felt the craving. But as soon as we were back in the car and returning to Paris, we'd really get jittery, sweating like mad [signs of withdrawal]. We'd stop in Lyons to go cop some dope. That was the best time, after a full month without using, it was really good ... I'd stop at other times too, three–four days just to get the feeling back. Otherwise after a while you just don't feel it (heroin) anymore ... Sometimes guys would be glad to be going to jail so that when they'd come out they could enjoy heroin again. But jail can also be a way of avoiding degradation, becoming an absolute junkie. My cousin, he never went to jail, that's why he's in such bad shape ...

Managing dependence is a way of remaining prepared for pleasure, that is, for being seized by the drug over a long period of use. Techniques of preparation, sophisticated vocabularies are made possible by the drug, and in turn renders it effective. The user and amateur are seized, attached, impassioned.

Conclusion: conditions for passion

If we were to describe the modalities of the action of drug use or the love of music we would ask 'what does it mean to take this drug/this music?' and thus 'what kind of subject does this use require?'. Instead, we have focussed on an unusual class of event in which users strive to be seized by objects of their passion. If we describe emerging sensations, the question is no longer 'how can this subject perform this action?' but rather 'how do certain events occur?' and 'how might certain people tentatively help them to occur?'. This is why the way of describing and qualifying these events of the passion

1) forces the sociologist and the amateur to use the same type of accounts, and to share the same specialized vocabulary, in the same tentative effort to characterize the 'event', and
2) cannot be separated from the modalities through which some moments and conditions are prepared in order to make these 'happenings' possibly occur.

Drugs, like music (or love, or wine tasting . . .) throw the user neither into of social construction and 'pure' ritual nor into chemistry or aesthetics (the mechanical effect of drugs or musical pieces themselves). Skilled gestures and techniques of the body, appropriate dispositions of the mind, obsessive tidiness in installation, organizational control of time and space, quasi-scientific expertise of the objects involved and adeptness at managing their passion as a collective construction of a 'connoisseur's practice' . . . these practical and social modalities are necessary but do not work by themselves. Our descriptions, observations and interviews constantly reveal a subtle interweaving between being abandoned to an external power and the virtuosity of practices, of manual, and of social skills. The user passes between active and passive. That is, between 'I am manipulated' (because I agree to it) and 'I manipulate' (an object which is stronger than myself). This 'passing' is at the heart of a theory of attachment. It emphasises the force of things as the locus of an event, of an emergence. There, in that encounter, the user is seized at those very points of asperity (or affordance) that are made possible and relevant by the sophistication of his/her own practices and vocabularies, as well as by the properties of the objects used.

The drug or the music is 'potentialized' as the user acquires the skills to condition the arrival of pleasure. The subject—expertly seized—passes between activity and passivity. The user strives tentatively to fulfil those conditions which will let him be seized and taken over by a potentialized exogenous force. 'Passivity' then is not a moment of inaction—not a lack of will of the user who suddenly fails to be a full subject. Rather passivity adds to action, potentializes action. The greater the strength of the constraints and the more she abandons herself to what can happen, the more strongly it can indeed happen and the more she feels herself. This is the classical paradox of passion—mostly described in the case of love: how can one act so intensely for something to arrive against which one can do nothing? The more passive the more active, the more active the more passive . . .

This takes us back finally to the notion of passion—to which drugs and music make good points of entry. So long, of course, that the analyst follows the protocols and the details of the technical dispositifs, the forms of the collective and the skills, mobilized by the participants. The paradox is that passion is entirely oriented towards an idea which is not the realization of the self, nor the realization of an intention, but the inverse: to let oneself be swept away, seized by some thing which passes. This active process of conditioning so that something might arrive is a central theme to passion. The impassioned's small gestures, obsessions, rituals, even if they are very active, are 'meta-gestures': they are aimed at framing or setting up conditions, and not on the mastery or control of what music or drugs make her feel. This mastery would be the negation of the power of these two objects. At the beginning they resist, and it is starting with this resistance that users let themselves be swept away—or not. What is at stake is not the consumption of an expensive white powder or the validation of an opera member's card, but the users' tentative encouragement of shifts between states of being. Music or drugs constitute their *beings*, transform them irreversibly, and thus lead them to happiness or distress.

This then is a theory of mediation in action. All the means are crucial. Users must pass through them, put them scrupulously to work, but they do not contain their end, they offer no guarantee. On the contrary, they are completely overwhelmed by the sublime moments which they can make arrive. This vocabulary of amateurs is a vocabulary of all passions, with its characteristic passings between, on the one hand, 'ordinary' terms of passion, terms that isolate, close, that refer to laborious activities, to the search of the addict for his dope, his nocturnal rituals of shooting up, to the work of the interpreter or the collector's lists, their methodical dispositifs and their meticulously described dispositions; and, on the other hand, the terms that evoke the appearance of that to which they abandon themselves, the total receptivity to that which arrives, when 'nothing else matters'. It is the 'good concert' for the rockers, the 'sublime' moments which words can only render banal. It is the 'ineffable' pleasure of the drug user which 'is so much stronger than sexual climax' that non-users cannot even come close to imagining what drugs might do. But these moments when users are swept away occur only after a conditioning, a disposition of oneself, uncertain, laborious, costly. The idea is common to experienced 'old addicts', for whom drug use can be the deft manipulation of whatever brings about forgetting, ecstasy or dependence. It is common to the young rocker or the fifty-year old classical music amateur. For all it is an instrumented technique, both personal and collective, that passes through sophisticated spaces and times and opens onto certain states in a non-necessary manner.

Notes

1 No English equivalent seems to exist. The term 'dispositif' is appropriate for our purposes as it focuses on objects, conditions and means through which entities in networks emerge.
2 This is the 'American' side of the coin; see eg a suggestive presentation of the debate with the methodological individualism in [Hirschman, 1977].
3 This is more the 'French' side: A. Hennion has shown how the idea of 'illusio', negative and critique in Bourdieu [eg 1980, 204], is already the unproblematic scientist and positive conception at work eg in the seminal theory by Durkheim [1912] of the cultural objects, seen as representation of an invisible social reality. For a summary of this, see [Hennion, 1993, 237–267].
4 Ethnomethodology and interactionism have helped to make this oscillation between the types of explanations less marked. However as Callon and Law remark, though these authors assume that 'interests' and 'norms' are not stable but arise in local situations, the gap remains because they remain concerned with describing the interaction between agent and structure, subject and object, human and non-human. Insufficient emphasis is put on the presence of objects inside the collective agencies.
5 See our discussion of S. Star and J. Griesemer [1989] below.
6 This is what music shows best, with its procession of objects, instruments, scenes, corporeal performances, all necessary and insufficient for it to emerge. When an interpreter says he 'plays music', 'music' is this score, in front of the performer, but it is just as much the very act of playing: unlike a cause or an effect, 'music' is not the 'object' of an action which might be external, instrumental, to it. From a long set of mediations (scores, instruments, gestures and bodies, stages and mediums), at certain moments, on top of it all—something might happen.
7 'Among all these acting entities no hierarchy is introduced: they have the same privileges and often play identical roles. This tolerance towards elements which people the world is taken to its extreme by semioticians when they use the notion of actant. [. . .] Actants are all the elements which accomplish or are transformed by the actions through which the narration evolves'. [our translation of Callon *et al.*, 1982, p. 92] With the notion of 'actants' semioticians can avoid the zero-sum game implied in causal explanations.
8 'We do not admire the Venus of Milo because it is beautiful, but it is beautiful because we admire it', said Charles Lalo in 1912.
9 See for example C. Hayles [1992].
10 Methadone treatment, for example, was deemed to be efficacious when the user asked for it and when its mode of use was close to the mode of use of heroin of the patient. Methadone is one of several opiates (moscontin, skénan, subutex . . .) prescribed for the treatment of heroin addiction in France, within institutional settings or with a close follow-up from the generalist. The drug prescribed then is caught in a web of social and technical relations. The goal of treatment is not to

make users abstain from methadone, not—immediately—from illegal drugs (anyway, they do not). It is rather to modify the mode of use. Methadone was thus allowed to become impure and entangled with the desires of the user for drugs. Indeed, we take this tolerance of impurity to be a characteristic of this philosophy of drugs: the more it is interpreted, projected upon, the more it is pharmacologically available, see E. Gomart [in preparation].

11 Antipsychiatrists and sociological critiques of medicalization were mobilized to illustrate the locking up (l'enfermement) of the patient; Foucault was literally referred to in several writings of treatment specialists. See M. Valleur [1992], A. Coppel [1993] and Thomas Sasz [1981].

12 Excerpt taken from a collection of one hundred transcribed interviews by a Belgian generalist, Marc Jamoulle, and gathered in a 1996 manuscript: 'Etre en roche'.

13 Prescribed medications used in non-medical doses in association with legal and illegal substances.

Bibliography

Becker, Howard S. (1974), 'Art as collective action', *American Sociological Review*, 39(6): 767–776.
Becker, Howard S. (1982), *Art Worlds*, Berkeley: University of California Press.
Becker, Howard S. (1985), *Outsiders: études de sociologie de la déviance*, Paris: Métailié.
Bourdieu, Pierre (1980), *Le Sens pratique*, Paris: Minuit.
Callon, Michel, Bastide, Françoise [et al.] (1984), «Les mécanismes d'intéressement dans les textes scientifiques», *Cahiers STS: Légitimité et légitimation de la science*, Ed. CNRS, Paris, 88–105.
Callon, Michel and Law, John (1997), «L'irruption des non-humains dans les sciences humaines: quelques leçons tirées de la sociologie des sciences et des techniques», in Reynaud, Bénédicte (ed.), *Les limites de la rationalité: Vol. 2, Les figures du collectif*, Paris: La découverte, 97–118.
Coppel, Anne (1993), «A la recherche de nouvelles régulations des drogues», *Transcriptase*, 22, 12–17.
Durkheim, Emile (1912), *Les Formes élémentaires de la vie religieuse: le système totémique en Australie*, Paris: Presses universitaires de France.
Foucault, Michel (1975), *Surveiller et Punir: naisssance de la prison*, Paris: Gallimard.
Gibson, J. (1977), *The Ecological approach to visual perception*, Boston: Houghton Mifflin.
Gomart, Emilie (in preparation), 'Surprised by methadone: an experimentation on constraint', doctoral thesis, CSI-Ecole des Mines, Paris.
Greimas, Algirdas-Julien and Courtès, Julien (1986), *Sémiotique: dictionnaire raisonné de la théorie du langage*, Hachette: Paris.
Hayles, Catherine (1992), 'The materiality of informatics', *Configurations*, 1, 147–170.
Hennion, Antoine (1993), *La Passion musicale. Une sociologie de la médiation*, Paris: Métailié.
Hennion, Antoine (1996), 'The History of Art—Lessons in Mediation', *Réseaux. The French Journal of Communication*, 3(2): 233–262.

Hennion, Antoine and Grenier, Line 91998), 'Sociology of Art: New Stakes in a Post-Critical Time', in *Sociology: Advances and Challenges in the 1990s*, ISA Research Council, Stella Quah (ed.), Sage Publications.

Hirschauer, Stefan (1991), 'The Manufacture of Bodies in Surgery', *Social Studies of Science*, 21(2): 279–32.

Hirschman, Albert O. (1977), *The Passions and the Interests*, Princeton: Princeton University Press.

Jamoulle, Marc (1996), «Etre en roche», *manuscript*.

Lalo, Charles (1912), *Introduction à l'esthétique*, Paris: Félix Alcan.

Latour, Bruno (1996), 'On Interobjectivity', *Mind, Technique and Activity*, 3, 228–245.

Norman, Donald A. (1988), *The design of everydaythings*, New York: Doubleday/ Currency.

Star, Susan Leigh and Griesemer, James (1989), 'Institutional Ecology, "Translations" and Boundary Objects: Amateurs and Professionals', *Berkeley's Museum of Vertebrate Zoology*, 1907–39.

Suchman, Lucy A. (1987), *Plans and Situated Actions. The Problem of Human Machine Communication*, Cambridge: Cambridge University Press.

Szaz, Thomas (1981), 'The Discovery of Addiction', in Saffer, Howard and Burglass, Milton Earl (eds), *Classic Contributions in the Addictions*, New York: Brunel/ Mazel, 36–48.

Valleur, Marc (1992), «Drogues et droits du toxicomane: le point de vue du praticien», Conférence «Drogues et Droits de l'homme», Université Paris X, Nanterre, 10 April 1992 [*roneo*].

Zola, Irving (1975), 'In the name of health and illness: On some socio-political consequences of medical influence', *Journal of Social Science and Medicine*, 9, 83–87.

Notes on contributors

Steven D. Brown is a Lecturer in Social and Organizational Psychology at Keele University and a member of the Centre for Social Theory and Technology. He has published articles on actor-network theory; the construction of stress; culture and technology and the history and philosophy of psychology. He is currently investigating Groupware and the mediation of memory within the ESRC Virtual Society programme.

Michel Callon is Professor of Sociology at the Ecole des Mines de Paris and a member of the Centre de Sociologie de l'Innovation. He is also President of the Society for Social Studies of Science. Together with Bruno Latour and John Law he was responsible for the early development of ANT. He is at present working on the anthropology of markets, and is editor of a book called *The Laws of the Markets* published by Blackwell which shows how economic markets are embedded in the discipline of economics. He is also working with Vololona Rabeharisoa on voluntary associations for those who are sick, and how these are contributing to new ways of creating and mobilizing scientific knowledge.

Rose Capdevila is a Lecturer in Psychology at Nene University College and is currently completing a PhD at the University of Reading. Within the context of social psychology, her work looks at the discourse and patterns around political participation. More specifically, her empirical research focuses on the construction of gender identities and identity politics within, outwith, and through the participation of women in social and political movements. She has published articles in social, discursive and feminist psychologies.

© The Editorial Board of The Sociological Review 1999. Published by Blackwell Publishers, 108 Cowley Road, Oxford OX4 1JF, UK and 350 Main Street, Malden, MA 02148, USA.

Notes on contributors

Anni Dugdale is a postdoctoral fellow in the Sociology Program of the Research School of Social Sciences at the Australian National University. Her writing and teaching focuses on feminism, sexuality, science and technology. Several articles on the IUD from the 1920s to the present are in press. She is currently writing a book with Zed Press tentatively titled *Devices and Desires: How the Making of a Contraceptive Technology Produced Postmodern Sexualities.*

Emilie Gomart is a doctoral student at the Centre de Sociologie de l'Innovation. After a Masters at Cambridge University in history and philosophy of science, she studied sociology of science at the Ecole des Mines in Paris. For her PhD dissertation ('Surprised by methadone: experimentations on material constraint') she has done fieldwork in a methadone substitution clinic. Her main topics are: 1) the variability of drug effects in relation to drug legislation, police measures and modes of use of the drug user; 2) debates about the legitimacy and efficiency in treatments of addiction of pharmacological substances as techniques of coercion of or collusion with the user.

John Hassard is Professor of Organizational Analysis at the University of Manchester Institute of Science and Technology. His publications include *Sociology and Organization Theory: Positivism, Paradigms and Postmodernity* (1993), *Postmodernism and Organizations* (1993), *Towards a New Theory of Organizations* (1994) and *Organization/Representation: Work and Organizations in Popular Culture* (1998). He is currently researching issues of representation, embodiment and organization in popular culture.

Antoine Hennion is Professor and Director of the Centre de Sociologie de l'Innovation de l'Ecole des Mines de Paris. He has published widely on the sociology of music and the arts, where his books include *Les professionels du disque* (Paris, Métailié, 1981), *Comment la musique vient aux enfants. Une anthropologie de l'enseignement musical* (Paris, Anthropos, 1988), *La Passion musicale. Une sociologie de la médiation* (Paris, Métailié, 1993), and *Music as Mediation*, Manchester, Manchester University Press (forthcoming).

Kevin Hetherington is Lecturer in Sociology in the Department of Human Sciences, Brunel University. He writes on space and identity and on museums and material culture. He is currently researching how the spaces of museums are (re)constituted

Notes on contributors

through touch by visually impaired visitors. He is author of *The Badlands of Modernity* (Routledge, 1977), *Expressions of Identity* (Sage, 1998), *New Age Travellers* (Cassell, 1999) and co-editor of *Consumption Matters* (Blackwell, 1996) and *Ideas of Difference* (Blackwell, 1997). He has also co-edited, with John Law, a forthcoming special issue of the journal *Society and Space* on actor-network theory and spatiality.

Bruno Latour is Professor at the Ecole Nationale Supérieure des Mines in Paris, and Visiting Professor at the London School of Economics. He has written extensively in sociology of science where his publications include *Laboratory Life: the Social Construction of Scientific Facts* (Beverly Hills, Sage, 1979), *Science in Action* (Milton Keynes: Open University Press, 1987), *The Pasteurization of France* (Cambridge, Mass.: Harvard, 1988), *We Have Never Been Modern* (Brighton, Harvester Wheatsheaf, 1993) and *Aramis, or the Love of Technology* (Cambridge, Mass.: Harvard, 1996).

John Law is Professor of Technology and Cultural Values at Lancaster University. He has written extensively on the sociology of technology, organizational sociology, and on actor-network theory, and is currently working on disabilities, medical technologies, materialities and subjectivities. His recent publications include *Machines, Agency and Desire* (co-edited with Brita Brenna and Ingunn Moser) (TMV, University of Oslo, 1998), *Organizing Modernity* (Oxford, Blackwell, 1994) and *A Sociology of Monsters* (ed.) (Oxford and Keele, Blackwell and the Sociological Review, 1991).

Nick Lee is Lecturer in Sociology and Deputy Director of the Centre for Social Theory at Keele University. He has previously written on Actor Network Theory, speed and stability, and the sociology of childhood and child protection. He is also a co-author with Paul Stenner, amongst others, of *Textuality and Tectonics: Troubling Social and Psychological Science* (B. Curt, 1994; OUP). His present research is concerned with the representation of children within adult-centred institutions.

Annemarie Mol is Socrates Professor of Political Philosophy at the University of Twente and research fellow of the Ethics and Policy program of the Netherlands Organization of Scientific Research. Her research concerns medicine, technology, the body, norms and normality. She is co-editor (with Marc Berg) of *Differences in Medicine: Unravelling Practices, Techniques and Bodies* (Durham,

Notes on contributors

N.Ca. and London, Duke University Press, 1998) and her book *The Body Multiple: Artherosclerosis in Practice*, will appear with Duke in 1999. Her email address is: a.mol@pobox.run.nl.

Ingunn Moser is a PhD student at the Centre for Technology and Culture, University of Oslo. She has been working on ICT and disability since 1994. In her current work she is focussing on how identity, subjectivity and agency is constituted in relation to bodies and technologies—and how different configurations of heterogeneous materials produce what we recognize as abled or disabled persons. She is co-editor—with Brita Brenna and John Law—of *Machines, Agency and Desire* (TMV, University of Oslo, 1998).

Paul Stenner is Lecturer in Psychology at the University of Bath. He received his PhD from the University of Reading in 1992 for research on the social construction of emotion with particular reference to jealousy. Since then he has published numerous scholarly articles in the field of critical psychology and has co-authored (with various members of the Beryl Curt Collective) two books: *Social Psychology: a critical agenda* (Polity Press, 1996), and *Textuality and Tectonics: troubling social and psychological science* (Open University Press, 1994). He and Nick Lee have worked together on several projects within critical psychology.

Marilyn Strathern is William Wyse Professor of Social Anthropology at the University of Cambridge. Her interests are divided between Melanesian (*Women In Between*, 1972) and British (*Kinship At The Core*, 1981) ethnography. *The Gender Of The Gift* (1988) is a critique of anthropological theories of society and gender relations as they have been applied to Melanesia, while *After Nature* (1992) comments on the cultural revolution at home. A monograph on comparative method is called *Partial Connections* (1991). Her most recent publications are the co-authored *Technologies Of Procreation* (1993) and the edited volume *Shifting Contexts: Transformations In Anthropological Knowledge* (1995).

Helen Verran is Senior Lecturer in the Department of History and Philosophy of Science, University of Melbourne. During the 1980s she spent many years as the lecturer in science education at Obafemi Awolowo University in Nigeria. The puzzles that the teachers who were her students set for her during those years are more fully explored in *Numbers, Judgement, and Certainty: Storytelling about African Logics* (forthcoming).

Index

The following abbreviation has been used in this index:
ANT actor network theory

abandonment, 226–30
accidents, 35
actants, 34, 41, 226
  as resources, 32, 36
action, 35
action theory, 222–4
actor, 18, 181–2
  Callon and, 158
  in market network, 193–4
  network and, 16
  see also actants; agency
actor network theory, 3–4
  fractionality of, 9–12
  naming of, 5–9
Addelson, K. P., 144, 154n
addiction, 222, 229, 230–1, 240
aesthetic judgement, 66
agency, 39–40, 211
Akrich, M., 23
anaemia, 77–85
anti-foundation, 93, 94, 95
Appadurai, A., 189
Ashmole, Elias, 61
assemblage, belonging by, 100, 105–6
attachments, 230–45
audit, teaching, 8–9
autobiography, 211–12

Bacon, Francis, 61
banishment, belonging by, 100, 101, 105–6
Becker, H. S., 238
belonging, 93, 94–5, 98–110
Berg, M., 23
boundary objects, 237–8
Brown, S. D., 11, 38, 45, 91
Bruno, Giordino, 64
Bryson, N., 56
Bunuel, Louis, 69

cabinets of curiosity, 60, 63, 64–5
calculative agents, 184, 186–7, 193
  framing, 190–2
Callon, M., 11, 29, 32, 33, 44, 158, 223, 226
Capdevila, R., 11
Carnap, R., 145
Cervical Screening Programme, 43–4
Charter of the Indigenous-tribal Peoples of the Tropical Forests, 177n
children, in legal system, 101–2
choice, 83, 85–6
circulation, 18–19, 20, 22, 23–4, 29, 104–5, 106
  as-essence, 30–45
classificatory table, 61–2
closure, 122, 125, 128–9, 131–2
comparison, 64–5, 172
compensation, in Papua New Guinea, 164–8
complexity, 8–9, 110
compromise, 124–5, 128, 131–2
conditioning, 227, 244
constraint, 221, 229–30
construction stories, 76
contingent contracts, 184
Convention on Biological Diversity, 160–4, 174, 176n
Cooper, R., 35
co-ordination of markets, 184–5
Cussins, Adrian, 20
Cussins, Charis, 20, 23
custom, 164, 171–2, 174
cyborgs, 155n, 214–15

Dadaists, 68–9
Dali, Salvador, 69
decentering, 92–4, 115
decision-making, 124–30
Deleuze, G., 2, 7, 36–7, 38, 96

Index

departure, 97-8, 106
dependency, 93
Derrida, J., 93, 104
description, 62, 228
difference, 81-2, 124-5, 161, 168-9, 174, 175
dis/ability, 198-215
discipline, 221
disconcertment, 141-2, 148
discontinuity, 213, 214-15
discretion, 207, 209, 211
disorder, 35-6
dispersal, 129
'dispositifs', 221, 222, 226
dissatisfaction, 16-17
drugs, 228-30
  pleasure of, 233, 235, 236-7, 239, 240-1, 242
Duchamp, Marcel, 68
Dugdale, A., 11
Dutch art, 60, 62

economic theory, 187-8, 192
embodiment, in quantifying, 148-50
emergence, and performance, 226
energy, 30-1, 37, 39
English language, quantifying in, 146, 147
entanglement, 189-90, 193
essence, 30
  circulation-as-, 30-45
ethical project, ANT as, 98, 106
Euclideanism, 6-7, 8
event-network theory, 225-6
exclusion, 91, 95, 98, 101, 105-7
expertise, 75-6, 120-1, 170
expression, 43, 44
externality, 187-8, 193

Fechner, Gustav, 39
Filer, C., 168
focal point, 185
force, 37-42
Foucault, M., 1-2, 58, 61, 62, 87n
  and comparison, 64
  and panopticism, 65
  and power, 38, 221
foundation, 91, 93-4, 95, 97, 142-3, 144-8
fractionality, 9-12
framing, 186-90, 193
  and construction of calculative agents, 190-2
French Academy of Sciences, 28, 30
Freud, S., 38, 68
functional blankness, 40

Garcia, M-F., 190-2
Garfinkel, H., 203
gaze, 57, 61
  of connoisseur, 66-7
  Renaissance, 58-9
Girard, R., 98
Gomart, E., 11, 23
Goodman, J., 169
Granovetter, M. S., 185-6, 187
Griesemer, J., 237
Guattari, G., 2, 7, 36-7, 38
Guesnerie, R., 183

Haraway, Donna, 11, 153n, 155n, 215
Heidegger, M., 109-10
Helmholtz, H. von, 30-1, 32, 39, 47
Hennion, A., 11, 23
heterogeneity, 5, 60, 170, 174, 175
  Bacon and, 61
  Dadaism and, 68-9
  gaze and, 57, 59
  internalization of, 65-71
  in museums, 51-4, 58, 62
  social, 164-5
Hetherington, K., 11, 39-40
homo economicus, 185, 193
Hooper-Greenhill, E., 58, 59
human/non-human divide, 4, 157, 158, 159, 223-4
Hutchins, 224
hybridity, 45, 95-6, 106, 109, 172
  enfranchisement of, 91, 95, 100
hyphen, in actor-network, 21-2

inclusion, 83-5
indigenous communities, 160, 163-4, 166-7
institution, modernity as, 94-5, 97
Intellectual, Biological and Cultural Property Rights seminar, 161, 172
intellectual property rights, 158, 159
  in Papua New Guinea, 160-71
intentionality, 40
interference, 81-3
interpretivism, 143, 144
IUDs (intrauterine contraceptive devices) 124-5
  committee on safety of, 116-18, 122-3
  leaflet on, 126-30

Kant, I., 39, 66
Kendall, G., 45
Kirsch, S., 168
knowledge, and technology, 161-2, 163, 175

Index

Krauss, R., 69

Latour, B., 7, 11, 107, 143, 154n, 157
   and hybridity, 96–7, 100, 106, 109
   and modernity, 94–7, 100
   and translation, 33, 34
Law, J., 20, 35, 38, 43, 44, 159, 182, 223
Lee, N., 11, 38, 91
legal system, 101
Leibnitz, G., 33–4
Lemmonier, P., 165
Levi-Strauss, C., 58
linear perspective, 54–7
Lynch, M., 19
Lyotard, J-F., 39

market, 182
   framing and, 186–92
   as a network, 183–6, 192
materiality, 4, 118
   practical, 116, 122
   relational, 4, 170
mediation, 96, 224–6, 244
Medici collections, 57–9
memory, 63–4
Michael, M., 43–4, 45
micro/macro, 16–17, 122
   Miller, P., 191
modernity, 21–2
   disappearance of heterogeneity in, 65–7
   Latour and, 94–7, 100
   Serres and, 107, 109
Mol, A., 11, 20, 23
monads, 34
moral project, ANT as, 91
Moser, I., 11
multiplicity, 75, 77, 83, 125, 128–9
museums, 51, 52–4
   modern, 67
   Renaissance, 58–9
   17th century, 60–5
music, 227–8
   pleasure of, 232, 234, 236, 238–9, 240, 241–2
Mutt, R., 68

natural contract, 107–9
negotiation, 122, 124–5, 131
network, 15–16, 34, 37, 106–7, 223
Nigeria, teaching quantifying in, 136–41, 148
Northern Ireland, 46–7

ontological politics, 74–87, 125
options, 79–80, 86

order, 67, 91, 98–9
   belonging and, 99–101
   museums and, 51–2, 58, 59, 67
oscillation, 125, 128
Other, 6, 105–7, 110
   nature as, 109, 110
overflowing, 188–9

Panofsky, E., 54, 56–7
panopticism, 65–6
Papua New Guinea, 157–75
passage, 57, 224
   disability and, 201, 203–4, 205–6, 207–8, 209
passion, 226–30, 243–4
passivity/activity, 227, 231–42, 243
Pels, D., 39
performance, 4, 7, 33, 77–85
   and emergence, 226
perpetuum mobile, 28, 30–45
perspectivalism, 75–6
philosophy, 33–5, 40–1, 45
pluralism, 76
policy-making, 114–16
Posey, D., 173, 174
power, 38–9, 115
presentation, 41
psychology, 45–7
purification, 96, 161, 163

quantifying
   as embodied, 148–50
   foundational accounts of, 144–8
Quine, W. V. O., 145

rationalization, 211–12
reality, 75
   multiple realities, 75, 77, 83
regionalism, 6
relationships, 158, 167–8, 169, 171
relativist account of quantifying, 145, 154n
Renaissance, 54, 55, 57–9
repetition, 37, 44, 46–7, 148–9
representation, 44, 61
Ribot, T., 39
ritual, 149
Rotman, B., 55–6, 59, 70
routine, 148–9

self-description, 172–3, 174–5
semiotics, 3, 4, 32, 226
Serres, M., 31, 32–3, 91, 97, 107–8
similitude, 58–9, 63, 64, 68–70
Singleton, V., 43–4
singularity, and multiplicity, 125, 128–9

© The Editorial Board of The Sociological Review 1999

Index

social continuity, 167
social contract, 107–8
social divisions, 171, 173–4
  through relations, 158–9, 168–71
social energetics, 37–8
society, 18–19
  technology and, 157, 159, 161–4, 170–1
  theory of, 19–20, 21–2
sociology of scientific knowledge, 114, 115
space, 21, 36, 55
  in between networks, 19
  museum as, 53–4
  theory of, 22
spatiality, 6, 7
specificities, 199–200
  movement between, 200–1, 207
Spinoza, B., 33, 34–5, 40–1, 43
Star, L., 39, 143, 207, 237
Stengers, I., 23
Stenner, P., 11
Strathern, M., 6, 8–9, 11, 215
strawberry market, 190–2
subject, 52, 70
  in Dadaism, 68–9
  in Dutch art, 62–3
  heterogeneity of, 66–7, 69
  in linear perspective, 56–7, 66
  as point of view, 52, 53, 56, 57, 62
  relationship with object, 53, 54, 60, 70–1
subject-networks, 220–1, 222–5
subjectivities, 23, 65, 71
  constitution of, 118, 119, 121–2, 127, 129
  dis/ability and, 198–215
substance, 30–7
Suchman, L., 223–4
summing up, 16–19
Surrealism, 69
symmetry, 38, 40, 159, 161, 171–5

Taxol, 169–70
technology and society, 157, 159, 161–4, 170–1

territory, 37, 41–2, 44, 45, 46–7
theology, 24
theory
  in actor network theory, 19–21
  of society, 19–20, 21–2
Therapeutic Goods Administration,
  subcommittee on IUDs, 116–18, 120–1
thermodynamics, 31, 32
Thomas, N., 189
time, 42–5, 146–7
topology, 6–7, 43
Traditional Resource Rights, 162
translation, 8, 10, 46, 172
  sociology of, 28–45
TSR2, 42, 44–5
Turner, J. M. W., 31, 32–3

universalist account of quantifying, 144–5
University of Ife, Institute of Education, 137

Velasquez, D., 62
Verran, H., 11
vocabulary of ANT, 20
Von Neuman, J., 146, 147
Vonnegut, K., *Hocus Pocus*, 27–8

Walsh, V., 169
Wiener, N., 34
will, 39–40
  to-connect, 40–1
Williamson, O., 183
Willke, H., 173, 174
World Intellectual Property Organization, 160
worldwide world, 107–8

Yoruba language, 146–7
  quantifying in, 146–7, 149–50

Zelizer, V., 190
Zermelo, E., 146, 147
zero, 55–6

Printed in Great Britain
by Amazon